Jain Community of Bundelkhand

Jain Community of Bundelkhand

Socio-economic and Cultural Change

Prakash C. Jain

Foreword by
Ravindra K. Jain

International School for Jain Studies

SHIPRA

Rs. 950; US$ 38

ISBN: 978-93-88691-41-3

First Published in India in 2020

Jain Community of Bundelkhand: Socio-economic and Cultural Change

Published by:
SHIPRA PUBLICATIONS
LG 18-19, Pankaj Central Market
I.P. Ext., Patparganj, Delhi 110092, India
Tel.: +91 11 2223 5152/6152, 9650028065
E-mail: info@shiprapublication.com
www.shiprapublication.com

Foreword

The area of the former Bundela Rajput kingdoms is still known by its indigenous name 'Bundelkhand' ('the domain of the Bundelas'). Besides designating the territory of former Bundela rule, Bundelkhand is the name of a linguistic region of India. The great majority of the people of seven southern districts of Uttar Pradesh and six northern districts of Madhya Pradesh speak Bundeli, a dialect of western Hindi. The Bundeli linguistic region is much larger (43,452.4 sq. kms.) than the area of former Bundela kingdoms and domains (22,180.7 sq. kms.).

In contemporary politics and economy, the Bundelkhand region is known for an incipient demand for political statehood and, at the same time, its teeming poverty and extremely drought-prone terrain. Its present day backwardness is in ironic contrast to its pristine historical glory that is amply recorded in legends and other oral sources. From the time of written records of this region's history Jain merchants alongside Hindu business castes of the Vaishya varna have played a prominent role in the rural and urban economy of Bundelkhand. The tradition continues to this day.

The focus on the Jains of Bundelkhand in this study is well chosen and timely. If we take a bird's eye-view of the Jain community in India there are pockets of this minority prominently in the western states of Rajasthan, Gujarat, Madhya Pradesh and southwards into Maharashtra. In the Indo-Gangetic plain proper there is a sprinkling of Jains, mostly in non-agricultural occupations in Punjab, Haryana, Uttar Pradesh and Bihar. In southern India there has been a long history of Jain settlements in Kannadiga and Tamilian regions. Here, along with the instance of Maharashtra there are some Jain agricultural communities. Historically, it is worth pointing out that whereas in much of northern and western India the Jains conform culturally to a Vaishya or trader model, the southern Jains have been inheritors of a kingly tradition, the Kshatriya model, which is mirrored even today in their being partly agriculturists and also organised around royalty-supported institutions like that of the Bhattaraka. Jains in Bundelkhand belong to the typical Vaishya model of north India with their roots in the rural communities and situated at an arm's length from the royalty. On the other hand, they have throughout been at the mercy of predator rajas, small and large estate-holders of Hindu castes, who are often depicted in regional histories as bandit-kings.

The spring-board for Dr. Prakash C. Jain's work on Bundelkhand Jains is these rural communities of small businessmen though many of their members have now attained mobility as wealthy merchants. Alongside the harnessing of wealth, they have contributed much to a variegated rural and urban elite status in terms of religion, philanthropy, legal profession, scholarship and literary accomplishment. Dr. Prakash C. Jain has eloquently recorded their story. However, set against the all-India profile of the Jains -- both rich and plebeian -- the Bundelkhand Jains exemplify par excellence the small change of commercial and ritual transactions that mark their day-to-day quotidian life. This feature is markedly manifest in the temple-related worship and festivities in the villages of Bundelkhand. The religious community consists of sets of specialists such as tyagis, pundits or vidwans and munis in regular interaction with lay Jains. I have provided a flavour of this community life through a detailed account of Bundelkhand rural Jainism contained in the autobiography of Kshullak Ganesh Prasadji Varni (Jain, Ravindra K., 1999, Chapter 5). It portrays what is to my mind, The Jain Path of Purification, (to use the title of Professor P. S. Jaini's noted book on the subject) for the laity and how it interacts with worldly demands. Let me in conclusion state what I have not done in introducing Dr. Jain's monograph. I have resisted from summarizing or even highlighting the substantive data contained in this comprehensive sociological text. There is a nuanced relationship and distinction between sociology and anthropology. It may be noted that my observations above and in my own monograph alluded to earlier, complement and supplement anthropologically the sociological insights of Prakash Jain's study. Ideally, one should have also raised the issue of comparative religion and society, especially the interface between metaphor and community in Jainism and Buddhism, for instance. But let that be our joint task for the future!

9th June 2019.

Ravindra K. Jain
"Anveshi", Village Hartola,
District Nainital, Uttarakhand.

Preface

I was greatly interested in doing some work on the Jain community since my post-graduation days, but circumstances did not allow me to do that for about four decades. So following my superannuation as Professor of West Asian Studies, when the opportunity came to me to submit a research proposal for a Senior Research Fellowship to the Indian Council of Social Science Research, I chose to work on the Jain community of Bundelkhand to which I myself belong. I was born and brought up in Saidpur village of Lilitpur district. My early schooling up to eighth grade was done in my village school and up to 10th grade at Shri Varni Jain Inter College, Lalitpur. My further studies and the subsequent employments at Varanasi, Ottawa and Delhi prevented me from staying in the region for longer periods of time, bur regular short visits in order to meet parents and other family members have kept me in touch with the region ever since.

My familiarity with the region, academic background of Sociology, and the working knowledge of Jain philosophy through basic texts such as *Tatvarth Sutra*, *Sarvartha Siddhi*, etc. that were taught to me by Pt. Kaiash Chand Shastri during my four-year long stay at Shri Syadvad Digambar Jain Mahavidyalaya at Varanasi prompted me to take up this theme for sociological investigation. The broad theme of Bundelkhand's Jain community was further delineated by putting focus on the socio-economic changes in the community to which I have been a witness since the late 1950s when I was growing up in my native village as a teenager. A vividly fascinating account of Bundelkhand's Jain community of the first half of the 20th century is also available in Kshullak Ganesh Prasad Varni's autobiography *Meri Jeevan Gatha*. Needless to say, there have been significant changes in various aspects of the Jain community of the region since then.

The present study attempts to sociologically examine the select aspects of socio-economic and cultural changes in the Jain community of Bundelkhand. More specifically, it focuses on changes in the community's educational and occupational profiles; social structural features, and the Jain way of life. The data were collected with the help of a questionnaire in the four core districts of Bundelkhand, namely Lalitpur, Jhansi, Sagar and Tikamgarh. Additionally, secondary material pertaining to certain Jain elite families, pandits, ascetics, vidyalayas, associations, places of pilgrimage, etc. was also collected.

Data collection would not have been possible without the active support of a large number of people of Bundelkhand. These included about 200 odd Jain respondents to the questionnaire including about a dozen or so key informants. I am thankful to all of them. Among the informants, mention must be made of Ms. Nikita Jain, Nirmal Kumar Jain, Sagar; Neelesh Jain, Lalitpur; V. K. Jain, BHEL, Jhansi; Shikhar Chand Jain and Chakresh Jain, Tikamgarh; Kailash Chowdhary, Mahroni; and Devendra Kumar Jain, Sadumal.

I am also thankful to Dr. Alok Kumar Jain of Delhi's Shri Vir Sewa Mandi for making me available a soft copy of Siddhantacharya Pandit Phoolchandra Shastri's book Parwar Jain Samaj ka Itihas, and to Surendra Kumar Jain of Bhagwan of Chhatarpur district for promptly sending to me his book Golapurav Jain Samaj: Itihas Evam Sarvekshan and a couple of other books relevant to the study. My thanks are also due to Dr. Deepak Jain and his wife Sunita Jain, editor and publisher of Bhopal-based monthly "Taaran Bandhu", for sending to me some useful material about Taaran Samaj, including privately-conducted population enumeration data of the community. My friend Dr. Ramesh Chand Jain, a well-known Jain scholar, loaned me a book by Doctor R. K. Jain of Kota that helped me in preparing the list of Jain monks and nuns who were born and brought up in the greater Bundelkhand region. I am thankful to him for this and for discussing the subject-matter of the book on a number of occasions. Needless to say, without these books, this work would have been incomplete, and perhaps much different than what it is now.

For writing the Foreword of the book I am grateful to Dr. Ravindra K. Jain, formerly Professor of Anthropology and Dean of the School of Social Sciences, Jawaharlal Nehru University, New Delhi. Even otherwise, as a senior colleague, he has always been a source of inspiration for me as we share the academic interest on Indian diaspora and the Jain community.

I am also grateful to Dr. Shugan C. Jain, Founding Chairman and Director, International School for Jain Studies, New Delhi for agreeing to co-publish the book as a part of the School's publications programme (www.isjs.in). At the ISJS, thanks are also due to Dr. Shrinetra Pandey, Shri Sushil Jana, Shri Shivam Saxena and Ms. Jyoti Pandey for various acts of help towards getting the Manuscript ready for publication. Shri D. Kumar, Shipra Publications, New Delhi deserves a word of thanks for readily accepting the book for publication. Last but not the least, I would like to thank my wife Dr. Renu Saxena and my daughters Dr, Rashi Prakash and Ms. Sanskriti Prakash for their love and support that made my academic pursuits a lot less arduous.

My going to Varanasi for post-High School studies and staying at Shri Syadvad Mahavidyalaya during 1962-66 happened within a certain pattern which has generally been discussed in Chapter Four: Accordingly, informed Jain parents/ guardians of Bundelkhand having moderate educational aspirations for their wards, and that too without having to spend too much money, used to send them to the community-run Sanskrit vidyalayas spread all over north India where liberal arts stream disciplines mixed well with Sanskrit and Indological/Jain Studies.

However, in my case, the difference was that being a Science srtream student I had no plan to study Sanskrit/Indological courses, and therefore had to pay a subsidized fee for my lodging and boarding in the hostel of the Vidyalaya. The only compulsion was to attend a daily class on Jainism and successfully pass out its annual examination for ensuring my next year's stay there. Apparently, all this was planned for me by my maternal uncles Shri Moti Lal Jain, M.Sc. (Technology) and Shri Kailash Chand Jain, B.E. (Electrical), who financially supported my stay for five years there. Both of them had also benefited from the Vidyalaya while pursuing their respective studies in Varanasi, particularly in the initial phases. And to repeat the pattern as it were, they were guided in this regard by their uncle Pt. Phoolchandra Shastri, who himself had studied at three-four Jain Sanskrit vidyalayas including Shri Syadvad Mahavidyalaya before settling down in Varanasi. During my stay in Varanasi from 1962 to 1978, I had many occasions to meet and take Panditji's guidance and help.

This book is dedicated to the fond memories of Siddhantacharya Pt. Phoolchandra Shastri (1901-1991), the doyen of Jain Pandits, and my younger brother Dr. Hukum C. Jain (1949-2013), Associate Professor of Adult & Continuing Education, University of Sagar who before his untimely death had begun to take serious academic interest in Bundelkhand's Jain community.

New Delhi **Prakash C. Jain**

Contents

List of Tables

1
Introduction

The study sought to analyse the nature of demographic, economic and socio-cultural change among the Jains in North India, with special reference to the Bundelkhand region. The region presently hosts about 150,000 Jains who mostly belong to conservative variant of Digambar Jainism called Terapanth. More specifically, the study attempts to focus on the demographic dynamics, educational and occupational changes, changes in structure and functioning of family and marriage and social stratification, and changes in the Jain way of life and values in the Jain community of Bundelkhand over a couple of generations.

Bundelkhand Region

Bundelkhand region, geographically located in central India, is spread over some part of Madhya Pradesh and some part of Uttar Pradesh. It lies between the Indo-Gangetic plain to the north and the Vindhya mountain range in the south. The general slop of the country is towards the northeast as indicated by the course of the major rivers which include Kali Sindh, Betwa, Ken, Tons, Pahuj, Dhasan and Chambal.

Bundelkhand gets its name from Bundela Rajputs who ruled the region from the early 16th century until 1950. Prior to that, from 10th to 15th century, Chandel Rajputs were the predominant rulers of the area. During the Chandel period, Bundelkhand was home to a flourishing Jain community. It was also during this period that the famous temple city of Khajuraho was built between the mid-10th and mid-11th centuries.

Bundeli dialect and its several sub-dialects constitute the spoken language of the region. Hinduism is the predominant religion of Bundelkhand. However, the presence of Jainism, especially Digambar Jainism has been historically significant in the area. A large number of Jain pilgrimage places are located in Bundelkhand. A large number of prominent Digambar Jain traditional scholars (*Pandits*) of the 20th century belong to this region.

Bundelkhand "officially" is comprised of thirteen districts—seven districts of the southern part of Uttar Pradesh and six districts of the northern part of Madhya Pradesh. These districts are Jhansi, Lalitpur, Jalaun, Hamirpur, Mahoba,

Banda, Chitrakoot in Uttar Pradesh and Datia, Tikamgarh, Chhatarpur, Panna, Sagar and Damoh in Madhya Pradesh. The Bundelkhand region covers an area of around 70,000 sq. km. with an estimated population of 18.2 million in 2011. Many people include a number of neighbouring districts of Morena, Bhind, Shivpuri, Guna, Ashok Nagar, Gwalior and Vidisha as part of the Bundelkhand region, but there is a larger consensus on only 13 districts being part of Bundelkhand. This definition is also generally used by the governments, media and civil society organisations when they refer to Bundelkhand. In any case, there is no doubt about the fact that the cultural influence of Bundelkhand extends up to the cities of Gwalior, Bhopal, Indore and Jabalpur. Thus, a distinction can be made between the "official" Bundelkhand and the "cultural" or greater Bundelkhand, the latter comprising 29 districts (*See* Map 2.4). In this study we would focus ourselves mostly on "official" Bundelkhand.

Bundelkhand is well known as an economically poor and backward region in India. Correspondingly, the Jain community of the region too appears to be sharing some of these characteristics, and therefore needs to be subjected to a sociological inquiry regarding its socio-economic status as well as the extent of socio-economic change and modernisation taking place in it. Before we outline the objectives of the study more precisely, a brief account of the Jain community in Bundelkhand as well as in India would be in order.

Jains in India and in Bundelkhand

The Jains are one of the oldest religious communities of India. Although the origin of Jainism is lost in antiquity, it was revived by Lord Mahavira during the sixth century B.C. Jainism as well as Buddhism belongs to the *Shraman* tradition, a tradition that is distinct from the Vedic tradition and is considered even older and indigenous (Folkert, 1993; Jaini, 1970; Jain, Ravindra K., 1999). As a social movement during Lord Mahavir's time Jainism was opposed to caste system, secondary status of women, dominance of the priestly class, ritual sacrifices, slavery and monarchical basis of polity (Jain, Prakash C., 2011).

At least since the late medieval period, the Jains have been a minority community in India (Sangave, 1980; Jain, Prakash C., 2011). Since the 1872 Census the Jains seldom constituted more than half a percent of the total population of India. The current population of Jains is estimated around 4.7 million (about 4.45 million in 2011 Census). About 300,000 Jains live in diaspora, mainly, in the U.S., the U. K., Kenya, Nepal and Canada (Jain, Prakash C., 2011: 86-112). The Jains in India are heavily concentrated in the western half of the country, particularly in Maharashtra, Rajasthan, Madhya Pradesh, Gujarat, Karnataka, Western Uttar Pradesh and Delhi. Close to 80 per cent of them live in urban areas. Other demographic features include very high level of literacy (95%), the lowest infant mortality rate and medium level of sex ratio (954 females per 1,000 males in 2011 Census compared to 903 for Sikhs,

939 for Hindus, 951 for Muslims, 1023 for Christians and 965 for Buddhists). In spite of the highest literacy rate among the Jain women, their work participation rate is the lowest compared to their counterparts in five other religious communities in India, namely Hindu, Muslim, Christian, Sikh and Buddhist.

Since 1981, the Jain population has been growing very slowly. The decadal growth rate during 1981-91 was only 4.42 per cent compared to 23.17 per cent for the previous decade. This only confirms the urban middle class character of the community. Although during the decade 1991-2001 the growth rate of the Jain population was 26.0 percent, this was mainly due to the fact that during the 1990s the Jains were exhorted by the ethnic media to return themselves as "Jains" and not as "Hindus". The decadal growth rate between 2001 and 2011 again came down to about 5.4 per cent (Jain, Prakash C., 2019: Chapter 7). Thus, the low fertility behavior continues to remain the characteristic feature of the contemporary Jain community (Census of India, 2001 (2005)); Jain, Prakash C., 2011: 48-85; *Times of India*, New Delhi, 26 August 2015). The Jains are relatively an affluent minority mainly engaged in trade, commerce and various professions (Jain, Prakash C., 2011; 2019; Mittal, 2006; Sangave, 1980).

Bundelkhand Jain community is largely made up of two of the three major Digambar Jain sub-sects, namely Terapanth and Taaranpanth. Terapanth sub-sect is the mainstream Digambar Jain tradition whose name was coined sometime during the early decades of the 17th century in contradistinction to the *Bisapanth* that supported the institution of *Bhattarak* and worship the idols of Tirthankars with flowers, sweetmeat, burning-incense, etc. (materials that are supposed to contain or kill micro life forms). The Terapanthis worship the same with dry fruits, husked rice, etc. Terapanth name is derived from the fact that its adherents are the followers of the naked ascetics who have to practise thirteen (*tera*) kinds of codes of conduct. Besides Terapanth, Taaranpanth is the other sub-sect of Digambar Jainism that inhabits the Bundelkhand region. Compared to Terapanthis, the followers of Taaranpanth are very small in number. Whereas the former are the murtipujaks (idol-worshippers), the Taaranpanthis are non-idolatrous sub-sect that emerged sometime in the 15th century A.D.

The total Jain population in Bundelkhand in 2001 was enumerated at about 142,351 that increased to 148,612 in 2011 census of India. Of this the followers of Terapanthi sub-sect constitute an overwhelming majority (about 94.0%), while Taaranpanthis constitute a very small minority (about 6.0%). The Jains represent about 0.8 per cent of the total population of the region. The economy of Bundelkhand is dominated by the Jains, both in wholesale and retail trading. An increasing number of them have also been joining modern occupations such as teaching, engineering, medicine, law, chartered accountancy, information technology, etc. (Jain, Prakash C. 2018b). The Jains also have the higher levels of literacy, urbanisation, income and religious orthodoxy. A vast majority of modern as well as traditional scholars of Jainology/Jain Studies belong to the Jain community of Bundelkhand since about the last quarter of the 19th century, though in recent decades an increasing number of them have been working outside the region (*See* Jain, Prakash C. 2018a; 2018b).

Research Problem

Social change is a universal phenomenon. Broadly speaking, it can be defined as significant alternations in systems of social interaction. These systems may range from friendship circle to family, neighbourhood, village community, economy and economic institutions or the whole society. The historical evolution of human societies has varyingly been traced by social scientists through a number of stages such as hunting-gathering, slavery, feudalism, capitalism, communism/socialism, etc. which are based on the dominant mode of production. Societies have also been classified in terms of traditional and modern/post-modern and developing and developed.

Ongoing process of social change and modernisation in India has been exerting considerable pressure on various aspects of the Jain community. It has affected the daily life of a large segment of the Jain community, particularly those who have been living in large towns and cities. There have been significant changes among the Jains in their daily routine, food habits, religious and life-cycle rituals, inter-personal relations, structure of the family and even that of the community. In most of these spheres one can notice a certain amount of dilution in the orthodox Jain way of life.

Increased individualism, competition and consumerism in the context of the growth of capitalism in India have disturbed the equilibrium of the traditional Jain way of life as indeed all other traditional ways of life. Increased incidences of economic crimes, corruption, dowry demands, feticide of girl children, use of alcohol and non-vegetarian food, and general disinterest in religion in the young generation have given rise to concerns in the Jain community leadership to arrest these trends.

How, why and to what extent these changes over two-three generations have affected the contemporary Jain community of Budelkhand is the main focus of this study. In order to do that, the data obtained through this study are compared to two sets of past/historical referents: (i) Autobiography "Meri Jeevan Gatha" (*My Life Saga*) of Ganesh Prasad Varni (1874-1961) which was written some time during the mid-1940s and first published in 1949. It details in narrative style the socio-economic and educational condition of the Bundelkhand Jain community of the late 19th and the second half of the 20th centuries; and (ii) author's lived experiences and observations as an adolescent and later on as a sociologist who was born and brought up in Saidpur village of Lalitpur district, and subsequently studied for matriculation examination at Shri Varni Jain Inter College, Lalitpur during 1960-62. Since then, although the author has been living outside the Bundelkhand region, scores of visits had been made during the past half a century to the various parts of the region in order to meet family members, relatives and friends, and attend marriage and death ceremonies, etc.

Ganesh Prasad Varni, born in a Hindu Vaishnav caste named Asati in Hansera village of district Lalitpur was greatly influenced by Jainism since his childhood. Subsequently he got converted into Jainism. He briefly taught at Madanpur, Agra, Jaipur, Indore and Baruasagar. In his early and mid-20s he again turned to studies of Sanskrit and Jainism at Jaipur and later on at Mathura. At the age of 30 he went to Benaras (Varanasi) for further studies where he was humiliated by a Brahmin scholar on the ground that Ganesh Prasad was a follower of Jainism, a religion that does not believe in the authority of Vedas and therefore is a *nastic* (non-believer). Subsequently, Ganesh Prasad was able to get another tutor for teaching him Indological subjects, particularly Grammar and Logic, but was determined to establish a Digambar Jain Sanskrit School and was eventually successful in his efforts. This was the beginning of the celebrated Shri Digambar Jain Syadvaad Sanskrit Mahavidyalaya at Varanasi in 1905 whose first student as well as the founder was Ganesh Prasad Varni himself.

The story behind the establishment of this college is quite interesting. As detailed in his autobiography (1949), with the first donation of one rupee from his friend towards the cause, Ganesh Prasad purchased 64 postcards and posted them the next day to a number of well-to-do and learned co-religionists with the request to help set up a Jain college at Varanasi. The responses were very encouraging and the pathshala got started with four students and as many teachers.

Ganesh Prasad's studies in Sanskrit and particularly in Jain Logic continued for over two decades, first at Banaras Hindu University and later at Calcutta (now Kolkata) and then again at Varanasi. The studies were interrupted by Bundelkhand calling and Ganesh Prasad returned to his native province of Bundelkhand where the Jain community was still educationally backward, and for which he wanted to do something.

Besides setting up Jain Sanskrit Vidyalayas at Varanasi and Sagar, Ganesh Prasad Varni and his two disciples Brahamachari Manoharlal Varni and Brahmachari Chidanand Varni were instrumental in getting established about three dozen Jain pathshalas, gurukuls, vidyalayas at different places in Bundelkhand. Many more schools and other educational institutions, both sacred and secular, were named after Ganesh Prasad Varni during and after his life time.

Ganesh Prasad Varni was not only a life-long learner, a student and a scholar, but also a social and educational reformer, an activist, a volunteer and a leader. As Ravindra K. Jain (1999: 74-75) put it: "If one goes by the mainly activist role of Varni in getting donations, establishing schools and boardings, learning and teaching the fundamentals of Jainism to lay Jains, participating in panchkalyanaka and panchayats, etc., he does not emerge as a leader but a volunteer. However, in the last phase of his autobiography there is a distinct impression of a *tyagi*-householder becoming a leader." On top of these he was also a *tyagi*, a spiritual seeker and practitioner of the Jain ethical principles. Because of all these qualities, he earned the honourific title of Varni—meaning a preacher of religion and morals. In Jain ascetics hierarchy he rose to become a *Kshullak* and died as a naked ascetic 108 Muni Ganesh Keerti at Isri (near the foothills of Sammed Shikharjee, the most revered pilgrimage place for Digambar Jains). Ganesh Prasad Varni travelled far and wide in north India and especially in the Bundelkhand region that he knew very intimately. The Bundelkhand Jain *Samaj* revered him like a saint. Not surprisingly, he is considered "the Mahatma Gandhi of the Jain community of Bundelkhand".

In Ganesh Prasad Varni's autobiographical account, the Jain community of Bundelkhand figures predominantly as a community of wholesale as well as retail traders of provision goods, hardware and jewelry items, grains and cloth merchants, money-lenders, etc. There is conspicuous absence of a service class, except an occasional reference to a teacher or a *lekhpal* (land record keeper). There is also no mention of Jains as cultivators. The top of the economic hierarchy was occupied by wealthy merchants locally known as Seths. Some of them who figure prominently in the autobiography are: Sir Seth Hulum Chand Kashliwal of Indore, brothers-trio Seth Braj Lal, Seth Chandra Bhan and Seth Laxmi Chand Jain of Bamrana/Sadhumar, Shrimant Seth Bhag Chandra Shobha Lal Jain of Sagar, Singhai Kundan Lal Jain of Sagar, Shrimant Seth Mohan Lal of Khurai, and Seth Mathuradas and Seth Parmeshthi Das Tadaiya of Lalitpur, and Sahu Shanti Prasad Jain of Dalmianagar and Calcutta.

Varni was greatly attracted by the religiosity of the Jains of Bundelkhand who mostly belong to Terapanthi sub-sect. Commenting on the daily routine and religious activities of the Jains of Bundelkhand, he (1949: 10-11) writes: "Why am I not born to a Jain family? Where drinking strained water, giving up night food, not eating food prepared by person of other religion, continuous praying and doing worship of Jinendradev by singing, doing self-study, organising *Shastra sabhas* in which men and women of neighbourhood get assembled, preaching of vratas and other codes of conduct, etc. are regarded as religious activities." Varni was greatly influenced by Jainism, and subsequently he got converted into it. Later on, he even requested his mother and wife to get converted to Jainism.

Varni, however, was not equally appreciative of wasteful and rituals-oriented religiosity of those well-to-do Jains who organized *panchkalyanaka* (ceremony that involves celebration of five auspicious events in the life of Tirthankars) and *vedi-pratishtha* (idol installation ceremony), and indulged in construction of new temples, etc. as he thought that the money spent on such activities could have been better utilised for educational purposes. Time and again he laments the fact that the Jains of Bundelkhand would spend thousands of rupees on *panchkalyanaka* etc. but would not like to give even five rupees for an educational cause. Pilgrimage often figured as a major religious activity which was performed in small groups either on foot or by trains. Jain dharamshalas invariably served as boarding and lodging places. It is interesting to note that there is hardly any mention of *Munis* (naked ascetics) in the autobiography which only suggests that following the revival of the institution of naked asceticism in early 20th century by Shantisagarji Maharaj (1871-1955) after a gap of about a millennium there were not enough of them available for circulation in the Bundelkhand region at that time. In the past few decades the situation has completely changed in this regard, and today scores of Digambar Jain *munis* are not only staying in cities and towns of Bundelkhand during the rainy season, but otherwise are also available almost year-round.

Thus, Ganesh Prasad Varni's autobiography about his life and work in Bundelkhand during the first half of the 20th century provides not only a reference-point but also a perfect backdrop against which socio-economic changes in the contemporary Jain community of the region can be compared and contrasted.

Survey of the Literature

There is considerable amount of literature on the Jain religion and philosophy. The social anthropological and sociological studies of the Jain community, however, continue to remain scarce. Sociological studies of Jainism begins with the German sociologist Max Weber's book *Religion of India* (1958) which contained a chapter on Jainism and Buddhism titled "Heterodox Soteriology of the Cultured Professional Monks". This small piece provides significant sociological insight into the structure and functioning of the Jain community and religion. However, his work remained virtually unknown to the world until its translation into English in 1920s. Meanwhile, in the late 1950s an Indian sociologist V.A. Sangave had published a major work on the Jains which was mainly based on scriptural material and a preliminary social survey. Surprisingly, Weber does not figure in this work.

After Sangave's work, no major sociological/anthropological work on the Jains was done for over a decade until 1971 when Balwant Nevaskar published his book on a comparative study of the Jains and the Quakers using some of the propositions of the Weberian Protestant Ethic thesis. During the late 1980s, the Anthropological Survey of India's People of India Project did collect some descriptive data on about one hundred "Jain Communities" (sic) across India but they are sketchy and repetitive (Singh, 1998). About the same time, a group of scholars at Oxford and Cambridge and other western universities began to publish research papers and books based on their fieldwork in India, particularly in Gujarat and Rajasthan (Babb, 1998; Banks, 1992; Carrithers, 1989; Carrithers and Humphrey, 1991; Cort, 1991; 2001; Dundas, 1992; Folkert, 1993; Humphrey and Laidlaw, 1994; Laidlaw, 1995). A cursory look at the literature reviewed above, which was published since the late 1980s suggests that much of it is concerned with the Jain religious themes such as renunciation, worship, rituals and role of the mendicants in the community. These developments have inspired some Indian scholars (Jain, Ravindra K., 1999; Jain, Prakash C., 2011; 2019; Jain, Shugan and Jain, Prakash C., 2013; Jain, Shalin 2017; Sethi, 2011; Mittal, 2006; Singhi, 1987; 1991) to undertake social scientific studies of the Jain community.

Some work on the Jain community from social sciences perspectives has also been done by some other Jain scholars which is written in Hindi language (e.g., Jain, Deepak, 2001; Jain, Kapoor Chand and Jain, Jyoti, 2006; Jain, Mahendra Kumar, 1986; Jain, Shital Chand and Phool Chand Jain Premi, 2012; Jain, Surendra Kumar, 1996; Shastri, Siddhantacharya Pt. Phoolchandra, 1992). As mentioned above the autobiography of Kshullak Ganesh Prasad Varni (1949) is the only major and comprehensive work describing quite a number of aspects of the Bundelkhand Jain community of the first half of the 20th century. Nevertheless, it can fairly be stated that no systematic study of socio-cultural change amongst the Jains has so far been undertaken. This study was aimed to partially rectify this situation.

Objectives of the Study

1. To investigate the nature of socio-demographic transition of the Jains in north India.
2. To study the changing occupational structure of the Jain community.
3. To analyse trends of inter-generational occupational mobility and future aspirations.
4. To examine the emergent status of women in the community, particularly in terms of education and occupational status, work participation rate and religiosity.
5. To highlight the salient features of social organisation among the Jains, including caste system, marriage patterns and the family structure.
6. To assess the overall impact of urbanisation and modernisation on the Jain community.

Rationale of the Study

1. There are very few anthropological/sociological studies on the Jain community, least of all on demographic, economic and socio-cultural changes. Moreover, most of the studies have been done on Shvetambar Jains living in urban areas of Gujarat and Rajasthan only (Banks, 1992; Cort, 2001; Humphrey, 1991; Laidlaw, 1995). Focusing on the Jains in Bundelkhand area would therefore counter-balance these trends. In other words, this is perhaps for the first time that a systematic study of socio-cultural change among the Digambar Jains living in rural as well as urban areas in India has been conducted.

2. As already mentioned, Bundelkhand is one of the most under-developed regions in India. The Jains are widely spread in the area as a trading community. Their class status and class relationship with the masses of peasantry and workers would help us understand the socio-economic dynamics in the region which has been suffering from poverty, illiteracy, corruption, bad governance and social injustice.

Conceptual Framework

Any sociological study of the Jains, or for that matter, any other minority community in India cannot be done in isolation. Socio-economic development, changes in value system, social structural changes, demographic changes, community's role in politics—all or any of these aspects can be studied only in the wider context of the Indian society, particularly in its regional-linguistic context. At the same time, the historical perspective should also not be ignored.

Sociology is a multi-paradigmatic social science, and as such a number of theories are available to analyse various social phenomena pertaining to the Jain community. However, I propose to use a political economy framework based on neo-Marxism. This choice is obviously personal in terms of my training as well as the efficacy of the proposed conceptual framework. Within this framework, the Jain community can be conceptualised not as a trading community (as in my opinion this is only a descriptive term), but as a segment of the trading and commercial petty bourgeoisie whose class interest and class behavior easily explain their relative prosperity. A very high degree of individualism, the Protestant ethic like elements present in Jainism, high level of urbanisation and literacy, and progressive occupational specialisation over the centuries—all have tended to add to the prosperity and relative modernisation of the Jains (Jain, 2011; Nebaskar, 1970; Weber, 1958). This prosperity is also reflected in the fertility rate of the Jains, whereby the birth rate has registered a sharp decline since the mid-1980s (*See* Jain, Prakash C., 2019).

Hypotheses

The following hypotheses were proposed to be tested in this study:

1. Jains have been undergoing the demographic transition with sharply declining death as well as birth rate vis-à-vis other religious communities in India, mainly due to their relative economic affluence and the middle class character.
2. Jains continue to be mainly a trading community in Bundelkhand with an increasing number of them taking up modern professional careers such as teaching, engineering, medicine, law, computer sciences, information technology, etc.

3. In spite of high literacy and education, lower than national average work participation rate among the Jain women can be attributed to their economic affluence.
4. Jain women in Bundelkhand display a very high degree of religiosity in terms of daily temple visit, observing dietary rules, reciting or listening to scriptures, and observing various religious rituals.
5. The overall impact of urbanisation and modernisation among the Jains can be summed up by concepts like relative affluence and consumer culture that clearly contradict some of the fundamentals of Jainism, particularly *aparigraha* (non-possession), thus creating the "Jain paradox" of ostentation and renunciation.

Locale of the Study

The locale of the study are the four core districts of Bundelkhand, namely Lalitpur, Jhansi, Sagar and Tikamgarh. Whereas the first two districts are located in Uttar Pradesh, the latter two are in Madhya Pradesh. The data were collected from both urban and rural areas. The urban areas consisted of all the four district towns. Two Tehsil level towns Mahroni and Madawra and three villages Saidpur, Sadumal and Birdha—all located in Lalitpur district constituted rural areas for our purpose. These field work sites are briefly discussed below.

Lalitpur: The district occupies an area of 5,039 km^2. Lalitpur District is a part of Jhansi Division and was carved out as a district in the year 1974. Lalitpur is divided into four tehsils, Lalitpur, Mahroni, Pali and Madawra. The population of Lalitpur in 2011 was enumerated at 1,218,882. The district has a population density of 242 inhabitants per square kilometre (630/sq mile). Its population growth rate over the decade 2001-2011 was 24.57 per cent. Lalitpur has a sex ratio of 905 females for every 1000 males and a literacy rate of 64.95 per cent.

The district forms a portion of the hill country of Bundelkhand, sloping down from the outliers of the Vindhya Range on the south to the tributaries of the Yamuna River on the north. The Betwa River forms the northern and western boundary of the district, and most of the district lies within its watershed. The Jamni River, a tributary of the Betwa, forms the eastern boundary. The Dhasan River forms the district's southeastern boundary, and the south-eastern portion of the district lies within its watershed.

The territory of the present-day Lalitpur district was part of the state of Chanderi, founded in the 17th century by a Bundela Rajput who descended from Raja Rudra Pratap of Orchha. Chanderi, along with most of Bundelkhand, came under Maratha hegemony in the 18th century. Daulat Rao Sindhia of neighbouring Gwalior annexed Chanderi state in 1812. In 1844, the former state of Chanderi was ceded to the British, and became the Chanderi District of

British India, with Lalitpur town as the district headquarters. The British lost the district in the Indian Rebellion of 1857, and it was not reconquered until late 1858. In 1861, the portion of the district west of the Betwa, including Chanderi, was returned to Gwalior state, and the remainder was renamed Lalitpur district. It remained a part of Jhansi district from 1891 to 1974. In 1974, the district was carved out from Jhansi district. There are two Uttar Pradesh Vidhan Sabha constituencies in this district: Lalitpur and Mahroni. Both of these are part of Jhansi Lok Sabha constituency. In 2006, the Ministry of Panchayati Raj, Government of India named Lalitpur one of the country's 250 most backward districts (out of a total of 640). It is one of the 34 districts in Uttar Pradesh currently receiving funds from the Backward Regions Grant Fund Programme.

Lalitpur is a major centre of trade and commercial activities of Bundelkhand. As it has a vast hinterland consisting of a large number of villages, it has developed a well-functioning credit system which has been a part of local folklore as expressed in the following saying: *Jhansi gale ki fansi, Datia Gale ka haar; Lalitpur na chhodiye, Jab tak mile udhar* (Jhansi is a snooze of neck, Datia is a garland of neck; Don't leave Lalitpur so long as things are available on credit). Though people differ on the origin and exact meaning of the saying about Jhansi and Datia, at least its meaning of the Lalitpur part is quite clear.

Jhansi: The city of Jhansi is the district headquarters. Lalitpur District, which extends into the hill country to the south, was added to Jhansi District in 1891, and made a separate district again in 1974. In 1861 the city of Jhansi and a dependent territory was ceded to Gwalior State and the capital of the district was moved to Jhansi Naoabad (Jhansi Refounded), a village without "cantonment" (military camp). Jhansi (the old city) became the capital of a "subah" (provínce) within the state of Gwalior, but in 1886 was returned to British rule as a district of the United Provinces of Agra and Oudh in exchange for the Gwalior Fort and the cantonment of Morar nearby.It had been given to the Maharaja of Gwalior, but came under British rule in 1886 as the result of a territorial swap. The population of Jhansi in 1901 was about 55,000 while Jhansi district's population had been about 407,000 in 1891. The main city in Jhansi district is Jhansi. Mauranipur, Garautha, Moth, Babina, Chirgaon, Samthar, Gursarai, Erich, are the other major towns in the district.

According to the 2011 census Jhansi district had a population of 1,998,603. This gives it a ranking of 231st in India (out of a total of 640). The district has a population density of 398 inhabitants per square kilometre (1,030/sq mile). Population growth rate over the decade 2001-2011 was 14.54 per cent. Jhansi has a sex ratio of 890 females for every 1000 males, and a literacy rate of 75.05 per cent.

Sagar: The Sagar district has an area of 10,252 km^2, and a population of 2,021,783 (2001 census), a 23 per cent increase from its 1991 population of 1,646,198. Sagar district is dominated by Sonis, Jains and Yadavs. According to the 2011 census, Sagar District had a population of 2,378,295· The district has a population density of 232 inhabitants per square kilometre (600/sq mile). Its population growth rate over the decade 2001-2011 was 17.62 per cent. Sagar has a sex ratio of 896 females for every 1,000 males, and a literacy rate of 77.52 per cent. As of 2011, it is the third most populous district of Madhya Pradesh (out of 50), after Indore and Jabalpur.

Tikamgarh: Tikamgarh district is part of Sagar Division. The district has an area of 5,048 km^2. The original name of Tikamgarh was Tihri. In 1783, the ruler of Orchha Vikramajit (1776–1817) shifted his capital from Orchha to Tihri and renamed it Tikamgarh (Tikam is one of the names of Krishna).

The area covered by this district was part of the Princely State of Orchha till its merger with the Indian Union. The Orchha state was founded by Raja Rudra Pratap in 1501. After merger, it became one of the eight districts of Vindhya Pradesh state in 1948. Following the reorganisation of states on 1 November 1956 it became a district of Madhya Pradesh. In 1901, the state had an area of about 2,000 sq miles (5,200 km^2), and population of 52,634. Vir Singh, Maharajah of Tikamgarh, merged his state with the Union of India on 1 January 1950. The district became a part of Vindhya Pradesh state, which was merged into Madhya Pradesh state in 1956. Today Orchha is reduced to a small town and its importance is maintained only due to its rich architectural heritage and tourism.

According to the 2011 census, Tikamgarh District had a population of 1,444,920. The district has a population density of 286 inhabitants per square kilometre (740/sq mile). Its population growth rate over the decade 2001-2011 was 20.11 per cent. Tikamgarh has a sex ratio of 901 females for every 1,000 males, and a literacy rate of 62.57 per cent. In 2006, the Ministry of Panchayati Raj had named Tikamgarh one of the country's 250 most backward districts (out of a total of 640). It is one of the 24 districts in Madhya Pradesh receiving funds from the Backward Regions Grant Fund Programme.

Since 26 April 2013 Tikamgarh has been connected by railways to Lalitpur under the Lalitpur-Singrauli Rail Project. The first train to travel between the two stations was Tikamgarh-Jhansi passenger train. The railway line between Tikamgarh and Lalitpur rail route is 40 kilometre long. The then Union Minister of State Pradeep Jain Aditya had flagged off the train at Lalitpur station.

Mahroni: It is a tehsil (sub-district) town in Lalitpur district with a population of about 10,000. There are about 350 Jain families consisting of about 2,000 persons. It has five Jain temples.

Madawra: It is also a small town in Lalitpur district which has recently been made a tehsil (sub-district). Madawara's population is also about 10,000. There are 13 Jain temples in the town serving about 2,000 members of the Jain community. The town serves a vast rural hinterland.

Saidpur: It is a large village of 1,200 families and 6,972 population as per 2011 census data. Sex ratio was 968. Literacy 67.67 per cent (Male: 80.31%, Female 54.45%). Number of Jain families: 27.

Sadumal: Population: 5,289; Number of families 967; Sex ratio: 927; Literacy: 69.72 (Male 84.06 per cent, Female 54.18 per cent); Number of Jain families: 37.

Birdha: A large village with a population of 6,137, Birdha is situated in the close proximity of Lalitpur. Sex ratio: 928; Literacy: 70.88 per cent (Male 85.30%, Female 55.34%); Number of Jain families: 20.

Research Methodology

A research problem like the one here required an intensive empirical fieldwork. As such, a carefully constructed Questionnaire was used for data collection. In order to have a comparative perspective on the theme a two-tier fieldwork was done at the levels of villages, small towns and cities. The size of the sample, names of the fieldwork sites and details about author's familiarity with the sites are given in Table 1.1.

Table 1.1: Details of Fieldwork Sites, Sample Size, etc.

Types of the field-work sites	*Names of the fieldwork sites*	*Sample size (House-holds)*	*Author's familiarity with the fieldwork sites*
Rural	Mahroni, Madawra, Saidpur, Sadumal, and Birdha—all located in Lalitpur district of U. P.	70 (about 31%)	Born and brought up at Saidpur village; considerable familiarity with other villages and towns
Urban	Lalitpur (U.P.), Jhansi (U.P.), Sagar (M.P.), and Tikamgarh (M.P.)	110 (about 69%)	Did High schooling in Lalitpur during 1960-62, and frequent visits to Lalitpur, Jhansi, Tikam-garh and Sagar since then.

This study was designed as an exploratory study as very little sociological/anthropological work has been done on the Jain community in India. This is perhaps the first sociological study of the community in the Bundelkhand region. Besides questionnaire, other ethnographic techniques such as observation, interview and oral history were also used for data collection. Even while administering the questionnaire a certain amount of flexibility, even at the cost of methodological rigour, was proposed to be observed so that important information about socio-economic change among the Jains was not left out.

Four fieldwork visits were made during 2014. The first two visits were particularly made in order to have an overall impression of the Jain community in the Bundelkhand region, and also for developing contacts with key informants in both rural and urban areas. In next two visits the Questionnaires were administered, and data were collected. The fieldwork was carried out in the months of February and March 2014 as per the following schedule:

1. During the first week of February 2014 data were collected from respondents in the Sagar city.
2. During the first and second week of March 2014 data were collected from Lalitpur, Tikamgarh and Jhansi cities, and the towns and villages of Mahroni, Madawra, Sadumal, Saidpur and Birdha of Lalitpur district.

Of the 210 questionnaires distributed, only 180 were found to be complete in all respects. Secondary source material such as ethnic newspaper clippings, biographical and autobiographical material, *abhinandangranths,* relevant brochures, etc. had also been collected. The data thus collected have been processed and tabulated.

Concluding Remarks

It is hoped that the study would fill a major gap in our understanding of the socio-cultural and economic changes in the Jain community of the Bundelkhand region as no anthropological/sociological work on the subject has so far been done.

2

Bundelkhand and Its Jain Community

This chapter highlights the salient features of Bundelkhand region and its Jain community. The regional profile of Bundelkhand is presented in terms of location in central India, geographical features, climate, population and demographic characteristics, religious and caste composition, economy and politics, etc. A brief historical account of Bundelkhand would also be presented. The Jain community of the region is profiled in terms of its demographics, educational and economic profiles, political contribution, social organisational features and religiosity and the Jain way of life.

Bundelkhand Region

Located in central part of India and comprising of six districts of Uttar Pradesh and seven districts of Madhya Pradesh, Bundelkhand region derives its name from two sources: (i) the indigenous Bundela scion of Rajput families who ruled the region since about the beginning of the 16th century until a year before India's independence, and (ii) Bundeli language/dialect which is spoken in the region and is of western Hindi variety (*See* Jain, Ravindra K., 2002). Perhaps more credible and historically logical explanation appears to be as follows: after the Vindhyagiri Mountains range the region was known as Vindhyelkhand that got corrupted to Bundelkhand, and its rulers came to be known as Bundelas. Similarly, the local language got corrupted from Vindheli to Bundeli or Bundelkhandi (*See* Shastri, Kamal Kumar, 1967: 17).

The region's central location in India and that of its 13 districts is presented in the following maps 2.1 to 2.4. The Bundelkhand region within these boundaries had an area of 70,000 sq. km., and an enumerated population of 15.5 million as per 2001 census, and 18.6 million in 2011. The current population is in the vicinity of 20.0 million.

History of Bundelkhand: Medieval and Modern Periods

History of Bundelkhand can be traced back to the Mahabharat period when the region was ruled by Chedi kings, and it was known as Chedi desh. However,

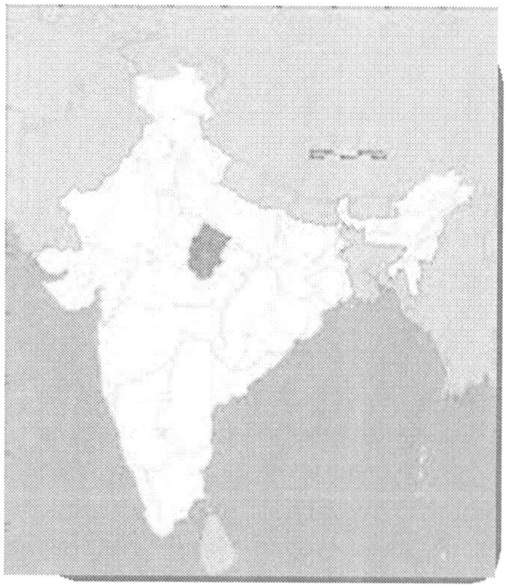

Maps 2.1 and 2.2: Location of Bundelkhand in India

here we shall confine our discussion to medieval and modern periods only. The Chandela Rajput clan ruled Bundelkhand from the 10th to the 16th centuries. In the early 10th century they were feudatories of the Pratiharas of Kannauj, and ruled from the fortress-city of Kalinjar. The Chandelas captured the strategic fortress of Gwalior c. 950. King Dhanga (c. 950–1008 A.D.) left many inscriptions, and endowed a large number of Jain and Hindu temples. Dhanga's grandson Vidyadhara (1017–29 A.D.) expanded the Chandela kingdom. The famous temple-city of Khajuraho was built by the Chandellas between the

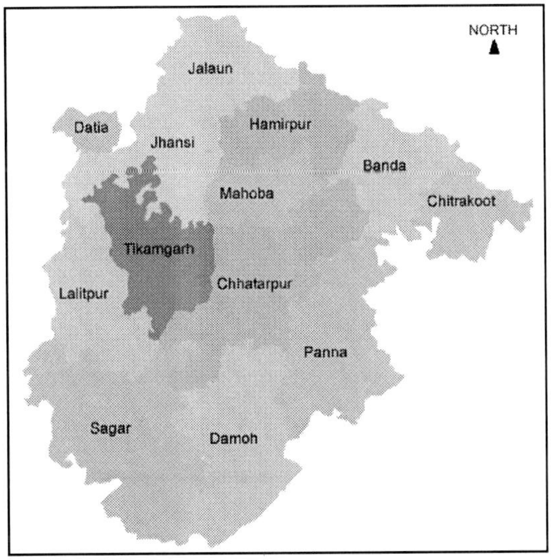

Map 2.3: Districts of Bundelkhand (Courtesy: www.bundelkhand.in).

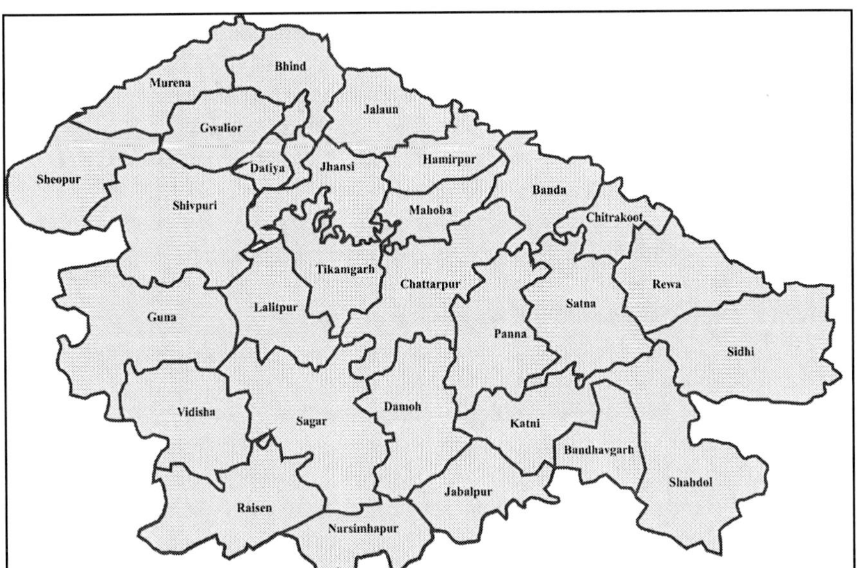

Map 2.4: "Greater", "Cultural" and/or Proposed Bundelkhand State

mid-10th and mid-11th centuries. During the Chandela period, Bundelkhand was home to a flourishing Jain community and numerous Jain temples were built in that period.

In the 12th century, the Chandellas were challenged by the Rajput Chauhan rulers of Ajmer challenged the Chandelas, and in the 13th century by the Muslim rulers, but they survived until the 16th century as minor chieftains. Bundela Rajputs grew to prominence starting in the 16th century. Orchha was founded in the 16th century by the Bundeli chief Rudra Pratap, who became the first Raja of Orchha. In 1545 Sher Shah Suri also failed to capture Kalinjar from the local Bundeli kings.

In spite of the nominal Mughal rule in the region from the 16th to 18th centuries, in 1671 Bundela chief Chhatrasal, with the help of Marathas, conquered the whole of Bundelkhand. On his death in 1732 he bequathed one-third of his dominions, including Jalaun and Jhansi, to his Maratha allies, who before long succeeded in controlling the whole of Bundelkhand, with the local rulers as tributaries to the Marathas.

The Marathas ceded parts of Bundelkhand to the British in the 1802 Treaty of Bassein. In 1818 the Peshwa in Pune ceded all his rights over Bundelkhand to the British at the conclusion of the Third Anglo-Maratha War. In 1853 the Raja of Jhansi died childless, and his territory was annexed to British Bundelkhand. Rani Lakshmi Bai, the widow of the Raja of Jhansi, protested the annexation because she was not allowed to adopt an heir, and because the slaughter of cattle was permitted in the Jhansi territory. Because of these reasons Jhansi joined the first war of Indian independence in 1857. A few men of the 12th native infantry seized the fort, and massacred the European officers of the garrison. Led by the Rani, the rebels captured several of the neighbouring British districts and princely states allied to the British. She died bravely in battle in Gwalior in 1858, and Jhansi was brought under British control.

After Indian independence in 1947, the princely states of Bundelkhand Agency were combined with those of the former Bagelkhand Agency to form the province of Vindhya Pradesh, which became an Indian state in 1950. On 1 November 1956, Vindhya Pradesh was merged into Madhya Pradesh. Similarly, the former United Provinces of Agra and Oudh were named Uttar Pradesh, and thus the Budelkhand region got divided into these two states.

Since the early 1960s, a political movement has been there to establish a separate state of Bundelkhand. In 2011, while the Bahujan Samaj Party government in Uttar Pradesh under Ms. Mayawati had proposed the creation of a separate Bundelkhand state from seven districts of the State, organisations such as Bundelkhand Mukti Morcha (BMM) wanted it to include six districts from Madhya Pradesh as well. Union Minister Uma Bharati of Bharatiya Janata Party during campaign for Lok Sabha elections of 2014 at Jhansi had promised to create a separate state of Bundelkhand within three years if her party was voted to power. A similar promise was made by Congress leader Pradeep Jain "Aditya" during the same election campaign. Nothing of this sort has happened so far. In spite of being rich in mineral resources, the region continues to be under-developed and under-represented in state and union level politics. The national as well as the local parties and organisations also continue to debate the issue—some promoting further development of the region and some seeking separate statehood.

Demographic Profile

Bundelkhand region is one of the most backward regions in India. It is sparsely populated. The total population of Bundelkhand was estimated at 18.3 million in 2011 census. During the earlier decades of the 20th century the population growth rate was quite low. However, in recent decades Bundelkhand has witnessed high population growth. The history of population growth of the region during the last 110 years has followed a multivariate course; besides the interplay of birth and death, in-migration and out-migration also contribute considerably to the population growth. The first phase (1901-1921) is that of progressive decline causing a very slow population growth—population decrease was mainly due to the influenza epidemic of 1918-19. The second phase (1921-1951) was a period of moderate population growth due to the great economic depression, two world Wars, national political movements and disturbances (Sub-continent's partition) together with some natural disasters. The third phase (1951-1981) is marked by a rapid population growth mainly due to the decline in the death rate. During the period 1901-1981, the total population of the Bundelkhand region increased from 3.45 million to 8.03 million—a net increase of 132.58 per cent. However, this change is not high when compared to the national average of 176.11 per cent (*See* Singh and Chaturvedi 1984: 53-65). The total population of the region in 1981 (8,037,206 persons) reached to 8,874,000 persons in 1991, and 15.5 million persons in 2001. In 2011 the total population of the region was enumerated at 18.3 million, out of which approximately 14 million of the population lived in rural areas. The distribution of the total population and some other demographic characteristics such as gender distribution and male and female literacy rates by districts is given in Table 2.1.

By Indian standards, the region is marked by low population density. As per the Census 2001 figures, the population density of UP Bundelkhand as a whole works out to 280 persons per sq km—less than a third of the state average. There is a clear variation in intra-regional distribution of population. There is higher population density in the Bundelkhand Plain areas (particularly in Jalaun and Banda), and Bundelkhand Intermediate region areas (particularly in Jhansi and Tikamgarh), and lower population density in Bundelkhand Upland (particularly in Panna and Chhatarpur) and the southern Damoh and Sagar plateaus.

Table 2.1: Population and Other Demographic Characteristics of Bundelkhand, 2011

	District	Total Population	Male Population	Female Population	Population Growth	Average Literacy	Male Literacy	Female literacy
1	Jhansi	2,000,755	1,061,310	939,445	14.66%	76.37	86.58	64.88
2	Hamirpur	1,104,021	593,576	510,445	5.78%	70.16	81.27	57.19
3	Mahoba	876,055	465,937	410,118	23.66%	66.94	77.72	54.65
4	Jalaun	1,670,718	895,804	774,914	14.87%	75.16	84.89	63.88
5	lalitpur	1,218,002	639,392	578,610	24.57%	64.95	76.41	52.26
6	Banda	1,799,541	966,123	833,418	17.06%	68.11	79.38	54.95
7	Chitrakoot	990,626	527,101	463,525	29.29%	66.52	77.42	54.03
8	Datia	786,375	419,432	366,943	18.40%	73.5	85.18	60.21
9	Tikamgarh	1,444,920	759,891	685,029	20.11%	62.57	73.3	50.71
10	Chhatarpur	1,762,857	935,906	826,951	19.54%	64.9	74.22	54.34
11	Sagar	2,378,295	1,254,251	1,124,044	17.62%	77.52	86.27	67.71
12	Panna	1,016,028	532,866	483,162	18.62%	66.08	75.63	55.55
13	Damoh	1,263,703	660,478	603,225	16.58%	70.92	80.96	59.9
	Total	18,311,896	9,712,067	8,599,829				

Courtesy: Ministry of Rural Development, Governmentof India.

Economy of Bundelkhand

1. Agriculture

In spite of only about half of the total land available for agricultural purpose, and vagaries of monsoon in Bundelkhand, agriculture continues to remain the predominant occupation in the region. Additionally, agricultural productivity is low mainly due to the unavailability of water and the lack of irrigation facilities. Until the1970s, only about 15 per cent of the cultivable land was irrigated in Bundelkhand. By 1980s, the irrigated area had more than doubled in Jhansi, Jalaun, Chhatarpur and Tikamgarh districts, trebled in Lalitpur district, and had increased by over five times in Panna, Damoh and Sagar districts (Tyagi, 1997: 167). Bundelkhand is predominantly a cereals, pulses and millets growing region, though for the past few decades there has been a huge drop in the cultivation of millets, particularly of jowar, bajra and barley. Both the UP and MP governments have been trying to promote the cultivation of jatropha to produce bio-diesel on a large scale in the region.

Notorious dacoits like Devi Singh, Malkhan Singh, Pooran Singh alias Puja Babba, Moorath Singh, Phoolan Devi and a number of other robber and kidnapper gangs ruled the area during the past half-a-century or so. Currently the area is economically and industrially one of the most backward areas in India (*See* NITI Ayog, 2018). Lack of resources, poor communications, and infertile land are some of the reasons for underdevelopment in the region. About 80 per cent farmers of the region have been in debt to banks and private financiers. Not surprisingly, some 3,280 farmers in Bundelkhand had committed suicide during April 2003 and March 2015.

2. Industry, Manufacturing and Service Sectors

Small-scale indigenous industries that existed in the region were destroyed by the British colonial rule after 1857. Subsequently there was no significant industrial development in the region. By the end of the 20th century there were only two large manufacturing units in the region: (i) Bharat Heavy Electricals Ltd., a public sector undertaking located near Jhansi since 1970s, and (ii) a cement plant of Birla Group set up in Damoh in the 1980s. Besides these two there are also a few medium-size industrial units in the region (*See* Table 2.2).

The largest non-agricultural employment is provided by Beedi industry in Sagar district, railways in Jhansi, and stone quarries in Lalitpur, Panna and Chitrakoot districts. Handloom works and tailoring are significant employers in Jhansi and some other districts of the region. Presently tourism sector is under-developed and is confined to spots in and around Jhansi, Orchha, Khajuraho, Chanderi, Chitrakoot and Devgarh. The Jain pilgrimage circuit with at least three dozens of Jain teerthkshetras in the Bundelkhand region has the greater potential to develop.

Table 2.2: Large and Medium Industrial Units in Bundelkhand

District	*Industries (Product/Process)*
Jhansi	Bharat Heavy Electricals (rail engines, transformers)
Sagar	Madhya Pradesh Agro Products (Super phosphate fertilizer), Central India Paper & Board Mills (straw boards), Arvind Foods (solvent extraction), Sanmati Forest Industries (Kattha), Sagar Soya Products (soyabean oil)
Datia	Gwalior Synthetics (cotton yarn, art silk), Agro Solvent products (solvent extraction), Kishori Pujari Granite (granite cutting)
Tikamgarh	K.P. Solvex (solvex extraction)
Damoh	Abhishek Cement (Portland cement), Diamond cements (cement, clinker), Shobha Soya (soyabean oil)
Panna	MP Carbide and Chemicals (calcium carbide), National Mineral Development Corporation (diamond mining)

Industrial development in Bundelkhand is also lacking due to the unavailability of skilled labour force, lack of infrastructural and locational disadvantage.

Migration

During the past few decades Bundelkhandhas emerged as a major migrating region. Much of this migration has been taking place in rural areas where employment opportunities in sectors other than agriculture are lacking. According to 2002 BPL Survey data, 50 per cent to 70 per cent of rural household across the region had at least one member who migrated annually for casual or seasonal employment, or migrated permanently or semi-permanently. The major determinant in such kind of migration is the size of the land-holdings. Studies suggest that compared to landless households, small and medium farmers have greater propensity to migrate. In terms of social groups, members of ST and SC migrate more than people from other categories. The major destinations of these migrants are towns and cities outside Bundelkhand such as Gwalior, Indore, Jabalpur, Bhopal and Delhi and the National Capital Region. A majority of outstanding Bundelkhand students, irrespective of caste/class background who receive higher education outside the region often tend to get employment there itself, thus depriving the region of top class talent. This is true not only about modern professions such as engineering and medicine, etc. but also true about traditional scholars including Jain pandits.

Castes in Bundelkhand

As in other parts of India, Bundelkhand region too has a large number of castes. In this region, the top of the varna/caste ritual hierarchy is dominated by Brahmins. These Brahmins belong to two main groups known as Jujhotias and Kanyakubjas—both of them claiming to have come from the ancient city of Kannauj, near Kanpur. Groups/castes claiming Rajput and Kshatriya lineage are ranked below the Brahmins. These include Bundela, Panwar, Chauhan, and Dhundhera. In Bundelkhand they are often referred to as "Thakurs", or "Thakras" (*See* Jain, Ravindra K., 2002). Thakurs are the biggest landlords of Bundelkhand, and own up to 30 per cent of the land followed by Brahmins who own between15 per cent to 20 per cent. The third in the varna/caste hierarchy are Vaishyas such as Agrawals, Asatis, Gahois, Guptas, etc. and Jain banias. Their traditional occupation being trading and money-lending, they did not own much land, but with increased agricultural distress over a period of time some money-lenders have come to acquire large landholdings in different parts of the countryside. Kayasthas (scribes) also belong to this category who were the first to get associated with land record-keeping and administration during the British period, and now are mostly in numerous professions such as teaching, law, engineering, medicine, administration, etc. Some of them in rural areas also own land.

All these caste groups are classified in official parlance as "General" category, and constitute about 15 per cent of the total population of Bundelkhand. Ranked below the general category are a number of castes collectively known as "Other Backward Class" (OBC). These castes form about 50-55 per cent of the total population of the region. Often named after their traditional occupations, the major OBC caste groups in Bundelkhand are as follows: Lodhis (landowners and cultivators aligned to ruling families), Kurmis (cultivators), Ahirs (Yadavas; traditionally catle-breeders and milkmen), Kachhis (vegetable cultivators), Koris (weavers), Sunars (goldsmiths), Telis (oil-pressers), Nais (barbers), Dhobis (washermen), Kumhars (potters), etc. The OBCs have acquired a political edge due to their numerical strength and post-independence land reforms.

Scheduled Castes (SC) and Scheduled Tribes are traditionally placed at the bottom of the caste hierarchy. Whereas the SCs constitute about 20 per cent to 30 per cent of the total population of the region, the STs proportion range from 5 per cent to 15 per cent.

Status of Women

The projection of Rani Laxmibai, the former Queen of Jhansi as a generalised symbol of empowerment of women in Bundelkhand bears no resemblance to the actual status of women in the region. The women of Bundelkhand are a much exploited lot. In rural areas they toil from dawn to dusk—cooking, drawing water from the well, collecting dung and firewood, grazing cattle and/or doing manual labour at construction sites. According to a study, farm women in Bundelkhand put in about 12 hours of hard work, whereas men work for less than five hours a day. On top of this, women labourers get lower daily wages. Moreover, domestic violence and discrimination within and outside the family is quite common. The overall status of widows, particularly those of poor and young is even worse. Force of traditional and feudal values, lack of economic opportunities, low levels of literacy and poor health condition of women—all these factors stymy any efforts in raising the status of women in Bundelkhand.

To sum up, Bundelkhand is one of the most backward regions in the country with a very large population (85% plus) of OBCs, SCs and STs. A majority of population is dependent on agriculture for livelihood, but agriculture has been a difficult occupation in the region due to lack of agricultural land, poor soil quality, erratic rainfall, lack of irrigation facilities and the cumulative indebtedness of small and marginal farmers. This economic scenario has led to massive out-migration of people as well as significant number of suicides among the farmers. Other sociological factors such as wide-spread corruption, caste-based inequality, discrimination and untouchability, low status of women and neglect of children's education, etc. have further added to the woes of the people of Bundelkhand (*See* NITI Ayog, 2018). It is against this socio-economic backdrop of the region that a brief profile of the Jain community of Bundelkhand is presented next.

Jain Community of Bundelkhand

Jains constitute an important community in the Bundelkhand region. They are mainly involved in whole sale and retail trading, banking and money-lending and various professions, and as such they have been vitally integrated into the regional economy which is largely based on agriculture and mining. Before we highlight the select features of the Jain community of Bundelkhand, a brief history of Jainism in the region would be in order.

Jainism in Bundelkhand

Nothing can be said with certainty about the antiquity of Jainism in the Bundelkhand region. According to Jain sources, Chandragupt Maurya after becoming a Jain monk had accompanied Acharya Bhadrabahu to Shravanbelagola in the wake of 12-year long famine in north India. Emperor Ashoka had appointed his grandson Prince Samprati, a devoted Jain, as the Governor of Ujjaiyni. After Ashoka's death Samprati became the ruler of Ujjaiyni. This is confirmed from an inscription from Vidisha dated 425 A.D. A group of Tirthanka statues from Saleha in Panna district also confirms the presence of Jainism in western part of Bundelkhand. After Maurya and Gupta periods, the Parmar period (7th to 8th century A.D.) is important from the viewpoint of the growth of Jainism in the region. During this period Devgarh emerged as a major centre of Digambar Jainism where a large number of temples were constructed. Bhattaraks of Devgarh were quite influential and they helped spread Jainism in Chanderi, Sironj, Thoobon and Vidisha. Besides Vidisha, temple construction also took place at Gyaraspur in 10th century A.D.

Chandela rulers (9th to 12th century), particularly Dhangraj, Madan Varma and Parmadird had quite liberal attitude towards Jainism and therefore a large number of temples were constructed at Ajaygarh, Mahoba, Khajuraho, Dudhai, Chandpur, Thoobon, Madanpur, etc. during this period. The Khajuraho Jain temples along with their Hindu counterparts are today very well known the world over for their grandure and beauty. Parmar rulers were quite helpful in spreading Jainism in the Malwa region with Ujjain as a major centre of Jain influence. Jainism took firm roots in Gopachal (Gwalior) area and up to Vidisha during the reigns of Kachchhap rulers (950-1125 A.D). Jabalpur as well as Vidisha also flourished as centres of Jainism during the Kalchuri regimes (9th to 13th century).

Thus, beginning with the late 4th or early 5th century A.D. Jainism had widely spread in Bundelkhand region by the 11th century A.D. In most parts of the region it was only Digambar Jainism that prevailed. Its followers were mainly trading castes/communities. The Bundelkhand Jain community was numerically further strengthened by the arrival of refugee members of the Jain Parwar caste from Gujarat who eventually left the region due to bitter sectarian conflict between two major sects of Jainism. This happened sometime in the 12th century A.D. when the Shwetambars had been successful in receiving royal patronage and favours from the then Gujjar ruler Siddhraj. According to Siddhantacharya Pt. Phoolchandra Shastri (1992: 53-54), the exodus was the final outcome of the prolonged and bitter doctrinal rivalry between Shwetambars and Digambars that had been going on since the 10th century A.D. As per

Shwetambar literary sources, the *shastrarth* (religious debate) took place between Shwetambar scholar Devsuri and his Digambar counterpart Kumudchandra on the issue of women's liberation in which the latter was defeated. The forced migrants were Parwar by caste. After the migration they initially settled in Chanderi and nearby areas from where they got spread to the other parts of Bundelkhand where members of Golapurav, Golalare as well as Parwar Jain castes had already been settled for at least a couple of centuries (Shastri, Jaganmohan Lal 1992: 20).

Demographics

In Bundelkhand, the Jains with less than one percent of the total population of the region constitute the third largest religious community after the Hindus (93.17%) and Muslims (5.58%). They are mainly involved in whole-sale and retail trading, banking and *mahajani,* and various professions, and as such they have been vitally integrated into the regional economy for centuries. The overwhelming majority of Jains in Bundelkhand are the followers of Terapanthi Digambar Jainism, and a tiny minority of them belongs to Taaranpanth who are also known as *Samaiyas.* The region's Jain community is divided into the following important Jain castes: Parwar, Golapurav, Golalare, and Samaiya. The 2011 census data suggest that there were about 150,000 Jains in the region whose district-wise distribution is presented in Table 2.3.

Table 2.3: Decadal Growth in Jain Population of Bundelkhand, 2001-2011

State/District	*District Population, 2011*	*Jain Population, 2001*	*Jain Population, 2011*	*Proportion of Jain Population, 2011*	*Decadal Growth Rate, 2001-2011 (%)*
MP-Bundelkhand					
Sagar	2,378,458	59,931	62,992	42.39	5.11
Damoh	1,264,219	23,818	25,005	16.83	4.98
Tikamgarh	1,445,166	14,604	15,569	10.48	6.61
Chhatarpur	1,762,375	9,766	10,409	07.00	6.58
Panna	1,016,530	4,534	4,734	3.19	4.41
Datia	786,754	499	453	00.30	-9.22
Sub-Total		113,152	119,162	80.19	5.30
UP-Bundelkhand					
Lalitpur	1,221,592	19,797	20,390	13.72	3.00
Jhansi	1,998,603	7,620	7,328	04.93	-3.83
Banda	1,799,410	884	916	00.62	3.62
Chitrakoot	991,730	283	285	00.19	0.71
Jalaun	1,689,974	344	256	00.17	-25.58
Mahoba	875,958	223	234	00.16	4.93
Hamirpur	1,104,285	48	41	00.03	-14.58
Sub-Total		29,199	29,450	19.82	0.86
Total	**18,335,044**	**142,351**	**148,612**	**100.00**	**4.4**

Source: Dheeraj Jain (2017).

Table 2.4: District-wise Distribution of Jain Population of Bundelkhand by Rural/Urban Residence, Gender and Sex and Child Sex Ratios, 2011

Region/District	*Rural*	*Urban*	*Male*	*Female*	*Sex Ratio*	*Child Sex Ratio*
MP-Bundelkhand						
Sagar	18,678	44,314	32,691	30,301	927	966
Damoh	12,523	12,482	13,180	11,825	897	917
Tikamgarh	5,215	10,354	8,156	7,413	909	896
Chhatarpur	3,867	6,542	5,450	4,959	910	1046
Panna	2,484	2,250	2,479	2,255	910	991
Datiya	342	111	223	230	1,031	722
Sub-Total	43,109	76,053	62,179	56,983	931	923
UP-Bundelkhand						
Lalitpur	6,026	14,364	10,636	9,754	917	879
Jhansi	908	6,420	3,798	3,530	929	884
Banda	795	121	483	433	896	1000
Chitrakoot	239	46	141	144	1021	1308
Jalaun	75	181	141	115	816	538
Mahoba	57	177	133	101	759	769
Hamirpur	22	19	24	17	708	1333
Sub-Total	8,122	21,328	15,356	14,094	864	959
Total	51,231	97,381	77,535	71,077	898	941

Source: Dheeraj Jain (2017).

Table 2.5: Jain Population of Bundelkhand: Literacy and Work Participation Rates (%) by Gender, 2011

District	*Literacy Rate*			*Work Participation Rate*		
	Person	*Male*	*Female*	*Person*	*Male*	*Female*
MP-Bundelkhand						
Sagar	96.80	98.1	95.39	33.65	55.39	10.2
Damoh	98.41	97.49	93.10	36.17	56.68	13.32
Tikamgarh	95.16	97.56	92.53	33.53	52.56	12.59
Chhatarpur	94.66	97.31	91.70	33.77	54.07	11.45
Panna	96.40	98.88	93.99	34.43	56.31	10.38
Datia	94.31	96.59	92.17	47.02	60.54	33.91
Sub-Total	95.45	97.65	93.15	36.42	55.92	15.30
UP-Bundelkhand						
Lalitpur	96.21	97.97	94.31	34.32	54.49	12.32
Jhansi	96.68	98.38	94.25	33.58	54.87	10.68
Banda	96.73	98.86	94.33	32.42	54.66	7.62
Chitrakoot	92.94	97.66	88.19	36.84	44.68	29.17
Jalaun	91.95	96.09	87.04	31.64	51.77	6.96
Mahoba	89.57	92.50	85.71	32.48	48.12	11.88
Hamirpur	91.18	90.48	92.31	19.51	29.17	5.88
Sub-Total	93.68	95.99	90.96	31.54	48.25	12.07
Total	94.56	96.82	92.05	33.98	52.08	13.68

Source: Dheeraj Jain (2017).

The data in Table 2.4 clearly reveal that in the 2011 census only 148,612 individuals were enumerated as the followers of Jainism in Bundelkhand. This figure amounts to about 0.88 per cent of the total population of Bundelkhand (18.5 million in 2011). In Bundelkhand, the Sagar district hosts the largest number of Jains followed by Damoh, Lalitpur, Tikamgarh, Chhatarpur, and Jhansi. Further on, much of the Jain population of Bundelkhand (about 80%) resided in the MP-Bundelkhand. The data in the Table 2.4 further suggest that with the exception of Lalitpur and Jhansi districts, the Jain population in the other UP-Bundelkhand districts, namely Banda, Chitrakoot, Hamirpur, Jalaun and Mahoba is miniscule—adding up to only 1,732 individuals in 2011 census.

The Jain population of Bundelkhand constituted about 3.4 per cent of the total Jain population in India which was enumerated at about 4.5 million in 2011. Of these 52 per cent were male and 48 per cent female. The level of urbanisation is 66 per cent which is significantly lower than the Jain national average of 80 per cent. The sex ratio in the Jain population of Bundelkhand is 898 which is much lower than the Jain national figure of 954 females per 1,000 males (*See* Table 2.5). The sex ratio for 0-6 age group, also called child sex ratio which is 941 females per 1,000 males appears to be much higher compared to the national Jain average of 887. Both these demographic indicators, however, seem to have been distorted mainly because of the very small population base of Jains in six districts of the region, namely Datia, Banda, Chitrakoot, Jalaun, Mahoba and Hamirpur. Thus, for example, if we take into account the rest of the districts of Bundelkhand, then the sex ratio averages to 914—still on the lower side of the national average of 954.

Our data suggest the small size family norm of 4-5 members. Age of marriage also appears to have gone up by a few years in recent decades. Our field work data also suggest a considerable number of boys beyond marriageable age remaining unmarried, particularly in villages and towns due to skewed sex ratio and other sociological factors. At the same time, late, inter-caste and inter-religious marriages are also on the rise.

Table 2.5 provides data about the level of literacy and work participation rates among the Jains of Bundelkhand. Both these demographic indicators appear to be satisfactory and in tune with the national level indicators of the Jain population. Literacy (94.18%) and education among the Jains of Bundelkhand have certainly gone up which is reflected in increased number of them working/getting employed as professionals in public as well as private sectors within the region and outside it. The work participation rate for Jain males in Bundelkhand is about 34 (52.08 for males and 13.68 for females).

There appears to be a fair amount of out-migration of Jains, particularly of highly educated professionals from Bundelkhand as many of them happen to be getting education outside the region and thereby easily getting suitable jobs there itself. Thus, a significant number of Bundelkhandi Jains have been living in Bhopal, Indore, Jabalpur, Gwalior, Nagpur, Pune, Mumbai, Ahmadabad,

Jaipur, National Capital Region of Delhi, and many more towns and cities in India. Even if some of these Jains are willing to come back to their native places, the region is not developed enough to provide them suitable employment. A number of Bundelkhandi Jains have also settled abroad, particularly in North America.

To sum up, about 150,000 Jain population of Bundelkhand is unevenly distributed across the 13 districts of the region—about 95 per cent of it living in only six districts, namely Sagar, Damoh, Lalitpur, Tikamgarh, Chhatarpur and Jhansi. Among the major demographic indicators, the skewed sex ratio has been the most problematic in that the shortage of marriageable-age girls has forced a considerable number of boys either to remain unmarried or opt for inter-religious marriage. Fortunately, the child sex ratio since the 2001 census has been improving as evident from the 2011 census data. Increased access to higher education has also been prompting many Jains not only to go for professional occupations, but also to migrate outside the region in search of better employment opportunities.

Table 2.6: Some Jain Demographic Characteristics in Select Districts of Bundelkhand, 1981

District	*Jain Population*	*Growth Rate, 1971-81*	*Urbanisation*	*Sex Ratio*	*Family Size*
Sagar	45,144	21.95	58.11	913	6.2
Guna	20,265	27.42	63.52	903	6.8
Damoh	18,639	23.40	33.31	929	5.7
Lalitpur and Jhansi	16,239	30.04	51.56	830	9.2
Vidisha	13,683	26.27	69.13	921	6.0
Tikamgarh	11,029	36.23	47.07	901	5.7
Ave/Total	125,219	27.55	53.8	899	6.6

Source: M.K. Jain (1986).

Economic Profile

For generations, most Jains in Bundelkhand continue to be small-scale traders, bankers, mahajans and adhatiyas. All over the region, general and provision stores and textile shops are particularly owned by the Jains. They are also into jewellery and sweets confectionary business. After India's independence, some of the Jains in the area were among the first to undertake certain entrepreneurial activities such as operating buses and trucks as means of transportation, setting up saw as well as flour, pulse and rice mills, running restaurants and small hotels, and occasionally owning a petrol pump station. A small section of Jains is also engaged in modern education-based professions such as teaching, healthcare, engineering, law, chartered accountancy, information technology and varying levels of government services.

Due to their involvement in trade and commercial activities, the Jains in Bundelkhand are generally called "Baania" or "Bania"—a label that carries both positive and negative stereotypical connotations. On the positive side, the Jains are regarded as "wealthy", intelligent, enterprising, and receptive to education and learning. Negative stereotypes, on the other hand, portray them as miser (*makkhichoos*), shrewd, exploitative, manipulative, and physically weak.

In any case, for at least a millennium the Jains have been very well integrated into the regional economy. In the villages they had been part of the now disintegrating *jajmani* system whereby they took services of a number of Hindu castes, namely Brahmin, barber, washerman, gardener, sweeper, etc. in exchange for cash and/or kind. For over a century now, out of the town and village based economy of Bundelkhand quite a few Jains could accumulate enough wealth to have been instrumental in getting performed certain religious rituals like *panchkalyanak* and eventually earn honourific titles of Singhai, Sawaisinghai, Seth and Shrimant Seth. All in all, the Jains in Bundelkhand can well be considered as economically well-off by Bundelkhand standard, a region which is not only economically underdeveloped but also patriarchal and caste-ridden. Not surprisingly, this situation until recently had attracted the ire of dacoits, and a number of wealthy Jains in the region had been the worst victims of dacoity for centuries.

Education and Occupational Structure

For centuries an overwhelming majority of Jains in Bundelkhand have been engaged in petty trade and commerce, their paternal or family occupation. The Sagar district survey of Jain youth conducted in 2011 by the author had found that about 49 per cent of the respondents were engaged in family shop-keeping business (Jain, Prakash C. and Jain, H. C., 2017). There appears to be stagnation in inter-generational occupational mobility from grandparents' generation to that of the respondents. Thus, 48 per cent of the grandparents also used to be engaged in shop-keeping. As far as the modern education and occupation was concerned, only two generations ago, most Jains preferred to go for conventional occupations such as teaching, banking and local government record keeping (*Lekhpal*). A privileged few became engineers, doctors and accountants. Very few Jains served in railways, police and army or Indian Administrative Services. Perhaps this is still true.

As already mentioned, Bundelkhand continues to remain educationally and industrially a backward region. Thus, for instance, Lalitpur district, the stronghold of Jains in UP-Bundelkhand, had only one-degree college until recently—and that too had not been functioning properly. There are only four universities at Sagar, Jhansi, Rewa and Chitrkoot. Due to lack of awareness and economic constraints, most Jain families do not send their wards to colleges and universities. Those who are economically a little better off end up in acquiring graduate and post-graduate education, mostly in arts, science or commerce subjects. Very few can afford professional education in subjects like engineering, medicine, law, business-management or information technology.

Most Jain families are deprived of quality education as they have access to only government schools, where the medium of instruction is Hindi and written or spoken English is not taught properly. Thus, in the Sagar district survey it was found that only 3 per cent of the respondents had gone to English medium schools (Jain, Prakash C. and H. C. Jain, 2017). Lack of knowledge of English not only hampers further education of most Bundelkhand Jain youth, they also succumb to long-standing family pressure for joining either the family shop-keeping business or go for lowly employment.

Historically, for more than a century now, Sanskrit Jain Vidyalayas have been an important avenue of getting education and employment. Given the significant level of poverty among the Jain families in the region two generation ago, many of them used to send their wards for getting educated to various Sanskrit Jain Vidhyalayas located regionally (e.g. Sadhumar, Papaura, Sagar, Morena), or as far away as Banaras, Arrah, Mathura, Jaipur, Mahavirji and Delhi (*See* Varni, 1949; Appendix-5). These *Vidyalayas* provided free boarding, lodging and tuition. It was also these *vidyalayas* that produced several generations of traditional Jain scholars (Pandits) as well as modern Jain scholars of Sanskrit, Prakrit and Jainology/Indology (*See* Appendix-2). Sons and daughters of these Pandits/Jainilogy scholars have often gone into modern professional occupations. This had been a general trend throughout the 20th century. It is only now that some of these *vidyalayas* have begun to decline in the absence of students and perhaps community financial support.

Jains from Bundelkhand have historically been migrating to numerous cities and towns outside the region. These include Indore, Bhopal, Jabalpur, Gwalior, Jaipur, Ahmedabad, Amarawati and Nagpur. Apparently, this must have been done for seeking better economic/employment opportunities at these places. They also provide better educational opportunities for the next generation of emigrants. This trickle migration over the years and decades has led to the evolution and consolidation of small Bundelkhandi Jain communities outside the region. Thus, Nagpur hosts a Parwarpura (neighbourhood) named after the Parwar Jain caste of Bundelkhand. In Cuttack (Odisha), there is a Digambar Jain temple and a market named after Manju Chaudhari, a Bundelkhandi Jain who was appointed Governor by Maratha rulers in the 18th century. Similarly, Ahmedabad hosts a significant number of Golalare Jains who have been migrating to Gujarat for quite some time now. A small number of Parwars are also settled in Ahmedabad. This migration trend has been continuing even today whereby highly qualified professionals (including traditional Jain scholars and Pandits) are migrating to numerous towns and cities outside the Bundelkhand region in India and abroad.

Socio-Political Contribution

Jainism is often considered as an "other-worldly" religion as it puts great deal of emphasis on salvation. On closer scrutiny, however, it can well be argued that "in-worldly" elements, that is, concern for social and human welfare are almost equally present in Jainism (*See* Jain, Shugan C. and Jain, Prakash C., 2014). Three aspects of the Jain socio-political contribution in the context of the Bundelkhand region that are highlighted in the following pages are:

1. Political participation,
2. Social work, and
3. Literary contribution.

1. Political Participation

During the ancient and medieval periods the existence and spread of Jainism, or for that matter of any religion, was dependent on the good will and patronage of various ruling dynasties in different parts of India. Getting patronised in itself is a political act, and the Jains can be considered to be successful in this regard. Even during the Mughal period, they enjoyed a considerable amount of good will and favours from the Mughals (*See*; Jain, Shalin, 2017).

In modern times Jains played an important role in India's freedom struggle. Thousands of them all over the country went to jail, and some of them were hanged to death for their patriotic acts by the British regime. Bundelkhand region was no exception on this count. In a study of Jains' participation in the freedom movement in North India, it was found that of a total of about 800 Jain freedom fighters, over 200 belonged to Bundelkhand region alone (Jain, Kapur C. and Jain, Jyoti, 2006; Appendix-6). Moreover, of the 20 or so Jain martyrs of north India's freedom struggle, four were from Bundelkhand: Amar Chand Banthia, Gwalior; Chaudhry Bhaiyalal Jain, Damoh; Singhai Prem Chand Jain, Damoh; Saboo Lal Jain Baisakhiya, Garhakota, Sagar (Jain, Kapoor and Jain, Jyoti, 2006).

After India's independence, six Jains were nominated to the Constituent Assembly of India. Of these, one member, namely Ramakant Malviya was from Sagar. Jains in Bundelkhand have also been active at various levels of electoral politics—parliament, state assemblies and local government bodies. While Bundelkhand has returned only a couple of Jain members of Parliament from its constituencies, it was only recently that Pradeep Kumar Jain "Aditya" from Jhansi could become a MP and Minister of State in Dr. Manmohan Singh's cabinet in the 15th Lok Sabha (2009-2014). The other MP was Shri Dal Chand Jain from Damoh/Sagar.

Madhya Pradesh is the only state in India which has the distinction of being served by six Jain Chief Ministers and a number of Cabinet Ministers—but none of them from Bundelkhand. Although very small in number, the Jains of Bundelkhand do have a considerable amount of political clout in about half a dozen districts of the region. Their role as opinion makers and and as election campaigners is particularly remarkable. A few of them have even won state level Assembly elections in both UP as well as MP—Bundelkhand. These include Dashrath Jain from Chhatarpur, Dal Chand Jain from Sagar, Dr. Arvind Jain from Lalitpur, Shailendra Jain from Sagar and Kapur Chand Ghuwara from Chhatarpur. A brief profile of these Jain politicians of Bundelkhand is presented below.

Dal Chand Jain. A freedom fighter since his early teen years, Dal Chand Jain (1928-2011) was elected to the Madhya Pradesh legislative assembly in 1967 and to the Lok Sabha in 1984 from Sagar and Damoh constituencies respectively on the Indian National Congress ticket. Dal Cand Jain was the son of well-known industrialist, Jain community leader and social worker Shrimant Seth Bhagwandas Jain of Sagar. Throughout his life Dal Chand Jain remained associated with a number of industrial, educational and religious associations including Madhya Pradesh Federation of Chambers of Commerce and Industries, All-India Beedi Industry Federation, Dr. Hari Singh Gaur University of Sagar, Shri Varni Jain Sanskrit Mahavidyalaya, World Ahimsa Sangh, All-India Digambar Jain Parishad (President, 1978-1992), and Shri Bhagchand Shobhalal Jain Charitable Trust (*See* Jain, Kapoor C. and Jain, Jyoti, 2006; www.jainworld/society/dalchand,htm). Like his father and uncle, Dal Chand Jain had a very soft corner for the poor, especially the members of the SC and ST communities.

Pradeep Kumar Jain "Aditya". Pradeep Jain was a member of the 15th Lok Sabha (2009-14) from Jhansi on Indian National Congress ticket. He was appointed the Minister of State for Rural Development in Dr. Manmohan Singh cabinet. Prior to this, he was a member of Uttar Pradesh Vidhan Sabha during 2007-09 from Jhansi constituency. Born (8 September 1962) and brought up in Jhansi, Pradeep Jain is advocate by profession. He is credited for getting installed a grand statue in Jhansi of the hockey legend Dhyan Chand. He again fought for the Lok Sabha seat from the Jhansi constituency in 2014 general elections, but lost it to Ms. Uma Bharati, a Bharatiya Janta Party candidate.

Dashrath Jain. Freedom fighter, Gandhian, lawyer, author and journalist, Dashrath Jain (1926-2018) of Chhatarpur was Home minister in the earstwhile Vindhya Pradesh government of Sambhu Nath Shukla (1945-52). Subsequent to the formation of state of Madhya Pradesh he was a deputy minister in the cabinets of Pt. Ravi Shankar Shukla and Dr. Kailash Nath Katju (1955-62). He was also elected MLA from Malahra in 1972 elections. He was an ardent advocate of clean politics and personal integrity. He has written a number of books in the fields of economics, sociology and Jainology.

Jayant Kumar Malaiya. Industrialist Jayant Kumar Malaiya (b. 1943), B. Com, LLB, is a veteran politician from Damoh. From the very beginning of his career he has been representing the Bhartiya Janata Party. He was seven-time elected to the Madhya Pradesh Legislative Assembly—first time in 1984 and the last time in 2013 when he was the Cabinet Minister of Finance, Water Resources, Housing and Environment. In his earlier stints he held a number of ministerial portfolios. He has travelled extensively across the world, and is married to Dr. Sudha Malaiya, an academic, social worker and activist.

Dr. Arvind Kumar Jain. Four-time member and one-time Minister of Health in UP Legislative Assembly, Arvind Kumar Jain represented Lalitpur on behalf of the Bhartiya Janta Party in 1989, 1991, 1993 and 1996 elections. An ABMS degree holder from Banaras Hindu University, he is a doctor by profession. He was born in Gauna village of Lalitpur district in 1935. A man of principles, Dr. Jain spent only about Rs. two lakh per election—the amount given to him by the Party for electioneering purpose. At the age of 83, he continues to look after his patients with the consultation fee of Rs. 10 only.

Shailendra Jain. Two-time elected as a member of Madhya Pradesh legislative Assembly (2013 and 2018), Shailebdra Jain continues to represent Sagar constituency as a BJP leader. He is a real estate businessman.

Kapur Chand Guwara. Guwara, a local Jain community leader, had won MP Legislative Assembly by-election in 2006 on Bharatiya Janata Party ticket from Malahra constituency in Chhatarpur district.

Compared to national and state level politics, the Jains' involvement at the local level politics is perhaps much better, but the representation of women even at this level is almost negligible.

2. Social Work

Philanthropy and social work have been an integral part of Jain philosophy and ethics. In the context of the Bundelkhand region, Jain Seths and Shrimant Seths, that is very wealthy individuals often used to get involved in the construction of temples and allied religious activities as mentioned in Chapter Four. Philanthropic and social work activities in the field of education and healthcare began to take place only after the arrival of Ganesh Prasad Varni (1949) on the scene around the turn of the 20th century. Subsequently, networks of Jain pathshalas/vidyalayas with free boarding and lodging facilities to the needy students, *dharmashalas* for the pilgrims, healthcare facilities, *gaushalas*, birds dispansaries, etc. were established during the first couple of decades of the 20th century. Since then some Jain monks, nuns and pundits have also been instrumental in inspiring these and other social work activities in the region.

3. Literary Contribution

Significant contribution has been made by a number of Bundelkhandi Jain literatis (*See* Appendix-3). Brief biographies of three of them are presented below.

Laxmi Chandra Jain. Combining in himself extra-ordinary qualities of a creative writer, poet, journalist and editor, an erudite scholar of Indian philosophy, religion, art history, literature, and Jain Studies, a great coordinator of cultural and literary events, an able administrator, and above all a near-perfect gentleman, Laxmi Chandra Jain (1909-1999) was truly a multi-dimensional personality. He was a double M.A. in Sanskrit and English from the University of Delhi. Apart from Hindi literature in which he himself was a distinguished participant, he also had a very good knowledge of Urdu, Bengali, Gujarati and Marathi languages and literatures (*See* Diwan 2000).

Laxmi Chandra Jain was born at Chhatarpur, Madhya Pradesh. He began his career with All India Radio as Radio Programme Officer in Delhi, to be followed by Publicity Officer of Bharat Insurance Company at Lahore, and as general Manager of a cement factory at Dalmianagar owned by industrialist Sahu Shanti Prasad Jain and his wife Smt. Rama Jain. After a brief spell at Lucknow, he moved to Calcutta to take over the responsibilities of Bhartiya Jnanpith founded by the Sahu Jain couple in 1944. Bhartiya Jnanpith was established with the following objectives: "To conduct research and publication of the extinct, rare and unpublished works of knowledge and to encourage the creation of original literature in the service of the people".

Bhartiya Jnanpith is one of the premier literary organizations and publishing houses of India nurturing modern Indian literature as well as Indological/Jainological Studies. For over half a century now, the organization is best known for the Jnanpith Award—the highest literary award of the country—that, since its inception in 1965 and until 2018, has been conferred on 54 literary luminaries of various Indian languages including English. Two more awards are given away by Bhartiya Jnanpith: (i) Moortidevi Award for a contemplative and perceptive literary work, and (ii) Navalekhan Award for young authors under 40 years of age. Needless to say, Laxmi Chandra Jain got so thoroughly involved in the conception and execution of the various activities of the Bhartiya Jnanpith that in due course of time he became synonym of Bhartiya Jnanpith. In spite of his extremely busy life, Laxmi Chandra Jain could find time to produce some experimental works like "Kagaz ki Kishtiyan", "Naye Rang, Naye Dhang" and "Gyrah Sapno ka Desh" (the last one written by 11 novelists). His wife Kuntha Jain and the eldest daughter Indu Jain were also reputed poets and authors.

Hukam Chand Bukharia "Tanmay". By any literarary standards, Hukam Chand Bukharia was a great poet—perhaps the greatest the Bundelkhand Jain community ever produced in modern times. Besides being essentially a romantic poet, he also wrote patriotic and spiritual poems with equal ease. He was very popular in *kavi sammelans* (poetic pulic gatherings). More often than not, his mere presence ensured the success of that kavi sammelan. His major works include "Ahuti" (1946), "Pakistan" (1946), "Pramad" (1948) and "Merc Bapu" (1951) (Sahitya Akademy, 1961: 54).

Born on 24 January 1921 in Lalitpur, Bukharia got involved in country's freedom movements early in his life. In 1940 and again in 1942 he was rigorously imprisoned for six months and 12 months (with a fine of Rs. 100) respectively. He was greatly influenced by Mahatma Gandhi and later on by Jain thinker-philosopher Acharya (Osho) Rajneesh. He was also a social reformer. In the local Jain community, he was instrumental in getting the Jain temples opened up for all, irrespective of caste or creed, worship rights to any Jain including women, and ban on death feasts within the Jain community. "Tanmay" earned his livelihood by teaching, practising law, putting up a wheat flour mill and an ice cream factory, and running a hotel. He was also a palmist and occasionally a planchantologist. He died on 26 November 1997.

Padma Shri Kailash Madbaiya. Hindi/Bundeli writer, poet Kailash Madbaiya is 2019 awardee of Padma Shri for literature and education. Born in a Jain family in Banpur village of Lalitpur district, Madbaiya (b. 1944) holds M.Sc., B.Ed. and LLB degrees. Initially he worked as a lecturer and later on joined the Madhya Pradesh Government public service, retiring in 2003 as a Joint Commissioner, Co-operatives. Presently he lives in Bhopal where he is the founder-president of Bundelkhand Literary and Cultural Parishad. Madbaiya has published more than two dozen books in Hindi and Bundelkhandi on literature, Jain history, culture and archeology. He has been a recipient of a number of awards and honours from literary, socio-cultural and religious organisations for his literary achievements. His major publications include *Bundelkhand ke Jain Tirth* (2004*), Bundeelkhand ki Lok Kathaen Bundeli Mein* (2014), *Saat Samundar Par* (2016), and *Mayur Pankh* (2018). Kailash Madbaiya has travelled widely in India and abroad including Nepal, Singapore, the UK and the USA. He is the first ever Jain reciepient of Padma Shri from Bundelkhand.

Social Organisation

In the Bundelkhand region, social organisational patterns of the Jain community are more or less akin to those of the wider Hindu community. Thus, the Jains too have a caste system along with well-defined family, marriage and kinship institutions. Not only the social organisational patterns, the life cycle rituals such as birth, child naming, marriage, death, etc. are also similar to those of the Hindus. Again, the food, festivals and recreational activities are more or less the same as among the Hindus, although of course the Jains are strictly vegetarian and teetotaller who would not like to indulge in hunting and gambling. The major religious function of the Jains in Bundelkhand is the ten-day long Paryushan Parva or Das Lakshan Dharm which is annually observed in the midst of the rainy season.

Sub-Sects and Castes

Two major Digambar sub-sects that prevail among the Jains in Bundelkhand are Terapanth and Taaranpanth.

Terapanth

The sub-sect is regarded as the mainstream one within the Digambar Jainism, and is named so because unlike Bisapanthis who believe in the institution of Bhattarak, Terapanthis continue to retain their faith in naked ascetics who follow the 13 kinds of codes of conduct prescribed for them—five *mahavratas* (great vows), five *samitis* (carefulnesses) and three *guptis* (regulations/controls). In north India the sect came into sharp focus with the emergence of the Adhyatma movement in Agra in 1626 A.D. Its main instigators were Banarasidas of Agra and Amar Chand of Sanganer (Jaipur). It was opposed to the domination of the institution of Bhattarak. The followers of Terapanth also opposed the worship of demi-gods and goddesses, and the use of flowers in worship. Today almost the whole of North India is Terapanthi as opposed to Western and Southern India which are by and large Bisapanthi. There are three major castes among Terapanthi Digambar Jains in Bundelkhand: *Parwar*, *Golapurav* and *Golalare*. These are briefly discussed below.

*Parwar***.** It is the majority Jain caste in Bundelkhand. In old Sanskrit inscriptions found in the region, the Parwars figure by the name Paurapatta or Puravaad. The earliest one such inscription in the region dates back to 11th century A.D. According to Pt. Phool Chandra Siddhantshastri (1992), the Parwars are the descendants of Parmar Kshtriyas. In ancient times they were known as "Pragvat" or "Paurpat" and were the followers of the Moolsangh established some 2100 years ago by Guptigupt, a Jain ascetic and grandson of King Chandragupta Maurya. The Parwars were initially spread in Gujarat and the Marwar region in present-day Rajasthan, and Central India, including Bundelkhand. Historically, Parwars are varyingly known as Pramar, Parmar, Panwar, Purwar, Porwar, Porwad, Porwal, Padmavati Porwad, Jangada Porwad, etc.—sometime as a separate caste/sub-caste.

During the ancient and medieval times, the Parwars as followers of Jainism were engaged not only in agriculture, animal husbandry and trade, but they also used weapons for self-protection (*vartashastropjeevee*). In due course of time with the disappearance of small democratic republics (*gana-rajyas*) there was no need to defend the territories and hence the use of weapons. Later on agriculture was also abandoned and the Jains relied only on trade, commerce and money-lending, and came to be regarded as Vaishyas.

Parwar is the only caste among Jains whose members are identified not only by their gotra but also by their "mur" (*mool*, that is the original place of residence). All the members of the caste are divided into 12 gotras and each gotra into 12 murs. Most of the 144 *mur* names of the Parwar caste are derived from village names in Gujarat and Rajasthan. Some of these such as Idar, Rakhiyal, Naradpuri, Patwara, etc. still exist even today.

As already mentioned, during the 12th or 13th Century a majority of Parwars had to leave Gujarat due to Shwetambar-sect instigated religious persecution at the hands of rulers who had patronized Shwetambar Jainism. The migrants took refuse in Malwa, Ujjain, Chanderi, Sironj, Tikamgarh, Panna, Chhatarpur, Orchha, etc. which were ruled by Parmar/Chandela or other Kshatriyas friendly to Jainism. They were also attracted by the fact that the followers of Moolsangh, namely Golapurav, Golalare, Golsinghare as well as Pawar caste Jains were already residing in these princely states and therefore their integration was relatively easier.

The Parwars are the numerically dominant caste among Jains in Bundelkhand. All India Digambara Jain Directory, 1914 estimated the total Parwar and Padmavati Parwar Jain population at 54,864 persons (*See* Table 2.7). According to the Parvar Directory published in 1924, there were 48,074 Parwar Jains in Bundelkhand. A majority of them were located in the vicinity of Betwa River, within a radius of 50 miles from Deogarh. According to the same source, they were spread in 1,438 villages and towns, notably in Lalitpur (1,122), Sagar (595), Khurai (503), Mungawali (481), Bamora (374), Bina-Itawa (358), Khaniadhana (320), and Madawara (304). Others were located in Jabalpur (1,058), Mandla (314), and Sivni (358). Since the 1924 estimates we do not have any idea about the distribution or total population of Parwars. Presently in Bundelkhand this figure must be around 100,000. A majority of Parwar population is still concentrated in towns and villages mentioned in the 1924 Directory, although since then the proportion of rural to urban has been reversed in favour of urban residents.

Table 2.7: Distribution of Jain Castes in Central Provinces and Other Parts of India, 1914

Province	*Parwar*	*Golapurva*	*Golarare*
Central Provinces	24,213	9,476	1,900
United Provinces	18,289	718	2,095
Rajputana and Malwa	11,707	376	1,565
Punjab	363	Nil	Nil
Bengal and Bihar	164	Nil	20
Bombay	60	Nil	02
Madras and Mysore	68	Nil	Nil
Total	54,864	10,570	5,582

Source: Adapted from Sangave (1980: 124-30).

Golapurav. Golapurav is the second largest Jain caste in Bundelkhand after Parwars. Scholars differ about the meaning of the word "Golapurav" as well as the place of its origin. Some assign its origin to Gwalior, others to Mahoba, and still others to an ancient South Indian territory "Gollarashtra", or "Golladesh" (*See* Malaiya, 1996; Jain, Surendra Kumar, 1996). "The other view is that they were a Golak Purana Brahmins born out of the union between a Brahman and a non-Brahman. It is from *Golak Purana* that the community name Golapurav is derived" (Samanta, 1998: 395).

Whatever may have been the story, or the place of its origin, the Golapurav (Sanskrit Golapurava) have historically been residing in Sagar, Damoh, Tikamgarh, Chhatarpur and Jabalpur districts of MP-Bundelkhand and Lalitpur district of UP-Bundelkhand. Estimatedly there were 10,570 Golapurav Jains in 1914 according to the All India Digambar Jain Directory (Table 2.7). Their population increased to 12,569 in 1941 and 35,074 in 1996 (*See* Kavyateerth, 1941; Jain, Surendra K., 1996). They were spread over in as many as 535 towns and villages, mainly of the MP-Bundelkhand region. Their district-wise distribution was as follows: Sagar (11,680), Chhatarpur (4,830), Damoh (3,812), Tikamgarh (3,701) and Jabalpur (2,861). Lalitpur distrct of UP had 1,100 Golapurav Jains, and 7,090 lived in the rest of India at 270 places (Jain, Surendra Kumar, 1996: 266). The current population of the caste may be estimated at around 50,000.

Golalare. Some scholars believe that the Golalare originally belonged to Bhind and Morena districts but today are spread in small numbers in all over the Bundelkhand region, and some other states of India. According to Nathuram Premi (1992: 160), in Surat district of Gujarat there is a caste known as: "Golarane" which following its migration to Bundelkhand sometimes during the medieval period came to be called "Golalare". The Golalare Jains numbered 5,582 in 1914 as per All India Digamber Jain Directory (Table 2.7). Their province-wise distribution was found to be as follows: United Provinces: 2,095, Central Province: 1900, Rajputana: 1,565, Bengal-Bihar 20, Bombay Presidency: 2 (Sangave, 1980: 124-29). Their present population is not known. Many of them are settled in Rajasthan (Jaipur, Sawai Madhopur and Bharatpur districts), Gujarat (Ahmedabad district) and in Maharashtra (Sirpur, Chopra, Faizpur, Khamgaon and Nandura districts). Quite a number of them are settled in Ahmedabad and other cities and towns of Gujarat

Taaranpanth

The sub-sect was founded sometime in the late 15th century A.D. The founder of Taranpanth was TaaranTaran Swami who was born in 1448 A.D. (v.s. 1505) in Pushpawati (Bilahri) village near Katni. His father Gadhasao was Chausakha Parwar and was a high official in the administration of Delhi's Lodi Sultan Bahlol (1451-1488). The impact of Islam is apparent on the sect as it does not believe in idol-worshipping. Instead they worship the Nirankar atman (formless soul). At the altar of their shrines called Chaityalaya they place and worship the *Samaysar* (an ancient Digambar Jain text written by Acharya Kundkund), and the 14 books written by Taaran Swami himself. The names of the 14 books are as follows: *Shravkachar, Pandit Pooja, Malarohan, Kamal Batteesee, Gyan Sammuchchaya Sar, Updesh Suddha Sar, Tribhangi Sar, Mamal Pahud, Chaubis Thana, Chhadmasth Vani, Nam Mala, Khatika Vishesh, Soonya Swabhav, and Siddhi Swabhav* (Swami, Kanji, 2010). Because of this, Taaranpanthis are also called Samaiyas or Granth Poojak (worshipper of the books). The Islamic influence theory about the emergence of the sect is contradicted by a more credible theory which suggests that Taran Taaran Swami as a young man was deeply hurt by day-to-day discrimination of Chausakha and Dosakha Parwars at the hands of Aathsakha Parwars. Between them there were no inter-dining and inter-marriage relations and they were not allowed to do worship in Jain temples. All this led Taaran Swami to have a break-away sect.

Taaran Swami's activities were mainly confined to the Bundelkhand region. He established a number of Chaityalayas in the region: 17 in Madhya Pradesh and four in Uttar Pradesh. Additionally four Chaityalayas were also established in Maharashtra. Presently the number of Chaityalayas is estimated at 100. The Taaranpanthis numbered only 1,107 as per the Digambar Jain Directory, 1914. During the early 1990s the total population of Taaranpanthis in India was liberally estimated at about 30,000 (Jain, Deepak, 2001: 108). It is reasonable to assume that it must have now gone up to about 40,000. Most Taaranpanthis are settled in Madhya Pradesh, and some in Uttar Pradesh and Maharashtra. Only about one-fourth of their population presently resides in the 13 districts of Bundelkhand. In terms of the caste composition Taranpanth consisted of six groupings: (i) Parwars (four sasan), (ii) Charnagar, (iii) Asati, (iv) Golalare, (v) Do Sasan Parwars, and (vi) Ayodhyavasi. Of the six caste groups, the Parwars have been numerically dominant. Osho Rajneesh (1931-1990) was a Taranpanthi by birth. Former member of Parliament late Shri Dal Chand Jain of Sagar was also a Samaiya.

Besides these castes, small number of Khandelwals and Agrawals also reside in the Bundelkhund region. According to Russell and Hiralal, there were 1,500 Khandelwals in Central Province as per the 1911 census. Agrawals, originating from Agroha in Hissar district of Haryana, are mainly settled in very small numbers in towns and cities of Bundelkhand.

All the Jain sects and castes in Bundelkhand were generally endogamous until about the end of the 20th century. Small size of them and the skewed gender ratio however have now forced them to break the sect/caste endogamy rule and go for inter-caste, inter-sect and even inter-religion marriages.

Kanji Swami Panth

During the past few decades, a new sub-sect called Kanji Swami Panth (KSP) in Digambar Jainism has emerged which is known after its founder Kanji Swami (1889-1981). A Shvetambar Jain Sthankavasi by birth, Kanji Swami who was based in the town of Songadh in Gujarat reinterpreted the first century Digambara Jain sacred text *Samayasara* written by Acharya Kundkund in a manner and perspective that gives more prominence to *Nischaya-Naya* (realistic/essential standpoint) than to *Vyavahara-naya* (practical standpoint). The *nischaya-naya* lays emphasis on understanding and contemplating on the true nature of the soul with a view of its purification, whereas the *vyavahar-naya* considered to be a temporary or transitory view-point helps us in adjusting with the practical issues in life. Emphasising the former the Kanji-Panth obviously wants to minimise the religious rituals in Jainism. The Panth is also not favourable to nudity in Jainism. It is, therefore, more popular with the educated class and the diasporic community, and its influence has been steadily increasing. However, another scholarly opinion is that "the poorer and lower caste Digambars tend to support the KSP" (Jain, Ravindra K., 1999: 117). In any case, the Kanji Panth has created a sharp division at the ideological level within the Digambar Jain community in north and central India, and particularly in Bundelkhand (Jain, Niraj, 2010). The critics believe that it violates the doctrine of *Anekantavada*—in this context the preference of one *naya* at the expense of the other. Besides Songadh, Jaipur, Ahmedabad and Mumbai are the other major centres of Kanji-Panth.

Social and Religious Conservatism

Bundelkhand is mostly inhabited by Terapanthi Digambar Jains, followers of most conservative sub-sect in Jainism. This particular sub-sect is characterised by the ideal-typical *moksha-marg* ideology, and abundance of religious rituals and overall orthodoxy (Cort, 2001; Jain, Ravindra K., 1999; Jaini, 1979). The prescribed codes of conduct for the four-fold order of the Jain society (samaj), namely sadhus (male ascetics), sadhvis (nuns), shrawak (layman) and shrawikas (laywomen) are rigorously followed by each component. In Ganesh Prasad Varni's accounts of Digambar Jain communities of Bundelkhand, the "doctrine and practice are closely tied up with each other" and that there is "a continuous and ever-increasing stress on the path of purification among Digambar Jain householders", which manifests in hierarchical differentiation of laity in the form of *brahmachari*, *kshullak* and *ailak* (collectively called *tyagis*). Along with *tyagis,* Jain pandits (teachers and scholars) form a significant intermediate layer between the ascetics and the laity in Bundelkhand region (Jain, Ravindra K., 1999: 51, *See* also Varni, 1949).

Thus, the householders' life is progressively imbued with spirituality and spiritual progress towards the salvation (*moksha*). A recently conducted preliminary survey of Jain youth in Sagar district highlights some of these features of social and religious conservatism of the Bundelkhand Jains. Thus, all the respondents make a daily visit to the temple for *Dev-Dharshan* and are in favour of imparting religious education to children in schools. Overwhelming majority of them is also in favour of giving *diksha* to young children. A great majority of them are not members of any Jain association. While all the respondents stay away from consuming alcohol and non-vegetarian food, about 50 per cent of them eat food after sunset (Jain, Prakash C. and H. C. Jain, 2017).

Of late, Jainism in Bundelkhand has been increasingly acquiring a fundamentalist tinge. The printing and publishing of Jain religious literature in the forms of magazines, books and pamphlets by various NGOs and associations and the introduction of exclusive Jain TV channels have been a contriburory factors in this regard. The moksha-marg ideology is being taken quite literally in practice by its most adherents. Religious congregations of the monks are not only well-attended, the laity-monk interaction is also frequent and intense. The number of tyagis (*brahmacharis, ailaks, chhullaks, munis and aryikas*) among the Jain laity is on the increase (*See* Appendix-7). Thanks to increased literacy among the women, the scriptures and other religious materials are widely disseminated among the Jains. This has resulted in increased indoctrination of the moksha-marg ideology among the Jains in Bundelkhand. In some Jain families even the school/college going boys and girls are so much indoctrinated by the ideology that they sometime find it difficult to adjust to the general behaviour of their class mates. Issues such as eating non-vegetarian food, questioning the existence of God, criticism of Jainism, particularly the nudity of Digambar Jain monks, etc. generally figure behind the inter-personal relations and the consequent temporary situations of maladjustment of the Jain youths in schools and work places. The religious orthodoxy, including the attendant practices and rituals are also on the rise. Thus, day-time marriages are in vogue in Bundelkhand as in the opinion of the moksha-marg ideologues this avoids night-time eating and associated himsa. Girls have been asked by a respected Jain nun in Damoh city not to go to temples in jeans; subsequently after a fortnight or so, there was a public bonefire of jeans as a mark of its rejection. To take up another important issue, although the region is dotted with a large number of pilgramige places and other kinds of temples, still newer temples are being built, while the older ones continue to suffer from neglect of upkeep and maintenance (*See* Appendix-4).

The Jain community of Bundelkhand does not seem to have a way out of this combined situation of social/religious conservatism, social (matrimonial) problems and problems of education and underemployment. A section of Jain population is resorting to urban migration in order to overcome some of these problems. In this context it must be noted that the Jains are the most urbanised (80% in 2011) community in India, as also in Bundelkhand (66% in 2011). Besides overcoming personal problems, the Jain youth donot seem to have a focused opinion on the improvement of the Jain community in Bundelkhand, except to suggest an overall economic development of the region. Can some social engineering be done by the Jain community at large?

Concluding Remarks

Bundelkhand is one of the most under-developed regions in India. This is quite evident in the region's socio-economic profile as well as its economy. The Jains are widely spread in the region as a trading community. Although small in number, they are vitally integrating into the regional economy. The region is dotted with scores of Jain pilgrimage places with impressive temple-complexes. It also has the distinction of having produced a large number of Jain pundits and modern scholars of Jainism in India during the 20th century. This was made possible by a network of Jain Sanskrit vidyalayas which provided alternative avenues for getting educated, especially for the poorer sections of the community. Taking advantage of modern education and associated occupational opportunities, the Jains in Bundelkhand today constitute relatively an affluent community. Unfortunately, the Jains in Bundelkhand continue to remain one of the least researched communities in India in terms of its dynamics of contemporary demographic, socio-cultural, political and economic changes.

3

Socio-economic Background of the Respondents

The chapter mainly focuses on the socio-economic background of the respondents in terms of their individual as well as community characteristics. These include age, gender, marital status, sect/sub-sect/caste, rural-urban background, education, occupation, land ownership, income, family size, use of gadgets at home, etc.

Gender

In our survey no direct question was asked about the gender status of the respondents. Instead the gender status was inferred from the first names of the respondents. Accordingly, a vast majority of respondents (96.0%) were male and the rest female.

Table 3.1: Gender of Respondents

Gender	*Percentage*
Male	95.6
Female	4.4
Total	100.0

Age

Age of respondents ranged from about 24 years to about 90 years. Age-distribution of respondents is presented in Table 3.2. It would be seen that more than 70.0 per cent of the respondents are in the age group of 51 years to 90 years. Only about 28.2 per cent of the respondents were in the 21-50 years age group. Thus, a great majority of respondents were elderly. This is obviously so because only heads of the households were requested to fill in the Questionnaire.

Table 3.2: Age of Respondents

Age Group	*Percentage*
21-30	6.1
31-40	5.6
41-50	16.5
51-60	35.0
61-70	22.4
71-80	11.1
80-90	3.3
Total	100.0

Marital Status

An overwhelming proportion of respondents (95%) was found to be married. Only 5 per cent were unmarried that also included a couple of bachelors, spinsters and a few widows as well as widowers.

Table 3.3: Marital Status of Respondents

Marital Status	*Percentage*
Married	95
Unmarried	5
Total	100

Sect/Sub-Sect

As already mentioned in the previous chapter, Jain community in the Bundelkhand region is dominated by *Terapanthi* Digambar Jain sub-sect. Therefore, the overwhelming majority of our respondents (93.9%) belonged to this sub-sect only. A few respondents (1.7%) were *Taaranpanthis*. In Bundelkhand the followers of this sub-sect are also known as *Samaiyas* who happen to be non-idolatrous.

Caste/Sub-Caste

As detailed in the previous chapter, *Terapanthis* are divided into three major castes: *Parwar*, *Golapurv* and *Golalare*. *Taaranpanthis*, or *Samaiyas* being the other subsect in Bundelkhand, and also being numerically very small, act as a caste for all practical purposes. In fact, formerly a majority of them belonged to *Parwar* caste. The distribution of our sample in terms of the four caste-groupings is as follows: *Parwar, Golapurv, Golalare* and *Samaiya*. All the four castes were traditionally endogamous but demographic dynamics in recent decades have forced them to practise inter-caste marriage within the Jain community.

Table 3.4: Caste of Respondents

Caste	*Percentage*
Golapurv	20.6
Parwar	70
Golalare	3.3
Samaiya	1.7
No Response	4.4
Total	100.0

Rural/Urban Background

Respondents were drawn from both rural and urban areas. Thus of the total respondents, 39 per cent were from rural areas whereas 61 per cent belonged to urban areas. This sample roughly represent the Bundelkhand reality in terms of rural-urban distribution of the Jains in the region. Incidentally, at the all-India level only about 25 per cent of the Jain population lived in rural areas in 2001 Census (Jain, Prakash C. 2011). In the 2011 census this figure came down to only 20.0 per cent. In this context it must be pointed out here that in the Bundelkhand region the divide between rural and urban areas should be conceptualised more on the lines of big towns and small towns than on the lines of city and village.

Home Ownership

Ownership of a home or otherwise is an important indicator of the socio-economic background of the respondents. Data in this study reveal that almost all the respondents (91.1%) in both urban and rural areas live in their own homes. Only 7.2 per cent respondents were living in rented houses. Three respondents did not reply to this question.

Table 3.5: Home Ownership of Respondents

Type of Residence	*Percentage*
Own	91.1
Rent	7.2
Other	1.7
Total	100.0

Agricultural Land Ownership

Although a majority of respondents live in urban areas, many of them also own agricultural land in rural areas which often happen to be their ancestral places.It is also very likely that most such respondents might be the recent immigrants into the urban areas who still continue to maintain land-ownership in those very villages from where they migrated.

Urban Immigration

Whereas one-third of respondents in our study in both rural and urban areas have declared themselves as native to their respective place of residence (non-immigrants), two-thirds of them (66.7%) have moved from villages to small towns or cities. This process of rural-urban migration has been going on for more than a century now. Responses to a question "since when did you immigrate into towns and cities?" are summed up in Table 3.6. Accordingly, about 63 per cent of the respondents said they moved more than 20 years ago, while 14.1 per cent moved between 10-20 years ago and 10 per cent less than 10 years ago. About 12.6 per cent of the respondents did not answer the question (*See* Table 3.7).

Table 3.6: No. of Respondents Immigrated into Urban Areas

Immigrated?	*Percentage*
Yes	66.7
No	33.3
Total	100.0

Table 3.7: When did the Immigrants Move?

No. of Years	*Percentage*
<10	10.0
10-20	14.1
>20	63.3
No Response	12.6
Total	100.0

Educational Background

Education happens to be an important indicator of the socio-economic background of the respondents in any sociological study. In modern times the level, kind and quality of education is directly related to the occupational status of the individual on the one hand and the class and prosperity of the community on the other hand. All the modern professions, trade and commerce require correspondingly better education, training and skill (*see* Table 3.8).

In terms of education two kinds of respondents in Bundelkhand Jain community have been *apriori* identified: (i) those who completed their schooling and/or higher education through normal channels of education in India, and (ii) those who graduated from community-supported Jain Sanskrit *vidyalayas* (colleges) which had been established during the first half of the 20th century in many cities, towns and villages of north India. In these *vidyalayas* boarding and lodging is provided free of cost, and along with the Sanskrit

Table 3.8: Educational Level of Respondents

Highest Education	*Percentage (%)*
Below Primary	0.6
Primary	5.6
Secondary	8.9
Higher Secondary	12.8
Graduate	26.1
Masters	42.7
No Response	3.3
Total	100.0

education (grammar, literature and other aspects of Indology), Jain philosophy and religion are compulsorily taught. Both students and Jain teachers are also supposed to be the practicing Jains in these institutions. In this study 23 per cent of the respondents were educated in these *vidyalayas*, whereas the rest of them (76%) were educated in mainstream or "normal" kinds of educational institutions.

Table 3.9: Respondents who Studied in Jain Vidyalayas

	Percentage
Yes	23.3
No	76.7
Total	100.0

When asked for the reasons for studying in Jain *vidyalayas*, 38.1 per cent of the respondents mentioned poor family economic conditions, while desire to study Jainism and Sanskrit was mentioned by 57.1 per cent of the respondents.

Most of the respondents who studied in Sanskrit *vidyalayas* were awarded Shastri or Acharya degrees, that is, degrees equivalent to graduation and post-graduation. In subsequent years some of them earned Ph.D. or even D.Lit degrees in Sanskrit, Prakrit, Pali, Hindi, Jainology or Indology disciplines.

Table 3.10: Reason for Studying in Jain Vidyalayas

Reason	*Percentage*
Poor condition of family	38.1
Wish to study Jainism and Sanskrit	57.1
No response	4.8
Total	100.0

Occupation of Respondents

A clear majority of our respondents (55.0%) are in wide variety of services, whereas only 38.9 per cent of them are engaged in business. Only 2.8 per cent of the respondents are engaged in agriculture (*See*Table 3.11). Among the rest, two respondents are housewives and the rest are either students or parents who do not fit into above mentioned occupational categories. Our sample survey also suggests that about 23 per cent of the respondents were engaged in family business which include general/provision stores, medical stores, hardware and jewellery stores, clothing and garment sales stores and purchase and sales of cereals, grams and pulses, etc. It is significant to note that 75 per cent of the respondents are not engaged in any kind of family business. This suggests that whereas the majority of respondents (55%) are employed in the formal service sector, about 20 per cent of them are engaged in non-conventional family businesses such as providing information and technology services, medical and legal services, accountancy and income-tax related services, small scale entrepreneurial activities and civil construction and contracting services.

Table 3.11: Occupation of Respondents

Occupation	*Percentage*
Agriculture	2.8
Business	38.9
Service	55
Housewife	1.1
Others	2.2
Total	100.0

Income

Jains of Bundelkhand are extremely prudent about disclosing their income and wealth. They often try to hide their wealth (in terms of gold, fixed deposits, land and other properties) and under-report the income even when it is obvious. Such obvious discrepancies had to be judiciously addressed while tabulating the income levels of respondents. On the whole our survey data suggest that about half of our respondents (49.4%) earn less than rupees five lakh per annum, whereas 28.9 per cent earn between rupees five to ten lakh. Further on, 10.6 per cent of the respondents earn between Rs. 10 to Rs. 15 lakhs, and 6.1 per cent earn between Rs. 15 to Rs. 20 lakh. There is also a group of respondents (3.0%) whose annual income exceeds Rs. 20 lakhs. This category also includes a few families whose business turn-over runs into crores of rupees.

In the Bundelkhand region, these income levels of the Jain community as a whole should be considered as quite comfortable given the fact that the people are living in smaller cities, towns and villages where transportation costs and other day-to-day living expenses are relatively low. Additionally, almost all the respondents live in their own houses.

Table 3.12: Annual Income of the Family of Respondents

Income in Lakhs	*Percentage*
<5	49.4
5-10	28.9
10-15	10.6
15-20	6.1
20 Lakhs & above	5.0

Family Size

The number of family members living with the respondents in our sample ranged from 1 to 23. However, the overwhelming majority of respondents (98.3%) had ten or less than 10 members in their families. The details of the frequency distribution of data about family size of the respondents are presented in Table 3.13. It can easily be seen that almost half of the total respondents (48.9%) had four to six members in their families, whereas 20.0 per cent of them had one to three members, and 21.1 per cent had seven to nine members. The remaining 10.0 per cent of the respondents had ten or more members in their families. Of these, only three families had 20, 22 and 23 members respectively.

Table 3.13: Size of the Family

Number of Family Members	*Percentage*
1-3	20.0
4-6	48.9
7-9	21.1
10+	10.0
Total	100.0

Gadgets Used at Home

The relatively high income levels of the respondents' families by Bundelkhand standards are also reflected in the various home appliances used by the respondents. Our survey data suggest that a vast majority of respondents own and use numerous home appliances such as cooking gas *choolah*, refrigerator, mixer/juicer, microwave ovens and coolers. Some of them also use air conditioners depending on the availability of electricity. Among the means of transport, bicycles and scooters, are widely used. Some of them also own cars or jeeps. Almost all the families own and use either telephone or mobile (see Table 3.14).

Concluding Remarks

An overwhelming majority of respondents were married, elderly male ranging in

Table 3.14: Gadgets Used at Home

Gadgets	*Percentage*	*Percentage*	*Percentage*
Gas Choolah	98.9	1.1	100
Fridge	91.6	8.4	100
Microwave Oven	36	64	100
Washing Machine	66.5	33.5	100
Scooter/Bike	86	14	100
Car/Jeep	49.2	50.8	100
Phone/Mobile	96.1	73.9	100
A.C./Cooler	78.2	21.8	100

age from 40 to 70 years. Almost all the Jains in Bundelkhand belong to *Terapanth* sub-sect of Digambar Jainism with microscopic minority being the followers of Taaranpanth sub-sect, also called *Samaiyas*. There are no *Shwetambar* respondents in our sample. The caste composition of the respondents is dominated by *Parwars* (75%) followed by *Golapurv* (20%), *Golalare* (3%) and *Samaiyas* (2%). The rural-urban break up of respondents is 31 per cent and 69 per cent respectively, significant majority of them being recent immigrants (20 years or less) into urban areas. Irrespective of living in rural or urban areas, the vast majority of respondents (91 per cent) own their houses. Some of them also own agricultural land in their native villages and towns.

A significant majority of respondents have graduate or post-graduate degrees. About 23 per cent of our respondents have stayed and studied in Jain Sanskrit *vidyalayas*—most of them simultaneously earning their graduate or post-graduate degree from a college or university. Occupation-wise, about 55 per cent of the respondents were working in service sector and only about 40 per cent doing business. Income levels of the respondents were found to be as follows—less than Rs. 5 lakh per annum: about 50 per cent, Rs. 5-10 lakh: about 30 per cent, Rs. 10-15 lakh: about 10 per cent and more than Rs. 20 lakhs: about 10 per cent. With these kinds of income levels and house-ownership, it is not surprising that most of the respondents could afford all kinds of home appliances. This study questions the stereotypical image of Bundelkhandi Jains being projected as a petty trading community. The study also suggests that the income levels of the community have been steadily on the rise for the past two decades or so.

4

Education and Occupational Changes

Jainism is a salvation religion. As followers of liberation-oriented cultured professional monks, Jains realise the importance of education not only for the other-worldly objectives, but also for the purpose of worldly affairs. In Jainism the combination of right perception, right knowledge and right conduct is considered as the means to liberation. Jainism also considers self-study as the supreme virtue/austerity (swadhyayparmamtapah). Thus, the other-worldly goals cannot be achieved without education and knowledge. As historical trading community the Jains also understand the importance of education for doing modern trades and commercial activities, and even for living a peaceful and meaningful life. It is against this backdrop that this chapter highlights the continuity and change in the occupational structure of the Jain community in Bundelkhand. The chapter attempts to explore issues and aspects like family business and entrepreneurship, accessibility of higher education to Jain students, and their professional/occupational choice, role of Jain Sanskrit *vidyalayas* (schools) in occupational mobility, inter-generational occupational mobility, and respondents' educational and occupational aspirations for the children/grandchildren. Wherever possible, arguments and analysis would be supplemented by relevant case studies.

Jains' Stake in Bundelkhand's Economy

Jains have been deeply entrenched into the economy of Bundelkhand for at least over a millennium now. They constituted predominantly a commercial and trading petty bourgeoisie. Their preponderance in these occupations is predicated on certain social structural features of the Bundelkhand society. Reports based on 1991 and 2001 census data clearly suggests that among the Hindu castes belonging to *Vaishya varna* such as Agrawal, Mittal, Bansal, Rastogi, Gupta, etc. are more or less absent in Bundelkhand. In fact, Bundelkhand society is dominated by Other Backward Castes (OBC) and Scheduled Castes/Dalits (SC). Thus, OBCs constituted about 53 per cent of the total population of Bundelkhand, whereas the share of SC/Dalits was about 25 per cent and that of Scheduled Tribes was around 10 per cent. The remaining 12 per cent consisted of Thakurs, Brahmins, Jains, Muslims and other religious communities. In terms of religious composition, the population of Bundelkhand consists of Hindus 93 per cent, Muslims 5 per cent, and followers of other religions 2 per cent, including Jains.

As the majority of the population in Bundelkhand is engaged in agriculture, mining and handicrafts, the Jains have acquired a pre-eminent economic niche in trade and commerce—and that too without much of a competition from any quarters. One exception in this regard has been the *Telis* (oil-pressure caste) who had initially opened provision shops and subsequently moved into other entrepreneurial activities such as flour mills, dal mills, etc., besides doing agriculture and their caste occupation of oil-pressing. In short, this conjecture of varna/caste composition and division of labour that evolved over centuries helps explain why the Jains have emerged pre-eminently and preponderantly as a trading and commercial community in the Bundelkhand region. It must also be mentioned in passing that this kind of historical conjecture with respect to Jains is unique to the Bundelkhand/Greater Bundelkhand region, and perhaps has not occurred anywhere else in India.

Since olden days Jain traders mainly supplied provision and household items such as rice, wheat, pulses, salt, sugar, jaggery, cooking oils, kerosene oil, ground nuts, dry fruits, spices and medicinal herbs, and pharmaceutical products. Additionally, textile was a major and mostly an exclusive item sold by Jain traders. Around the middle of the 20th century soaps, detergents, hair oils, shampoos, tooth powders and pastes, shoes, stationery items, school-books, etc. also began to be used by a small number of people in rural as well as urban areas. Tobacco and bidi were already consumed by a large section of peasantry and labour classes. Later on, cigarettes became a newer and fashionable item among the tobacco products. This list of items sold by traders kept on increasing as per the availability and demand of newer and modern products. Thus, a whole range of plastic goods such as buckets, mugs, chairs, tables, stools, toys, etc. flooded the market. Since about the last decade of the 20th century processed food items, particularly snacks and soft drinks, and bottled water, have swept the market, and the Bundelkhand region was no exception to the trend. The beginning of 21st century has also ushered in the era of transport revolution and mechanization of agriculture in rural areas which has given rise to boost in merchandising spare-parts of motor cycles, tractors and other agricultural implements along with their repair and servicing business. The latest to join the consumer market products are the mobile phones.

Most shops in rural as well as urban areas sold assorted items mentioned above. However, some also sold specialised line of products such as textiles, ready-made garments, hardware, jewellery, shoes, etc. Some idea of the economic activities of Jains in the region can be had from the 1986 unofficial "census" of Chhatarpur district Jain population numbering 8,127 spread over 104 towns and villages. The total number of families was 1,188. The occupational distribution of these families was reported as follows: *Kirana* (Provision) stores: 513 (43.2%), Textile shops: 152 (12.8%), Service 149 (12.5%), and others 374 (31.5%) (Jain, Mahendra Kumar, 1986: 95). Thus, as late as 1980s only 12 per cent-15 per cent Jain population of Bundelkhand was involved in services, and the rest mainly in business—particularly in *Kirana* and textiles related businesses.

During the third quarter of the 20th century, there were still a few Jain shopkeepers in villages who were dependent on *banji* (literally trade or business) for living. Each morning they would collect a number of provision goods in jute sacks, carry them on their own back or horse-back and rush to nearby small village(s) for selling the goods on barter basis. The business would last for four-five hours whence the shopkeepers would return home carrying back the unsold items and several kilogrammes of food grains they collected in exchange. During the 1950s and '60s, of the 16 Jain families living in Saidpur village of Lalitpur district, four did *Banji*—three of them used horses for transport as well as conveyance. Today this economic institution no longer exists in the Bundelkhand region.

Besides trade, commerce, money-lending, etc., some Jains in rural areas were also engaged in agriculture and animal husbandry. More often than not, they got the agricultural work done by the paid labourers, or on the share-cropping basis. Typical of the agrarian economy, most Jain families also kept domestic animals as per their requirements. These included cows, buffalos, oxens and horses. The rich ones usually had a large stock of such animals. Seth Laxmi Chand of Bamrana/Sadumal, for example, reportedly had a herd of about 200 such animals during the early decades of the 20th century. While cows and buffalos supplied milk and other dairy products, oxen were used for tilling the agricultural land and/or pulling the cart, thereby called the bullock-cart. Horse served as a means of transportation of goods and family members. As already mentioned, horse was also used by a few Jains to do *Banji.* Today, very few Jains in Bundelkhand are engaged in agriculture and animal husbandry.

In Bundelkhand villages, Jains never lived in segregated or separate areas. They were dispersed all over the village, and shops owned by them were generally located in their respective residences. Market places were generally located in the centre of the villages. During the past few decades this situation has changed in most road-side villages, and the market places have shifted to the main road/highway near the village bus stop. All the four villages included in this study have undergone this change. In fact, it is the country-wide trend following the economic and infra-structural development in rural areas. Weekly *haats* (markets) have also shifted to these new venues.

Jains' pre-eminent economic position as a trading community has bestowed them with certain public honour and respect in the wider society of Bundelkhand which was historically strengthened by philanthropic and benevolent acts of Jain economic elites, that is the Seths. The Seth is a generic term equivalent to *dhanik varga*, that is, wealthy and financially very well-off individuals. Often this class also included individuals who had been decorated with the traditional honourific titles of *Singhai, Sawai Singhai, Seth and Srimant Seth* on account of their sponsoring *Panch-kalyanak Mahotsav* (celebration of five auspicious events associated with the life of a Tirthankar, namely conception, birth, diksha, omniscience and nirvan) and/or *Gajarath Mahotsav* (elephants-drawn chariot procession).

The word *Singhai* is the distorted form of the Sanskrit word *Sanghpati.* In the Bundelkhand region, this title is given to those who have sponsored one *Panch-kalyanak* and/or *Gajarath.* Those who sponsor two *Panch-kalyanak* and/or *Gajarath* are given the title *Sawai Singhai*, in case of three *Gajarath,* the title is *Deodhria (Deodhe Singhai),* in case of four *Gajarath,* the title is Seth, and in case of five *Gajarath*, the title given is *Srimant Seth.* Later on, even in case of four *Gajarath,* the title of *Srimant Seth* was given. These titles are given by the community members on the completion of the function and are hereditarily used as prefix to their names or as surnames by the recipients.

The tradition of *Gajarath* is unique to Bundelkhund and it is from here that it spread to other parts of the country. According to Siddhantacharya Pandit Phoolchandra Shastri (1992: 539), some 200 years ago, a grand *Panch-kalyanak* was organised at Chanderi in which the chariot was drawn by elephants. Before this, there was no custom of using elephant-drawn chariot in P*anch-kalyanak.* Subsequently, the practice became commonplace in the entire Bundelkhad region, and spread to some other parts of the country.

Some idea of the strength of this *dhanik varga* can be had from the fact that as per *1924 Directry of Parwar Jains*, there were as many as 1,022 *Singhais*, 161 *Sawai Singhais*, and 130 *Seths* in the Bundelkhand region (Shastri, J. 1992: 15). The comparable figures for the Golapurav caste for the year 1941 was *Singhai* 1,183, *Sawai Singhai* 281, *Seth* 478, *Sawai Seth* 8 (Jain, Kavyatirth Mohan Lal 1941: 166). Needless to say, until about the middle of the last century, this *dhanik varg* functioned as community leaders and as such wielded considerable power among the Jains and non-Jains alike. In this context, a few case studies highlighting the status and role of the traditional economic elites in the Bundelkhand region would be quite illustrative.

Raibahadur Shrimant Seth Mohan Lal, Khurai

Shrimant Seth Mohan Lal (1863-1926) was a relative and adopted son of Seth Nand Lal Jain of Khurai who had migrated and settled at Khurai from Delwara village near Lalitpur town in 1798 A.D. In due course, of time Seth Nand Lal earned wealth from agriculture, business and money-lending, etc., and eventually earned the honourific title of Seth after getting performed three *Gajarath Panch-kalyanak Pratishthas* in 1834, 1839 and 1862. Seth Mohan Lal himself got performrd the fourth *Gajarath* function in 1893 and was bestowed with the title of Shrimant Seth.

Seth Mohan Lal who had inherited substantial amount of wealth was also a *malguzar* (land revenue collector) of 84 villages in the Khurai area. He was extremely popular in the Bundelkhand region on account of his leadership qualities and kind-heartedness. During 1899-1900 famine in the region he had generously opened his food-grains stock for distribution to the public. On another occasion he headed a delegation of 150 Jain pilgrims to Girinarji in Gujarat on his own expenses (Shastri, Pt. Phoolchandra, 1992: 336-37). Seth Mohan Lal was invited to participate in the Delhi Durbar on the occasion of the coronation ceremony in England of King George V in 1911, folloing which he was honoured with the title of "Raibahadur". In 1920 his persistent efforts led to the cancelation of a government-sponsored slaughter-house project in Ratona village near Khurai. Seth Mohan Lal was associated with a number of Jain institutions and associations including Shri Bharatvarshiya Digambar Jain Mahasabha and Parwar Sabha. For several years he was Secretary-General of the Mahasabha.

Seth Laxmi Chand Jain, Bamrana/Sadumal

Seth Laxmi Chand Jain (1856-1920) was a zamindar, businessman and money-lender at Bamrana and Sadumal villages of present-day Lalitpur district. He also had properties at Lalitpur town. He was a progressive person and had leadership qualities for which he was very well known all over the Bundelkhand region. He was the first president of Parwar Sabha at the Ramtek convention. He was the founder of Sadumal Jain Sanskrit Vidyalaya whose first principal was Pt. Ghanshyam Das of Mahroni. A promoter of Jainology, Sethji motivated and financially helped a number of students in getting them educated at Morena Jain Sanskrit Vidyalaya, an advanced institution for Jain Studies in those days. These included Pt. Ghanshyam Das, Pt. Phoolchandra Siddhantacharya, Pt. Hira Lal Siddhantashastri and Pt. Kishori Lal, to name only a few. In case of Pt. Ghanshyam Das, Sethji had additionally taken on himself the financial responsibilities of his family. His eleder brother's name was Seth Brij Lal Jain and that of his younger brother was Seth Chandra Bhan Jain who rose to become the president of Shri Bharatvarshiya Digambar Jain Mahasabha in 1932. Seth Laxmi Chand had no child and had an adopted son named Seth Sanat Kumar. The descendants of Sethji and members of the extended family are mostly in various professions now.

Seth Mathura Das Taraiya, Lalitpur

Taraiya family is a very well-known and illustrious family of Lalitpur. The family has been mainly into money-lending as well as trading business of textile and jewellery. Among the well-known family members, mention must be made of Mathura Das, Hukum Chand and Jineshwar Das. Seth Mathura Das (1872-1920) had leadership qualities and was known for these in the Jain community of Bundelkhand along with Seth Mohan Lal of Khurai and Seth Laxmi Chand of

Bamrana. He was involved in the renovation work of Shri Digambar Jain Atishaya Khetra, Khetrapalji, Lalitpur.

His son Seth Hukam Chand Taraiya (born 1917) had donated land for the construction of a Kanjipanthi temple Shri Seemandhar Jinalaya at Lalitpur. His cousin Seth Jineshwar DasTaraiya (1916-1998) had made financial contribution towards the construction of the same temple through Kamlabai Jineshwar Das Taraiya Trust. Seth Jineshwar Das was president of Lalitpur Digambar Jain Panchayat, and was the first chairman of the managing committee of Shri Varni Jain Inter College, Lalitpur that was established in 1946 in the wake of a *chaturmas* of Kshullak Ganesh Prasad Varni in the town. He was also an honorary District Magistrate for 38 years. The Taraiya family continues to be a respected family in Lalitpur, although its former glory is on the wane. Besides business and other traditional economic activities, a few of its family members have also moved into professional vocations. A couple of them are settled abroad.

Shrimant Seth Bhagwan Das Jain, Sagar

Second son of Seth Pooran Chand, Bhagwan Das was born in Airan village of Sagar district in 1899. His elder brother was Mohan Lal and the name of his younger brother was Shobha Lal. In 1930, he established a *bidi* (Indian cigarette made up of a tree leaf and tobacco) manufacturing enterprise under the name M/s Bhagwandas Shobhalal that turned out to be a great success. Subsequently, the family ventured out into a number of other businesses with overall turn-over running into several crores of Rupees. Seth Bhagwan Das was a great philanthropist. In 1940 he had established Mohan Public Charitable Hospital in memory of his elder brother, and in 1980 he donated a sum of Rs. 250,101 for setting up diagnostic centre for mental patients at the University of Sagar. In order to mitigate the sufferings of victims of Bhopal Carbide gas leak he had donated a sum of rupees one lakh to Prime Minister's Relief Fund. His widely known philanthropic act, however, was to give up in 1985 the ownership of 25 residential plots near his residential quarters on which Dalit families had been living for a number of years. This was done in the presence of the then Chief Minister of Madhya Pradesh.

According to Siddhantacharya Pt. Phool Chandra Shastri (1992: 372), Seth Bhagwan Das "was a devout follower of Taaran Taran Swami. He also had unbroken faith in Bundelkhand's great soul Kshullak Ganesh Prasad Varni and Songarh's saint Gurudev Kanji Swami. In order to listen to the discourse of the latter, Sethji used to go and stay in Songarh for months." As already detailed in Chapter Two, his son Seth Dal Chand Jain was two-term elected member of Indian Parliament from Damoh Lok Sabha constituency.

Nagarseth Gulab Chand, Damoh

Nagarseth Gulab Chand belonged to a rich Seth family of Damoh whose ancestors got constructed two temples at Kundalpur and one each at Damoh and Nainagiri—all accompanied by *Gajarath Panch-kalyanak Pratishtha Mahotsav*. His father Seth Dalchand was a zagirdar of 40 villages. When Gulab Chand was born, people of Abhana village requested and demanded Seth sahib Dal Chand for getting constructed a temple of Lord Ram to which he happily agreed by donating suitable land for the same and additionally getting constructed a pond as well (Shastri, Phoolchandra, 1992: 366-67). He was given the title "*Nagarseth*" by the public and is reflective of the fact that as chairman of the Debt Board during the great depression of 1930s, he had waved off the debt of rupees one lakh ninety thousand.

Nagarseth Gulab Chand donated 40 acres of land to a local government hospital in Damoh. For a number of years, he was Vice-President of Damoh Municipality. He was survived by three sons who like their father were active in public life. He was generous to the core of his heart. He would often help poor families on the marriage occasions. Each year on completion of the *Paryushan Parv* he used to invite all the Jains of Damoh town for a feast.

These are only a few illustrative names. There have been scores of others such as Shrimant Seth Laxmi Chand, Vidisha; Seth Chandra Bhan, Sadumal; Jatibhushan Singhai Kundan Lal, Sagar; Shri Shiv Prasad Malaiya, Sagar; Sawai Singhai Garibdas Jain, Jabalpur; Singhai Panna Lal Jain, Amravati; Seth Jineshwardas Tadaiya, Lalitpur; Sawai Singhai Kanhaiya Lal and Girdhari Lal Jain, Katni; Sawai Singhai Dhanya Kumar Jain, Katni; Shrimant Seth Dal Chand Jain, Sagar; Singhai Nathuram "Babba", Bina; Nagarseth Lal Chand Jain, Damoh; Sawai Singhai Ganpat Lal, Bhaiya Lal and Jinendra Kumar Gurha, Khurai; Dashrath Jain, Chhatarpur; Kapoor Chand Jain Potdar, Tikamgarh; Singhai Shikhar Chand Jain, Panna (*See* Shastri, Phoolchandra Siddhantacharya, 1992: 229-504).

With the passage of time the business activities of the older generation of Jain Seths and Singhais have undergone a number of transformations during the past half-a-century. Thus, a few legendary families have disappeared from the scene, mainly due to their being childless, or due to the incompetence of their descendants. Some of their descendants have expanded and modernized their businesses and have been doing very well. Still others have abandoned business and commercial activities altogether and have turned into families of educated modern professionals. Needless to say, education has played a major role in transforming not only the class of old elites but also the ordinary members of the Jain community in Bundelkhand. The present economic and professional status of the Jain community as per the sample of our study is highlighted next.

Education and Occupation of Respondents

In Chapter Three, we discussed the educational level and occupational background of our respondents. As per our data, there is a preponderance of respondents (68.8%) with graduate and post-graduate degrees. Not surprisingly, and correspondingly, a majority of respondents are engaged in service sector (55%) followed by business (38.9%). Very few respondents (2.8%) from our sample are pursuing agriculture. This only suggests that the majority of Bundelkhandi Jains have moved away from petty trade and commerce to the service sector. Therefore, the stereotypical image of them as petty traders and merchants is no longer sustainable. Even if we allow due concession to bias in our sample, the trend of moving away from trade and commerce to service sector appears for the time being to be irreversible. This is, however, not to suggest that business is no longer an attractive proposition for the Jains in Bundelkhand or that the trend is an absolute one. The rationale behind such an assertion is simple in that the business sector is not only diversifying and modernizing itself but many educated young boys are also getting attracted to it. Moreover, the possibility of earning wealth through business is far more real than through professional jobs.

Education and Occupational Mobility

Education and training play an important role in the choice of an individual's occupation. In traditional Indian society, education was neither universally imparted to all castes and classes nor was it easily available; it was restricted to only Brahmins and a few Kshatriyas. Moreover, only varna/caste-specific education and training was allowed to be given. The lower caste members were not allowed to get any general education. Since most occupations were caste-bound, the requisite education and training was imparted only within the family. Industrialisation and modernisation have changed all this: modern occupations are not only far more numerous and highly diversified, they also require extended modern education and specialised training which can be done only in a separate and now well-developed social institution, called school. Certain modern occupations do require as many as 5-10 years or more specialised education and training beyond at least 12 years of schooling. One can easily recall here the number of modern occupations such as university teaching, engineering, medicine, law, management, information technology, etc. in this context. In short, education is the best avenue in getting employment in modern occupations and for occupational mobility.

In our study, data presented in Tables 4.1 and 4.2 clearly bring out the changing educational profile of the respondents' fathers. A majority of respondents in our study are well-educated with graduate and post-graduate college/university degrees (68.8%), whereas the comparable figures in case of their fathers was 14.6 per cent only. This figure is further reduced sharply when we compare the educational level of grandfathers of the respondents (Table 4.3). In their case, a majority were educated up to sixth standard or less. Only 8.9 per cent had up to higher secondary level education, and graduation was a rare phenomenon.

These educational levels of the three generations of Jains had direct bearing on their respective occupational profiles as well. Tables 4.4, 4.5 and 4.6 present data on occupational status of three generations of Jains in Bundelkhand. In grandfathers' generation, 54.4 per cent were engaged in business and 13.9 per cent were engaged in agriculture; only a tiny minority (3.9%) was engaged in service sector. In fathers' generation, there was a slight reduction in dependence on agriculture (7.8%), and a little more dependence on business (58.9%). Here, service sector emerges as the second important avenue for employment (19.4%) after business. In respondents' generation, agriculture provides employment to only a miniscule minority (2.8%), whereas service sector has emerged as the pre-eminent employer (55.0%) followed by the business sector (38.9%). These data raise doubts about the stereotypical image of Bundelkhandi Jains being still labelled as a trading community.

The data also underscore the clear case of generational occupational mobility among the Jains in Bundelkhand, mainly on account of acquisition of modern education and skills by them. All this further underline the role of secular educational institutions that are universally available to the Jains and the members of other communities in India. However, in the case of Bundelkhandi Jain community, the role of Jain Sanskrit Vidyalayas as mentioned in Chapter One cannot be ignored. In fact, they have played a major role in educating and mobilising the community in numerous ways.

Table 4.1: Educational Level of Respondents

Highest Education	*Percentage*
Below Primary	0.6
Primary	5.6
Secondary	8.9
Higher Secondary	12.8
Graduate	26.1
Masters	42.7
No Response	3.3
Total	100.0

Table 4.2: Educational Level of Respondents' Fathers

Education	*Percentage*
Illiterate	1.1
Below Primary	15.2
Primary	34.7
Secondary	14
Higher Secondary	9.6
Graduate	11.8
Masters	2.8
No Response	11.8
Total	100.0

Table 4.3: Educational Level of Respondents' Grandfathers

Education	*Percentage*
Illiterate	3.9
Below Primary	13.4
Primary	29.6
Secondary	6.1
Higher Secondary	2.8
Graduate	1.1
Masters	0.0
No Response	38.0
Total	100.0

Table 4.4: Occupation of Respondents

Occupation	*Percentage (%)*
Agriculture	2.8
Business	38.9
Service	55.0
Housewife	1.1
Others	2.2
Total	100.0

Table 4.5: Occupation of Respondents' Fathers

Occupation	*Percentage (%)*
Agriculture	7.8
Business	58.9
Service	19.4
Other	2.2
No Response	11.7
Total	100.0

Table 4.6: Occupation of Respondents' Grandfathers

Occupation	*Percentage (%)*
Agriculture	13.9
Business	54.4
Service	3.9
Other	1.7
No Response	26.1
Total	100.0

Educational Aspirations for Children

What educational/occupational aspirations respondents have for their children? This open-ended question elicited too many multiple responses to classify them into a few clear-cut categories. No-responses were also unusually very high at about 32.0 per cent of the total respondents. About 40.0 per cent of the respondents expressed their opinion in favour of higher/modern/technical education. About 10.0 per cent wanted to get their children employed in business/family business. Other occupational aspirations included government services, teaching, banking, etc. (For details, *see* Table 4.7).

Role of Jain Sanskrit Vidyalayas

Bundelkhund region is dotted with a number of Jain Sanskrit P*athshalas/ vidyalayas*. The current research on the subject suggests that perhaps the first Jain pathshala in Bundelkhand was established at the Tirth Kshetra Nainagiri in 1902 by Shri DaulatramVarni. It was named Baba Daulatram Varni Pathshala

Table 4.7: Educational/Occupational Aspirations for Children/Grandchildren

Aspirations	*Percentage*
Higher Education	11.1
Modern Education	25.0
Technical Education	5.6
Family Business	1.7
Business	7.8
Government Service	3.3
Teaching	2.8
Medical	1.1
Banking	0.6
Doctor, Engineer	1.7
Basic Education	2.2
Engineering and Agricultural Education	0.6
Sportsman	0.6
Administrative officer	2.2
Family Business and Teaching	0.6
Religious Education	1.1
No Response	32.2
Total	100.0

to be changed later on as Baba Daulatram Varni Digambar Jain Pathshala. About the same time, he had also founded another one at Jakhaura, district Lalitpur (*See* Jain, Suresh, 2018: 19). Other pathshalas/vidyalayas have been located at Moraji (Sagar), Bina (Sagar), Paporaji (Tikamgarh), Sonagiri (Datia) Aharji (Tikamgarh), Baruasagar (Jhansi), Sadumal (Lalitpur) and dozens of other places. Even bigger and more prestigious ones that attracted students from Bundelkhand were located at Ayodhya, Varanasi, Morena, Hastinapur, Katni, Indore, Jabalpur, Sanganer/Jaipur and Mahavirji (*see* Appendix-5). Most of these pathshalas/vidyalayas were established during the first half of the twentieth century. The following four case studies of Morena Vidyalaya, Sagar Vidyalaya, Sadumal Vidyalaya and Syadvad Mahavidylaya of Varanasi would highlight the historical significance of Jain Sanskrit vidyalayas.

1. Shri Gopal Digambar Jain Sidddhant Sanskrit Mahavidyalay, Morena

This is one of the oldest running Jain Sanskrit vidyalayas in North India. It was established in 1902 by Pt. Gopaldas Baraiya as a Jain *pathshala* in order to teach the philosophical principles of Jainism. After the untimely death of Pt. Baraiya in 1917 at the age of 51 years, the *pathshala* acquired its present name. At one time this vidyalaya was the only authenticating institution for becoming Jain pandit/scholar. It produced a number of first generation Jain pandits in India. Prominent among these were: Pt. Manik Chandra, Nyayacharya; Pt. Devkinandan; Pt. Sumerchand Diwakar; Pt. Bansidhar, Nyayalankar; Pt. Makkhanlal Shastri; Bhattarak Shri Charukeerti; Pt. Jaganmohanlal Shastri; Pt. Bansidhar, Vyakarnacharya; Pt. Kailash Chand, Siddhantacharya; Pt. Phoolchandra, Siddhantacharya; Pt. Hukum Chandra Bharill; etc. Additionally, a number of Digambar Jain ascetics also graduated from this Vidyalaya. Some of these are Acharya 105 Vimalsagar Maharaj, Acharya 108 Sumatisagar Maharaj, Acharya 108 Sambhavsagar Maharaj, Pattacharya 108 Gyansagar Maharaj, Muni 108 Ganeshkeerti Maharaj, Muni 108 Chinmayasagar Maharaj, Muni 108 Vardhmansagar Maharaj and a dozen more. Presently the institution imparts Sanskrit education from *Prathma* (6th standard) to *Uttar Madhyama* (12th standard) and is affiliated to Maharshi Patanjali Sanskrit Institute, Bhopal. The Vidyalaya has accommodation facilities for about 60 students.

2. Shri Ganesh Varni Digambar Jain Sanskrit Mahavidyalay, Sagar

This educational institution was founded by Shri Ganesh Prasad Varni in 1905. Initially it was known as Shri Sattark Sudha Tarangni Digambar Jain Pathshala. This Vidyalaya has produced a large number of pandits, scholars, teachers and *pratishthacharyas* in the past. The main buildings of the Vidyalaya located at Moraji were constructed with the generous donations of two wealthy Jains named Rajji Lal Kamarya and Sukhlal Pannalal Kamarya and their family members. Quite a few members of the Jain community of Sagar have been deeply involved in the affairs of the Vidyalaya. Among these two need special mention here who gave their life-long services to this institution: Pt. Daya Chandra Siddhantacharya who served as a principal, and Pt. Munna Lal Samgorya who as a pracharak collected millions of rupees by way of donations for the institution.

3. Shri Mahavir Digambar Jain Sanskrit Vidyalay, Sadumal

This institution was founded sometime in the early 1917 by Seth Shri Laxmi Chand Jain of Bamrana/Sadumal who was greatly inspired by Kshullak Ganesh Prasad Varni. Presently the School has about 200 students on its rolls. Of these about 40 students stay in a hostel named after Shri Ganesh Prasad Varni which provides free boarding and lodging. The school's Sanskrit course examinations are conducted by UP Secondary Sanskrit Education Board, Lucknow and the Jain studies examinations by the Kundkund Gyanpith Examination Board, Indore. It is the oldest Sanskrit vidyalay in UP-Bundelkhand and has been instrumental in shaping the early career of the following pandits and scholars over a period of about a century: Pt. Phoolchandra Siddhantacharya; Pt. Hiralal Siddhantshastri; Pt. Parmeshthidas Nyaytirth; Prof Khushal Chandra Gorawala; Pt. Darwarilal Kothia, Nyayacharya; Pt. Amritlal Shastri, Jain Darshanacharya; Pt. Gulab Chandra Pushpa, Pratishthacharya; Dr. Ramesh Chand Jain; Dr. Shital Chand Jain; Dr. Surendra Kumar Jain "Bharati"; Dr. Ashok Kumar Jain; Dr. Kamlesh Kumar Jain; etc. (*See* Jain, Narendra K. 2017).

4. Shri Syadvad Digambar Jain Sanskrit Mahavidyalaya, Varanasi

Though located about 500-700 km away from the Bundelkhand region, Shri Syadvad Mahavidyalaya of Varanasi has been for all practical purposes a Bundelkhandi institution. In fact, for more than a century now it has been a mini Bundelkhand (*See* Jain, Prakash C, 2005: 54-56). We have already briefly narrated in Chapter One the story of the establishment of this *Vidyalaya* on 12th June 1905. Besides Ganesh Prasad Varni, two more individuals that were instrumental in establishing the Syadvad *Pathshala*, as it was known until 1910, were late Bhagirath Varni and late Pandit Pannalal Wakliwal. All the three gentlemen got commitment of funds mostly in Bundelkhand of Rs. 100 per month supplemented by further donations of Rs. 20 per month from Seth Dev Kumar of Arrah and Rs. 30 per month from the Jain community of Varanasi. The total amount of Rs. 150 per month was considered sufficient for supporting 10 students. Seth Dev Kumar also gave away his Bhadaini-located Jain temple, *Dharamshala* and other nearby buildings for the *Pathshala* and the hostel (*See* Siddhantshastri, Kailash Chandra 2014: 19),

In 1910 the *Vidyalaya* got its present name. In December 1913 the Syadvad Mahavidyalaya celebrated its annual day with great fanfare that made it famous overnight, as it were. The function was attended by a number of Indian and foreign Jain scholars, namely Pt. GopaldasVaraiya, Nyayacharya Pt. Manikchand, Kunwar Digvijay Singh, Seth Surajbhan, Pt. Jugalkishor Mukhtar, Lala Bhagwandin, Jugmandirdas Jaini, Barrister Ajit Prasad Jain, German scholar Dr. Herman Jaicobi, Dr. Strauss of Calcutta, Dr. Satish Chandra Vidyabhushan (Principal of Sanskrit College of Calcutta), and Theosophist Mrs. Anne Beasant. Representatives from all the provinces and cities and town of India were also present in the function. By then the number of students had risen to about 40. By mid-1920s Sanskrit Studies up to the Acharya level had started. At the same time teaching of English and the mainstream higher education degrees like B.A. and M.A. (taken simultaneously from other educational institutions such as Banaras Hindu University, Kashi Vidyapith, etc. in the city) were also attracting an increasing number of Jain students. In 1941, Sahu Shanti Prasad Jain Trust began to give scholarships to support such studies with the result that a number of them got employed as college professors after earning their M.A. degrees along with Acharya degrees and degrees in Jainology.

Besides academics, students of Syadvad Mahavidyalaya had also played a major role in India's independence movement, particularly in the Quit India Movement of 1942, and the political activities of Netaji Subhash Chandra Bose through Indian National Army. The students as well as teachers through various means sought to raise the awareness in the public about the British rule and its ill effects on the economy and society of India and the need to overthrow it. Thus, Ganesh Prasad Varni, the founder of the Vidyalaya, in the early 1940s in a public meeting at Jabalpur chaired by Pt. Dwarka Prasad Mishra, the then Chief Minister of Vindhya Pradesh, donated a sheet of cloth to the Indian National Army which when auctioned fetched Rs. 3,000.

All these *vidyalayas* are run by Jain community's donations made by wealthy individuals (Seths) and other well-to-do members of the community. Since all the *vidyalayas* are invariably located in Jain temples complexes or adjacent to them, the visiting pilgrims also give small donations. During the ten day long *parvushanparv* the principal or Jain teachers of the *vidyalayas* are also sent in far off towns and cities for delivering religious discourses and for collecting funds on behalf of these *vidyalayas*. The funds thus collected go in running these institutions in such a way that the faculty and staff members get paid their salaries, and the students enjoy the facilities of free boarding, lodging and schooling. On top of all this, the needy students are also given scholarships or loan scholarships of modest amount (e.g., Rs. 5 or Rs. 10 per month during 1960s) by charitable Jain trusts or such organisations. Thus, the parents of the students are quite substantially spared of spending much money on their education as well as living during the stay in Sanskrit *vidyalayas*. It must be mentioned here that except one at Mahavirji, most of these *vidyalayas* are open only to boys. Also an overwhelming majority of students come from Bundelkhand region—a region that has been relatively underdeveloped and poverty-stricken for centuries and continues to be so even today. The vast majority of Jains of Bundelkhand too were in tune with the overall condition of the region till very recently.

In Jain Sanskrit *vidyalayas*, two different kinds of courses are offered: (1) Courses about Jainism, (2) Sanskrit language courses. Teaching of Jainism often involves scriptural learning, generally one text a year. Courses in Sanskrit language include teaching of Sanskrit literature, grammar and Indian philosophy and sometimes elementary English. Classes for these courses are often held in the morning until about 10:00/10:30 a.m. after which most students pursue secular/regular academic studies that begin with high school or intermediate college course and go up to B.A., M.A. and Ph.D. programmes. In some Indian states Sanskrit courses and regular academic courses, particularly at school levels are deemed equivalent.

Studies in Jainism and Sanskrit courses go well with arts stream academic courses of colleges and universities. In fact students in Bundelkhund who go for Sanskrit courses come from relatively poor economic background and thus already lose the option of science stream schooling at the very beginning. The end result is that the Jain Sanskrit *vidyalayas* have been flooded with Bundelkhundi students since the beginning of the twentieth century when some of these *vidyalayas* were established. Not surprisingly, a number of such *vidyalayas* like Shri Syadvad Mahavidyalaya, Varanasi are these days on the decline in terms of the total number of students registered in an academic year, mainly because the flow of students from Bundelkhand has almost dried due to the improved financial conditions of Jains there who prefer to send their wards to get educated in academic disciplines like engineering, medicine, business management, information technology, etc. The Syadvad Mahavidyalaya presently has only 8-10 students compared to its heydays in 1960s and 1970s when it had about 60 students on its roll.

Jain pathshalas/vidyalayas played a number of important roles in the lives of the students and their families. To begin with, they partially mitigated the economic burden of those families which could not have otherwise afforded to send their wards to post-secondary educational institutions. This was particularly true about families located in rural areas where schooling was not available beyond primary (fifth standard) or secondary (eighth standard) level. There is no denying the fact that in vast majority of cases of the Jain families of Bundelkhand, free boarding, lodging and tuition were a great attraction in sending their wards to these vidyalayas. The process was not only a chain reaction in villages and towns, in some cases all the male siblings and their cousins were sent to Sanskrit *vidyalayas*. This was indeed a great community self-help programme as far as the Jains of Bundelkhand were concerned. This programme, though still continuing, had slowed down by the end of the 20th century.

If traditional Jain vidyalayas with their exclusive emphasis on teaching Jainology, Sanskrit and Indological subjects have not been able to attract contemporary Jain youth, some of them have been tryting to adjust with the changing times not only in terms of the contents of education but also the pedagogical experimentation. The Jain vidyalayas at Sadumal, Sagar and Morena clearly reflect this trend. Some newly established Jain schools like Patibhasthali Gyanodaya Vidyapith, Jabalpur—a girls' school affiliated to Central Board of Secondary Education, Delhi, is one such institution which was inspired by Acharya Vidyasagarji Maharaj. Vidyasagar Institute of Management of Bhopal was also established in 1997 in order to meet the then emergent needs of the Jain community of the greater Bundelkhand. Among those who played a key role in establishing this institution mention must be made of Shri Suresh Jain, IAS (Retd) (born at Nainagiri, Chhatarpur in 1945, the founding chairman and managing director).

Rise of Jain Pandits

Dispensing free education to poor and needy students of the community was, as it were, the latent function of these Sanskrit *vidyalayas.* Their manifest function obviously was to produce a large number of scholars in order to study and conduct research on the vast body of Jain scriptural and literary works that was preserved in temple complexes and Shastra *bhandaras* for centuries. The idea was to strengthen Jainology or Jain Studies on the line of, or as part of, Indology. Additionally, scholars were needed to correctly understand the Jain way of life, codes of conduct for lay persons as well as ascetics and to gain knowledge about, and to learn to perform various religious rituals and activities such as construction of a new temple, *bedi-pratishtha, siddhachakravidhan,* regular worship, *panchkalyanaka,* Jain style marriage, etc. Needless to say that historically the Jain vidyalayas have been successful in producing a large number of Jain pandits and scholars who performed these various functions for over a century now (Appendix-2).

Life and work of earlier generation of pandits was a difficult one as most of them had irregular source of income. Many of them had to move from place to place in search of suitable employment—sometimes leaving behind their families in their native places or in towns/cities where they planned to stay permanently. Some of them worked for wealthy Jain Seths as latters' guide and philosophers. Quite a few of them worked as teachers in Jain Sanskrit *vidyalayas.* Most of the pandits would often go to distant places in Gujarat, Maharashtra, Karnataka, Delhi, etc. to do *pravachan* (religious discourse) in order to collect funds for their respective Jain vidyalayas. By way of honours bestowed upon them they would also have some monetary gains for themselves. In any case, the pandits lived a simple and austere life as per Jain ethical principles. Pandits' role as a link between ascetics and *tyagis* on the one hand and the Jain laity on the other required them to publicly perform a conservative and *status quoist* role. In this context, it is surprising and interesting to note that while most pandits lived up to this role-model, the same was not acceptable to them for their children. Very few pandits sent their children to Jain Sanskrit *vidyalayas* to become pandits. In fact a majority of Pandits' sons were educated and trained to become engineers, doctors, professors, etc. The following three case studies clearly put the roles and profiles of the Jain pandits in proper perspective.

Late Pt. Phoolchandra Siddhantacharya

Pt Phoolchandra Siddhantacharya (1901-1991) was one of the foremost Jain scholars of the 20th century who hailed from Bundelkhand. He was born and brought up in Silawan village of present-day Lalitpur district. His initial education was done at a school ln the neighbouring village Khajuria and Sadumal Jain pathshalas from where he was sent for higher studies in Sanskrit and Jainism to Morena Jain Sanskrit Vidyalaya by Seth Laxmichand of Bamrana/Sadumal on his personal initiative and expenses, as Panditji was not from an economically well-off family. He also studied and taught at Shri Syadvad Jain Mahavidyalaya of Varanasi during 1920s. Later he and his younger brother migrated from his native place Silawan to Bina, from where he again migrated and finally settled in Varanasi.

In his social and political career, Pt. Phoolchandra Shastri was associated with quite a few movements, some of which he himself started. Before India's independence, he was not only an active member of Indian National Congress but also the office bearer of its district level units in Bina/Sagar, Solapur and Amravati. During Quit India movement he was imprisoned in 1941. After independence he quit politics and continued to devote himself to social causes as well as Jain Studies—activities in which he was already deeply interested.

As a social activist, Panditji was opposed to many social evils prevalent in Bundelkhand Jain community until the middle of the 20th century. Among these child and incompatible marriages, *Bissa-Dassa* issue, wastage of money on *Gajarath* functions, educational backwardness among the Jains, particularly women, etc. were the prominent ones, which he tried to ameliorate in his own way. Thus, for example, he supported the widely opposed *Harijan* Temple Entry Bill of 1949 on the ground that Jainism was opposed to the Hindu Varna system based on the criterion of birth.

The doyen of Jain pandits, the major contribution of Pt. Phoolchandra Shastri lies in editing, translating and interpreting several parts/volumes of Jain canonical works such as *Shatkhandagam, Kashaypahud and Mahaband (Jayadhabla)*, besides about a dozen other Jain philosophical treatises (For a brief introduction and a list of his publications, see Jain, Prem Chandra and Asha Jain, 2018: 1-18). His authored books include *Varna, Jati and Dharma* (1963, Second Edition), *Jain Tatwamimansa* (1960/1978), and *Parwar Jain Samaj ka Itihas* (1992).

Shastriji was a great institutions-builder as well. He founded several organisations such as All-India Digambar Jain Vidwat Parishad (founder joint-secretary, 1944), Shri Ganesh Prasad Varni Jain Granthmala (joint secretary and series editor, 1944), Shri Varni Jain Inter College, Lalitpur (founder-member, 1946), Shri Varni Digambar Jain Shodh Sansthan, Varanasi (1971), etc. Presently, the Varni Granthmala and the Shodh Sansthan are looked after by his son Dr. Ashok Kumar Jain, Professor of Nuclear Physics at Indian Institute of Technology, Roorkee. He has also established at Roorkee Siddhantacharya Pt. Phoolchandra Shastri Foundation in his father's memory.

As early as in 1962 on the occasion of the diamond jubilee celebrations of Jain Siddhant Bhawan, Arrah, the then Governor of Bihar Dr. Anant Shaynam Ayengar had bestowed upon him with the title of "Siddhantacharya". Subsequently he had been given several awards and honours including an "Abhinandan Granth" (commemoration volume) by various institutions and associations.

Pandit Dr. Hukam Chand Bharill

Dr. Hukam Chand Bharill was born at Barodaswami village in Lalitpur district on 25 May 1935. For over half a century now he lives in Jaipur. A prominent exponent of Kanji Swami Panth ideology in Digambar Jainism, Dr. Bharill is a traditional Jain pandit/scholar and spiritual preacher par excellence. He has authored 88 books, including his well-known work *Krambaddhaparyay*, originally written in Hindi and published in 1980. Since then the book has gone into 14th edition in 2016 with a total sale of over 52,000 copies. It has also been translated into English, Marathi, Gujarati, Kannada and Tamil. In all, over 100,000 copies have been sold. Dr. Bharill's spiritual discourses are very well attended and they are also run regularly on Jain television channels. He has made scores of visits to foreign countries in connection with his discourses.

Dr. Bharill edits a monthly magazine "Veetrag Vigyan", simultaneously published in Hindi, Marathi and Kannada. Secretary General of Pt. Todarmal Smarak Trust, he is also associated with a number of Jain associations and organisations including Mangalayatan University, All India Digambar Jain Vidwat Parishad and Digambar Jain Mahasamiti.

Prof. Bhagchandra Jain 'Bhaskar'

Professor Bhagchandra Jain 'Bhaskar' is presently a leading scholar of ancient Indian languages and Shraman culture. He was born on 11th September 1936 at Bamhori village of Chhatarpur district in Madhya Pradesh. After the early schooling at his village school, he moved for further education to Jain Sanskrit Mahavidyalaya of Sagar, and then to Shri Syadvad Mahavidyalaya, Varanasi. Prof. Bhaskar holds three M.A. degrees in Pali, Sanskrit and Ancient Indian History, Culture and Archaeology and as many D. Litts. In Sanskrit, Pali-Prakrit and Hindi, in addition to a Ph.D. from Colombo University of Sri Lanka on "Jainism in Buddhist Literature" for which he was awarded a Commonwealth scholarship. During 1965-96 he served as a faculty member at the Deaparment of Pali and Prakrit of the Nagpur University. Following his superannuation from there, he has been associated with several educational institutions as visiting/honorary/emeritus professor/director/research fellow, etc.

A prolific writer, Prof. 'Bhaskar' has authored about 50 books and 200 research papers in the fields of (i) Prakrit and Jainism, and (ii) Pali and Buddhism. Additionally, he has also got published 40 more books based on editing and translation of ancient manuscripts in both these fields. For his mammoth contribution Professor 'Bhaskar' was honoured with a number of awards including President's commendation and award in 2004. In spite of his old age he is still actively engaged in research and writing, in addition to editing a few journals and magazines, notably *Prachin Teerth Jeernoddhar*. He is also the founder director of Sanmati Research Institute of Indology and founder-president of Smt. Tulsa Devi Gore Lal Jain Charitable Trust. On his 75th birthday Prof. Bhaskar was honoured and facilitated by Shri Bharatvarshiya Digambar Jain Mahasabha with a commemoration volume (*Abhinandan Granth*).

Education and Employment of Women

Women of Bundelkhand have been taking full advantage of education as shown by the data in Tables 4.4 and 4.5. Data pertaining to educational qualification of respondent's spouses clearly reveal that a significant number of women (38.2%) are highly qualified with graduate and post-graduate degrees, whereas 26.4 per cent of them have secondary and higher secondary level of education. A small group of spouses has education up to the level of primary or less but none of them are illiterate. Unfortunately the percentage of respondents not reporting the educational qualification of their spouses (22.4%) is considerably high. On the whole, however, this scenario regarding education of Jain women is quite encouraging given the fact that Bundelkhand is educationally as well as economically a backward region.

The same cannot be said about the employment scenario of the Jain women in Bundelkhand. Only about 11.1 per cent spouses are employed in service sector while only 2.2 per cent of them are running their own business. A vast majority of them (66.4%) are housewives. These data about work participation rate of Jain women in Bundelkhand are in tune with the 2011 census data in which case the Jain women's work participation rate is only about 12 per cent compared to an all India women average of 26.0 per cent. Most observers agree that it is only due to relative affluence of the Jain community that relatively fewer women tend to seek paid employment in spite of the fact that they are highly educated and well qualified for varied employment. Notwithstanding some anomalies regarding Jain women's status in education and employment sectors, Jain women are accorded much better status in religious/spiritual matters. This issue is discussed at some length in Chapter 5.

Table 4.8: Educational level of Respondents' Spouses

Education	*Percentage*
Illiterate	0
Below Primary	4.1
Primary	14.7
Secondary	13.5
Higher Secondary	12.9
Graduate	14.1
Masters	24.1
No Response	22.4
Total	100.0

Table 4.9: Occupation of Respondents' Spouces

Occupation	Percentage
Agriculture	0
Business	2.2
Service	11.1
Other	0.6
Housewife	64.4
No Response	21.7
Total	100.0

Higher Education and Out-Migration from Bundelkhand

Apart from rural-urban migration resulting in the increased urbanisation of the Jain community within the Bundelkhand region, a considerable number of them has also been migrating to major towns and cities of India outside the region. These include Gwalior, Indore, Bhopal, Jabalpur, Nagpur, Amravati, Ahmedabad, Mumbai, Pune, Bengaluru, Varanasi, Jaipur, Delhi and the NCR region, just to name a few. The process has been historical dating back to at least the late nineteenth century, and has been continuing unabated (*See*Varni, 1949; Shastri, Phoolchandra, 1992). Whereas in earlier times the migration of Jains from Bundelkhand was confined to small-time entrepreneurs and traders, contemporary Jain migrants mostly happen to be highly educated professionals who study in colleges and universities outside the region and end up with better employment opportunities there. A number of Jains from Bundelkhand have also been working abroad and are active members of the Jain diaspora, particularly in North America. Here mention must be made of some prominent Jain emigrants who are settled in USA: Mahendra K. Pandya, MD, New York (Guna); Late Mahendra K. Jain, Professor Emeritus of Chemistry and Bio-Chemistry, University of Delaware (Sadumal, Lalitpur); Duli Chand Jain, Prof. of Physics, City University of New York (Ashoknagar); Yashwant K. Malaiya, Prof. of Computer Science, Colorado State University (Damoh); Anil Jain, Software Engineer, White Plains, New York (Sanodha, Sagar); Ashok Jain, MD and Asha Jain, MD, West Bloomfield, MI (Bina, Bhopal).

In this over-all context of "brain drain" from the region, there is an apt saying in Bundelkhand which goes like this: "*Kam padhe so har sain gaye, aur jyada padhe so ghar sain gaye*", meaning if you are less educated, you get away from the plough, and if you are more educated, you go away from the home. Thus, a significant number of prominent traditional as well as modern Jain pandits/scholars have gone and settled outside Bundelkhand. Mention may be made here of a number of scholars who worked and settled in cities and towns outside Bundelkhand as indicated against their respective names in the bracket. These included Late Pt. Devakinandan Siddhantshastri (Karanja/Indore), Late Pt. Siddhantacharya Pt. Phoolchandra Shastri (Bina/Varanasi/Roorkee), Late Pt.

Nathooram Premi (Bombay), Late Dr.Mahendra Kumar Nyayacharya (Varanasi), Late Pt. DarwarilalKothia (Varanasi), Late Prof. Khushal Chandra Gorawala (Varanasi), Late Dr. Raj Kumar Sahityacharya (Agra), Late Pt. Amritlal Shastri (Varanasi), Prof. Rajaram Jain (Arrah/NOIDA), Pt. Hukum Chand Bharill (Jaipur), Prof. Bhagchandra Jain "Bhaskar" (Nagpur), Prof. Gokul Chandra Jain (Varanasi/Indore), Prof. Prem Suman Jain (Udaipur), Dr. Ramesh Chand Jain (Bijnor/Delhi), to name only a few. Similarly a considerable number of Jain engineers, doctors, chartered accountants, IT Professionals, managers, bank officials, professors and teachers, temple priests, etc. have been permanently residing in different parts of India outside Bundelkhand.

One oft-repeated name of a historical person as prime example of out-migration from Bundelkhand is that of Manju Chowdhry (1720-1785) who was born and brought up in Kumhaidi village of Lalitpur district. He was orphaned in his childhood. As a young man he left his village in search of livelihood and after doing several odd jobs here and there finally reached Nagpur where in due course of time he became a courtier of Raja Mukund Dev. Subsequently on behalf of the Bhonsle rulers of Nagpur, Manju Chowdhry organised an army and attacked Orissa and was victorious in the battle. As a reward, he was appointed the administrator of Cuttack and was authorised to collect taxes from a market which is presently known as Chowdhry Market. Dewan Manju Chowdhry got constructed a Digambar Jain temple and hundreds of mountain caves for the travelling Jain monks to stay in them. The well-known Khandgiri-Udaigiri caves-complex is one of them. His sixth-seventh generation descendants still live in Cuttack.

Another region where Jains, mainly Parwars migrated outside Bundelkhand in the past was Mahakoshal (Jabalpur region) where they maintained their distinct identity and are still known as "Bundelkhandi Parwars" as opposed to another immigrant group known as "Gadha Parwars" whose place of origin was Gadha, a nearby town/area (*See* Shastri, Phoolchandra, 1992: 167). Immigrant Gahois from Bundelkhand are similarly identified in Jabalpur area.

A third destination of migration of Jains from Bundelkhand has been Ahmedabad where the Parwar Jains sought employment in textile mills and the Golalare Jains were involved in small-time business of door-to-door selling of kerosene oil. The descendants of these early and subsequent migrants are today very well settled in Ahmedabad and some other cities of Gujarat.

To sum up, economic migration of Jain castes/communities of Bundelkhand and the adjoining areas has been a historical process spread over more than a century. Marriage of Jain girls to different places from Bundelkhand has also been a factor in this regard. The net result is the fact that today the Bundelkhandi Jains are found almost all over the country. There is an urgent need to do more systematic research on the migration dynamics of the Bundelkhandi Jains, both inside and outside the region.

Jains in the Wider Society

Being an indigenous and one of the oldest religious communities, Jains are very well integrated into the Indian society. We already mentioned about the minority, and "socially partial" nature of this community which is highly dependent on the members of other communities for their day-to-day as well as business activities. Given these predicaments, the Jains have historically maintained quite cordial inter-ethnic relationships. So much so that a scholar has gone to the extent of calling the Jain community an "assimilative minority" (Schermerhorn 1978).

Problems of Education and Employment

Young Jains of Bundelkhand face a number of problems in getting themselves a suitable employment. This problem is directly related to the availability of good education in Bundelkhand. The quality of teaching in government schools is poor and the medium of instruction is generally Hindi. The poor knowledge of English on the part of many of them proves a major initial hurdle in getting suitable jobs as well as carrying on further studies. Although during the past couple of decades a number of English medium schools in the private sector have been established in most towns and cities of the region, the quality of education in them is not above average. In fact, most of them have turned out to be the commercial enterprises to make as much money as possible. The standard of teaching and work culture is poor. In such a scenario, in response to an open-ended question "Please state two-three major problems of the Jain community in Bundelkhand", a majority of respondents underlined the lack of quality education as the number one problem followed by lack of employment opportunities as number two problem. Problems of marriage and disunity within the community were mentioned as the third and the fourth important problems.

The above discussed educational situation of Jain students of Bundelkhand has drawn the attention of some Jain NGOs which have been trying to improve it. One such organisation is Digambar Jain Mahasamiti. Shri Vijay Kumar Jain, Ahmedabad-based industrialist and philanthropist, and the past-President of the Mahasamiti, had launched a programme called "Siksha Sahyog Yojana for Bundelkhand Jain Samaj" for upgrading the educational standards of primary and lower secondary students and improving their English language. The programme was launched in 2011-12 at 19 centres in Chhatarpur and Tikamgarh districts and covered about 650 students. Since January 2013, this programme changed its name to "Jain Siksha Samruddhi Yojana" and is presently doing more or less the same kind of work at 14 Centres of Bundelkhand in Chhatarpur, Sagar and Tikamgarh districts of Bundelkhand. In Bundelkhand, English medium schools are few and far between, and the medium of instruction in regular government schools is mainly Hindi. Additionally, the students who graduate through Sanskrit *vidyalayas* also face the problem of English.

In certain situations, the Jain youth are also discriminated against in job-hunting due to the perceived image of the Jain community being wealthy. Thus, slightly more than 50 per cent of the respondents in the Sagar district youth survey felt that they were discriminated against by other communities (Jain, Prakash C. and Jain, H.C., 2017). In spite of cordial inter-ethnic relations between Jains and other religious communities, the Jains are discriminated against by the wider Indian society. This discrimination is usually done in the field of employment, and the discrimination is rationalised by the stereotypical argument that the Jains happen to be an affluent community. In our sample survey, as many as 70.0 per cent of the respondents answered in the affirmative to the question whether the Jains were discriminated against socially, or in employment opportunities. About 28.3 per cent answered this question in the negative, and only 1.7 per cent did not make any response to the question (*See* Table 4.10)

Table 4.10: Discrimination against Jains Socially and/or in Job Opportunities

	Percentage
Yes	70
No	28.3
No Response	1.7
Total	100.0

The problem of unemployment among the Jain youth also looks grave although literacy and education among them is the highest. The Sagar district survey data suggest that 35 per cent youth were either unemployed or underemployed for which they cited the following reasons: (i) Lack of appropriate education and training (30%); (ii) Involvement in family business (19%); (iii) Lack of "approach" (13%). About 38per cent did not respond to this question.

In the fast changing times when the meaning and contents of education rapidly is being redefined, it is important to be up to date and competitive. Unfortunately, the Bundelkhand Jain Samaj is not yet prepared for that. It is not surprising, therefore, that Jain youth from this region rarely figure in various kinds of competitive examinations such as Indian Administrative Services (IAS), Indian Foreign Services (IFS), Indian Economic Services (IES), Indian Police Services (IPS), etc. Representation of Jains in the Indian Railways services is also inadequate, although Jhansi for a long time has been the headquarters of the North Central Railways. In this context it is heartening to note that one organisation that has been helpful to the Bundelkhand Jain youth aspiring to compete for state as well as central level Civil and allied services examinations is Mumbai-based JITO Administrative Training Foundation (JATF) whose training centres are located at Delhi, Jaipur, Indore, Pune and Chennai (*See* www.jitoatf.org). JATF is meant for 21-28 year old graduates/post-graduates in any academic stream, and provides all the necessary facilities including free boarding and lodging with concessional tuition fee and library facility.

Minority Status to Jains

People, including many Jains, consider Jains as a rich and advanced community, not in need of any government support or benefits like reservation. However, this is not the complete truth. It is, indeed, true that mainstream Jain communities likes of Oswal, Shrimal, Agrawal and Saraogi are rich business communities and comparatively advanced; but there is a large population of Jains belonging to communities that are socially and economically deprived. Such communities can be found in Bundelkhand, Karnataka, Odisha and West Bengal. Thus in Karnataka state, about 10 per cent of the Jain population is engaged in cultivation. Lesser known fact is that a large number of Jains belonging to such groups are even below poverty line (BPL Jains). The Sarak community living in the border areas of West Bengal, Bihar, Jharkhand and Odisha is a prime example of such a Jain community. Almost an unknown fact is that some Dalit, OBC, and tribal communities also follow Jainism. These deprived communities which follow Jainism are badly in need of central and state government schemes for minority communities.

It is against this background that the Jain community had been demanding the Union Government of India for the minority status for its members. Although the Jains have been recognised as a distinct religious community since the late nineteenth century British days and recognised so by the authorities since the first ever systematic census of India in 1881, they were arbitrarily denied this status in 1993 when the Government of India legally accorded the minority status to other five religious communities of India, namely Muslims, Sikhs, Christians, Buddhists and Parsis. Finally, the Indian Government conceded to the demand in January 2014. It needs to be mentioned here that by this time more than a dozen states in India had already accorded the minority status to Jain community.

Benefits and Advantages of Minority Status

Government can take over majority community temples and religious organisations but cannot take over any minority worship places and other organisations. Hence, the religious minority status would help the community in protecting Jain temples, pilgrimage centres, educational institutions and other socio-cultural organisations which are in dire need of attention, particularly in the Bundelkhand region. Some other benefits and advantages of religious minority status are listed below.

1. Religious Minority status for Jains will ensure protection of one of the oldest live religions of the world—Jainism as well as the unique Jain way of life. Jain community will be eligible to conserve its religion, languages, culture, etc. as per provisions of article 25 to 30 of Indian constitution.
2. Government cannot take over Jain religious places such as temples, dadabadis, samadhis, pilgrimage centres, trusts, etc. Moreover, government has to take initiative for safety and security and development of such centres.
3. Properties owned by Jain religious trusts will be exempted from rent control act.
4. Jain educational Institutions will have the right to teach Jainism and its philosophy.
5. Government will provide various benefits in opening and running schools, colleges, hostels, research institutes, hospitals, etc. Government land will be obtained at subsidised rate. Government interference will be minimised in opening and running educational and other institutes.
6. Jain institutions will be able to reserve 50 per cent seats for Jain students.
7. Meritorious and BPL students will get full exemption in tuition fees in schools.
8. Jain students will be eligible for free or subsidise coaching in coaching colleges run by universities.
9. Jain students will be eligible of grants for training in business and administrative courses.
10. Jains will have access to cheaper and subsidised loan for technical and other education and also for business.
11. Government will pay grant and scholarship to promote cultural and games and sports activities to Jain students and youth.
12. There will be wealth tax exemption for donations for charitable and religious causes.
13. Jain community will get special benefits in government employment.

Against this background, it is unfortunate to note that a vast majority of Jains in Bundelkhand do not seem to be aware of the notion of "religious minority status" as discussed above. In our sample, very few of them could highlight the benefits of minority status given to the Jains. In view of this, the appointment of Anil Jain Anchal, President of the Jain Panchayat of Lalitpur, as state chairman of the Uttar Pradesh Minority Welfare Cell in December 2015 was a well-come news (Jain Gazette, 14 December 2015).

Problem of Disunity within the Jain Community

Besides education and employment, lack of unity was also mentioned as a problem within the Jain community of Bundelkhand by a number of respondents. While saying so they must be having in mind a number of issues of the past as well as present times, namely sub-sectarian divide, caste and class differences, *Bisa-Dassa* issues, marriage and dowry problems, ideological divide due to the emergence of Kanji Panth and also the party politics. Some of these issues would be addressed in Chapter Five, while others need some elaboration as also the account of remedial measures taken from time to time to overcome them.

In Bundelkhand, as already mentioned, there are very few Shwetambar Jains and therefore the sectarianism has never been an issue. Sub-sectarian divide between Terapanthis and Taaranpanthis had been an issue for past few centuries, but now the *roti-beti* relations that were stopped have resumed due to the marriage imperatives prevalent in the region. Similarly, inter-caste marriages have also begun to take place due to skewed sex ratio. In lower-middle class segment of the community in the region, the dowry levels have come down significantly. The *Bisa-Dassa* issue that prevailed in the Jain community of the region since the consolidation of the caste system was already resolved socially around the middle of the 20th century. Kshullak Ganesh Prasad Varni and Br. Sheetal Prasad and a number of other tyagis and pandits had taken initiative in resolving a number of cases in the Bundelkhand region.

Table 4.11: Major Problems in Jain Community

Problems	*Percentage*
Marriage	30.0
Lack of quality education	41.1
Poverty/employment opportunity	35.6
Lack of unity	26.7
Other problems	26.7
No response	9.4
Total	100.0

Table 4.12: Grading of Burning Problems in Indian Society

Problems	*Percentage (%)*				*No Response*	*Total (%)*
	I	II	III	IV		
Socio-economic inequality	17.2	14.4	21.1	30.6	16.7	100
Poverty	13.3	19.4	28.3	23.3	15.6	100
Corruption	30.6	24.4	18.9	9.4	16.7	100
Illiteracy-ignorance	23.9	24.4	15	20	16.7	100

Besides the question about the problems of the Jain community in Bundelkhand, a question was also asked about the major problems in the Indian society. The respondents were asked to grade the four options, namely socio-economic inequality, poverty, corruption and illiteracy-ignorance. Data in Table 4.12 clearly suggest that corruption was rated as the most pressing problem of the Indian society by a majority respondent. The second place was jointly accorded to corruption and illiteracy-ignorance. Poverty and socio-economic inequality were voted by our respondents as the third and fourth most pressing problems of the Indian society.

Concluding Remarks

For centuries, Jains in Bundelkhand have been into trade and commerce, moneylending and banking, and even agriculture. During British period, some of them also rose to become *zamindars, malgujars,* and tax collectors. So much so that the Jains had monopolised trading and banking activities, and their stake in the regional economy was substantial. This scenario began to change with the availability of sacred as well as secular education from the early decades of the 20th century. Whereas by the last quarter of the past century, secular education gave rise to a class of modern professionals consisting of professors, engineers, doctors, lawyers, chartered accountants, etc., and later on the IT and management professionals, the sacred education, through a network of Jain Sanskrit *pathshalas* and *vidyalayas* spread inside and outside of Bundelkhand, produced a large number of Jain pandits, teachers, *tyagis,* authors, editors, journalists, publishers and distributors, and ascetics. In fact, the region is unique in producing the largest number of Jain pandits during the past 120 years or so. While very few Jain women have followed this particular set of professions, their access to modern education has been significant. However, as is quite common among the Jains of other parts of the country, only 10-15 per cent of the Jain women of Bundelkhand are employed today.

As is evident from the above discussion, the spread of education has certainly brought about unprecedented inter-generational occupational mobility in the Jain community of Bundelkhand. This is also reflected in the increased levels of income and prosperity among the Jains in the region. Declining attraction of Sanskrit education among the Jains of Bundelkhand is only an indirect proof of this economic transformation and prosperity.

This orientation towards higher education and modern professions in the Jain community of Bundelkhand, however, has accelerated the process of out-migration from the region with the result that both traditional scholars and modern professionals have been settled in different parts of the country and abroad. The out-migration as well as relative affluence in the Jain community of Bundelkhand might well be responsible for the lower decadal growth rate of population (4.4%) during the 2001-2011 decade as discussed in Chapter Two.

5

Social Structural Changes

This chapter attempts to analyse the process of continuity and change in the social structural features of the Jain community in the Bundelkhand region. These features include population and demography, kinship, family and marriage, caste system, status of women and youth, regional and caste associations, inter-ethnic relations, etc. As already detailed in Chapter One, the continuity and change in the social structural features would be examined in terms of the span of two-three generations—a duration sufficient enough for the changes to manifest and crystalise themselves.

Jains have been an integral part of the Indian society since ages. The religious and demographic structure of the Indian society and the position of the Jain community therein is presented in Table 5.1 (For demographic details, *see* Jain, Prakash C., 2019; Jain, Deeraj, 2017). The cultural affinity of Jainism to Hinduism and later on to Buddhism has also been immense. So much so that until about a century ago, Jainism was regarded a sect of Hinduism and/or an offshoot of Buddhism. The Jains have often been regarded as part of the Hindu *Varna vyavastha* (system). This is so in spite of the fact that Jainism is a separate religion. Accordingly, the Jains are often placed in the Vaishya category of the *Varna* system. This situation also arises from the fact that the term Vaishya denotes business and commerce and a large majority of Jains have traditionally been into these vocations. In fact, in Bundelkhand the Jains are often called as "*Baanias*" or "*Banias*".

This situation of Jains being considered as Hindus has significantly been changing since about the end of the 19th century when following the Hindu reform movements such as Brahmo Samaj, Arya Samaj, etc., the exclusive Jain associations such as Shree Bharatvarshiya Digambar Jain Mahasabha (1895) and Dakshin Bharat Jain Sabha (1896) were established, and the Jains began to take note of their community affairs in different parts of the country (*See* Kothari, 2004; Sangave, 1980; Patil, 2014). Simultaneously, Digambar Jain monastic tradition of ascetic nudity was also revived by Shree Shanti Sagarji Maharaj (1871-1955), the first Digambar Jain monk of the 20th century ("Diwakar", 2006). He was initiated into the monkhood in 1919.

Table 5.1: Demographic Indicators of the Six Major Religious Communities of India, 2011

Religious Communities	*Total Population*	*Percentage of Total Population*	*Population Growth Rate (2001-2011)*	*Urbanisation (%)*	*Literacy (%)*	*Sex/Child Sex Ratio*
Hindus	96,62,57,353	79.80	16.76	29.20	73.27	939/913
Muslims	17,22,45,158	14.23	24.65	39.91	68.54	951/943
Christians	2,78,19,588	2.30	15.53	40.12	84.53	1023/958
Sikhs	2,08,33,116	1.72	8.42	28.33	75.39	903/828
Buddhists	84,42,972	0.70	6.13	42.97	81.29	965/933
Jains	44,51,753	0.37	5.37	79.68	94.88	954/889
Others	79,37,734	0.66	NA	9.31	NA	NA
Not Stated	28,67,303	0.24	NA	42.68	NA	NA
Total/Average	**121,08,54,977**	**100.00**	**17.72**	**31.14**	**72.98**	**943/918**

Source: Census of India, 2011.

These developments were also accompanied by the rise of Jain ethnic press that began to publish weekly, fortnightly or monthly newspapers and magazines, and occasionally books and brochures on Jain religious or community affairs (*See* Jain "Bharati", Surendra K., 2004). A number of Jain publication houses began to bring out age-old Jain scriptures including philosophical-religious texts, and their translations and commentaries on them in vernacular languages, narrative literature and introductory and popular books on Jainism. Wide-scale translation and editing of Jain scriptures was made possible by the production and availability of traditional Jain scholars (Jain Pandits) who graduated from various Jain Sanskrit *pathshalas/vidyalayas* (colleges) located mostly in northern India. The means of transportation and communication facilitated people to people interaction and pilgrimages across the country. At the same time, the Jains as a community were also acquiring through trade and commerce a relative affluence—quite a few of them establishing modern industries and businesses. The Jains were also ahead of other communities in India (except Parsis) in taking advantage of modern education and producing a number of professionals in different walks of life.

All these developments tended to consolidate a separate identity of the Jain community over a period of time. Writing on this theme during the middle of the 20th century, a major sociological study concluded that the "Jains no longer regard themselves as Hindus and ardently wish themselves to be known as Jains and not as Hindus for any purposes" (Sangve, 1980: 308-09). In the context of the Bundelkhand region the basic identity of the Jains emerged and consolidated around their sub-sect, that is Terapanthi Digambar Jainism. This is particularly so in view of the fact that Shwetambar Jains and members of other sub-sects of Digambar Jainism (Taaranpanthis and Bisapanthis) are very few in numbers.

Social Structural Changes

As among the Hindus, the social structural features of the Bundelkhand Jain community are marked by kinship, marriage and family institutions on the one hand, and caste and class systems on the other. Whereas the former set of institutions can be termed as micro social structure, the latter ones can be classified as macro social structure. The characteristic features of these social structural elements of the Jain community in the Bundelkhand region and the social changes taking place in them is the major focus of the discussion in the following pages.

Kinship, Marriage and Family

In Indian society, institutions of kinship, marriage and family have been shaped by the respective community's personal law. The Jain community is no exception in this regard as would be seen in the following pages. As already mentioned, legally as well as traditionally, the Jains along with Buddhists and Sikhs have been treated as Hindus, and all the laws enacted for the Hindus since the British days are automatically applicable on these communities.

Kinship

Kinship is a basic institution in any human society. Kinship system can be defined as the system of relations between "kin", that is, persons related by real, putative or fictive consanguinity. Kinship encompasses not only all kinds of social relationships, patterns of expectations, belief and values within and outside the family but also the way of transmitting status and property from one generation to the next. Thus, kinship system encompasses a whole way of life of a particular community or society. In Bundelkhand region the Jains as well as the Hindus generally follow the northern zone pattern of kinship as suggested by Iravati Karve (1953). The main features of this pattern are: (i) territoriality, (ii) genealogy, (iii) incest taboo, and (iv) local exogamy. These also included caste endogamy and clan (*gotra*) exogamy. Presently four-*gotra (sasan)* rule, that is, avoidance of the *gotras* of father, mother, grandmother and maternal grandmother is generally practised in marriage alliance, but until only a couple of generations ago eight-*gotra* rule was quite common (Shastri, Pt. Phoolchandra, 1992). During the past few decades the kinship system has considerably weakened due to education, occupational mobility and migration, as a result of which members of a caste, sub-caste or a clan are now spread over a wide area. The rule of local exogamy is still practised in villages, but no longer in cities and big towns.

Along with weakening of kinship relations, primary kinship terminology has also undergone significant changes. Thus, the address terms for father in

Bundelkhand Jain community as diverse as *kakka, dada, dadda, nanna, pitaji, bade*, etc., are being increasingly reduced to only papa and in some cases to daddy. Similarly, address terms for mother have changed from *bai, aai, ma, matai* to now only 'mummy'. The address term in Hindi for father's elder brother is *Tau*, but in the Bundelkhand region this has been distorted to '*dau*'. The word *dau* is also used for an elderly unknown person of visible rural background. The terms *chacha, kaka, kakku* or *kakka* earlier used for father's younger brother(s) are being increasingly replaced by a single term 'uncle' not only in Bundelkhand but all over India. Ironically, the term uncle is also used for all the elderly looking acquaintances or strangers alike (eg. a neighbour, bus driver, shop keeper, milkman, etc.). Similarly, the word 'aunty'is likewise used for strange women as well as near or distant relatives. Compared to significant changes in terminology used for parents, there are hardly any change in case of brothers and sisters. Thus, as in previous generations, terms like *bhaiya, bhai sahib, bade/manjhle/chotebhaiya*, Ramesh *bhaiya,* etc.for brother(s) and *bain, bahin, jiji, Jijy, didi, badi/majhli/chotibahin*, etc. for sister(s) continue to be in use even now. Similarly, grandfather is addressed as *dada* and *babba* and grandmother as *dadi* and *Bau* and *badi ma*, etc. Also remaining unchanged are terms like *mama, mami* for maternal uncle and aunt respectively, and *bua* and *fufa* for father's sister and her husband respectively.

Before moving on to discuss changes in family and marriage institutions it would be interesting to briefly discuss the changes that have taken place in the naming of individuals, both males and females.

Name

People are generally named as per their parents' religious background, nationality and regional-linguistic context or local customs. Often the three factors go together in naming the individuals. In this study, the respondents were asked to state their full name. The responses show a wide variety of naming practices in Bundelkhand. These names when compared with the names which used to be given to Jains about two generations ago as we encounter them in Varni's autobiography, clearly suggest that there have been significant changes in the naming practices in the region. These changes can more systematically be discussed in terms of the first, middle and surnames of both males and females.

Old-style Male names (First and Middle): Asharfi Lal, Banshi Dhar, Bansi Lal, Bhaiya Lal, Brij Lal, Brindavan Lal, Bhure Lal, Chandra Bhan, Chunni Lal, Deva Kumar, Devaki Nandan, Dhanna Lal, Ganesh Prasad, Ganga Prasad, Gopal Das, Gulab Chand, Jambu Prasad, Jamuna Prasad, Jhamman Lal, Karode Lal, Kanchedi Lal, Kanhaiya Lal, Laxmi Chand, Mathura Das, Moti Lal, Mool Chand, Nand Kishor, Nannu Lal, Pancham Lal, Panna Lal, Pyare Lal, Ratan Chand, Sheetal Prasad, etc.

New Names: Abhishek Kumar, Anil Kumar, Amit Kumar, Anurag Kumar, Bimal Kumar, Chandra Kumar, Dhanya Kumar, Devendra Kumar, Kailash Chandra, Mahendra Kumar, Parimal Kumar, Prakash Chandra, Shubhas Chandra.

It would be seen that whereas first names are now more Sanskritised, the middle names are invariably either Kumar or Chand/Chandra. Middle names such as Dhar, Mal, Lal, Prasad, Rai, etc. have almost disappeared. There is no practice among Jains of Bundelkhand to use place's or father's name as middle name. As far as surnames are concerned, most Jains prefer to use the word "Jain". In some cases, family/*gotra* names such as Choudhry, Modi, Nayak, Bukharia, Taraiya, etc. are also suffixed after the Jain surname.

Old-style Female First Names: Asha, Bandna, Champa, Chameli, Chironja, Chironji, Angoori, Gajra, Geeta, Imarti, Jamuna, Kamla, Kusum, Laxmi, Madhu, Maya, Malti, Manorama, Nirmala, Pushpa, Parvati, Shanti, Sheela, Sudha, Usha, etc.

New Female Names: Abha, Anita, Aparna, Archana, Akriti, Kritika, Kalpana, Nidhi, Nikki, Neeti, Preeti, Rashi, Rashmi, Sanskriti, Sheena, Shuchi, Shruti, Shrutika, Tanuja, etc.

As in the case of male names, female names too are now more Sanskritised. Sometimes old names also reappear. Old-style first names were often suffixed by "Rani", "Bai", "Devi" as middle names which are no longer used. In some cases, the word "Kumari" is used as a middle name. Last name is invariably either "Jain", or family and/or *gotra* name.

It would not be out of place to also mention in passing that the term of greeting of one Jain by another in Bundelkhand region until only a generation ago, particularly in rural areas, was "*Juhar*" which is no longer in use; instead it has been replaced by a Sanskritised term "*Jai Jinendra*" which is now universally used among the Jains in India and abroad.

Family

The structure and functioning of Jain family closely resemble that of the Hindu family in different parts of India. In spite of the prevalence of patriarchy and emphasis on jointness common in both, the contemporary Jain family is perhaps a little more liberal and egalitarian than its Hindu counterpart, mainly because Jainism not only puts emphasis on individualism as well as gender equality, but also accords considerable space to religious and spiritual freedom to women. High level of literacy and education among the Jain women and relative affluence of the Jain community have also been helpful in this regard during the past half-a-century. In this context, the notion of *varnalabh* (attaining the quality of life) coming from the Jain scriptures is also handy in contributing to the higher status of Jain women. As already explained, *varnalabh* suggests that a newly married son is not independent in his parents' home and therefore must live separately with obligatory financial help and blessings of the parents (*see* Acharya Jinasena, *Mahapurana*, parv 38, shloka 136-142).The following changes can be seen in the Jain families in Bundelkhand during the past half-a-century or so.

1. **Smaller Size of the Family:** Though the data are not exactly comparable and also not comprehensive, there appears to be some change towards the smaller size of the family in Bundelkhand over a period of about three or four decades. In an unofficial census of Chhatarpur district Jain population conducted during the mid-1980s, the family size was found to be 6.8 persons (*See* Jain, Mahendra Kumar, 1986). The average size of the Jain family in select districts of the region as per 1981 census was found to be 6.6 members (Jain, M. K., 1986; *see* also in Jain, Prakash C., 2019: Chapter 5), whereas for the entire Bundelkhand region as per our study, it is 4.8 persons. The corresponding family size figures in a recent survey of the Jain community were found to be 5.0 for Madhya Pradesh and 4.7 for the country as a whole (ISJS, 2019). A sociological study of Jain women entrepreneurs (sample size 120) conducted in Pune in 2011 also points towards the small size of the contemporary Jain family in India. More precisely, the study found that about 60 per cent of these women lived in nuclear family and the rest in joint family. The overwhelming majority of them (96.2%) had children: 18.9 per cent had one child, 62.8 per cent had two children, and the rest (18.3%) had three or four children (Dhakle, 2011). None had more than four children. It must be pointed out here that the size of the family is mainly dependent on the structural cycle of the family. Thus, when the school/college-going children remain dependent on the parents the family size is also large, but the same family gets reduced in size when the children no longer live with the family due to employment or marriage and thereby start independent settled family life of their own.
2. Democratisation of family relations.
3. Decrease in discrimination against girl child.
4. Decrease in domestic violence.
5. Assertion of individuality in regard to choice of education and career, and marriage partner.
6. Daughters turning out to be more reliable and dependable than sons.
7. Daughters also giving *mukhagni* (lighting the pyre) to the dead body of parents during cremation.

Most of these changes are self-explanatory and do not need elaboration. Most of these changes are also taking place in varying degrees in the Jain communities of other regions as well as other religious communities of India.

Marriage

For the Jains, like the Hindus, *vivah* or marriage is one of the sacraments sanctifying the body (*shareer-sanskaras*) "through which every person must pass at the proper age and time" (Sangave, 1980: 139). Accordingly, marriage is considered an obligatory social act for every person. But the Jains and Hindus differ in their basic outlook towards the marriage institution. Whereas for the Jains it is a social act, a civil contract, for the Hindus it is a religious sacrament, which is necessitated by their belief that the birth of a son is must in order to gain moksha or salvation. According to Jainism, the presence, or absence of a son does not make a man spiritually meritorious or otherwise.

There are two-fold objectives of marriage in Jainism: (1) "to give legitimate outlet of sexual feelings so that human beings may rightly live a useful life, enjoying the fruits of Dharma, Artha and Kama, and thus be entitled to attain the great object—*Moksha*; and (2) to promote the cause of Dharma (Law) by generating righteous and chivalrous sons and daughters (Sangave, 1980: 141). Thus, it is a duty of the householder to be contented with his own life and to contrive for the continuance of the human race.

Given the socio-cultural diversity in India, the institution of marriage is based on local customs and tradition, and not necessarily on religious scriptures. So, although the Jain women are spared by scriptures the burden of bearing the son, in practice the need for the same has been as strong among the Jains as among the Hindus. Similarly, the prevalence of child marriage was quite common among the Jains until a few decades ago (*see* Sangave, 1980: 142). Cousin marriage among the Jains which is practised in Gujarat, Maharashtra and South Indian provinces is another example of regional or local variation in Jain marriage institution. Similarly, the rules of endogamy as well as exogamy observed by the Jains differ from place to place as per local customs. Within these parameters the institution of marriage has been undergoing considerable changes in the Jain community of Bundelkhand since at least the middle of the 20th century. These changes can be discussed systematically one by one under the following heads:

1. Disappearance of "Bad" Marriages

Until around the middle of the 20th century three kinds of bad or poisonous marriages (*vishvivah*) existed among the Jains in India in general and in the Bundelkhand region in particular. These were: (i) child marriage, (ii) polygamy, and (iii) age-incompatible marriage, which are briefly discussed below.

(i) *Child marriage.* Until a few decades ago, the Jains were also an early-marrying community. As among the Hindus, child marriage was quite a common feature of the Jain community as can be seen from the data in the following table.

Table 5.2: Married Females Aged 0-15 Years per 1,000 Females of that Age in Different Communities, 1881-1931

Community	*1881*	*1891*	*1901*	*1911*	*1921*	*1931*
Hindu	208	193	186	184	170	199
Muslim	153	141	131	123	111	186
Jain	189	172	164	130	117	125
Sikh	120	143	101	88	72	80
Christian	33	37	38	37	32	43

Source: Sangave (1980: 28, Table 25).

Professor Vilas A. Sangave (1980: 28) has shown that in the Bombay Presidency also "the Jains had the highest number of infant girls married and that both Hindus and Jains had very high figures for marriage of girls under the age of 15."

(ii) *Polygamy.* In independent India Jain marriages are governed by the Hindu Marriage Act of 1956 and therefore monogamy is the widely prevalent norm today. But as late as the mid-20th century polygamy was the most widespread custom among Jains" (Sangave, 1980: 163). An idea of this can be had from the 1931 census data which suggest that compared to 415 Jain males, 442 females per 1,000 Jain female population were married. In other words, 27 Jain females per 1,000 Jain female population were involved in polygamous marriages. In absolute terms, out of a total of Jain female population of about 564,000 in India in 1931, 15,228 Jain women were living in polygamy. It was for this reason that the proportion of widows among the Jains was unusually large of all the religious communities in India. Thus, according to the 1931 census report, 221 per 1,000 Jain women were widows as against the India average of 157. Comparable figures were 169 for Hindus, 129 for Muslims, and 114 for Sikhs. The 1931 census data on Jain widows show similar trends for the Bombay presidency and Rajputana (*see* Sangave, 1980: Table 24).

Thus, "in a very complex demographic dynamics of child marriage, widowhood and religious sanction on widow remarriage (except in South India), the Jain community had considerably reduced the proportion of females in the reproductive period" and thereby the rate of increase in the Jain population until at least the 1950s (Davis 1951: 183-84). These factors also reflect very clearly on the status of Jain women who additionally suffered from a very high level of illiteracy (99% in 1906) until about the last quarter of the 20th century (*see* Kothari, 2003; Sangave, 1980: 172).

(iii) *Age-Incompatible Marriage.* The age-incompatible marriage invariably was a union between a younger female and a much older male with an age gap of say twenty years or more. Again, invariably such marriages involved economically rich or well-off males and poor females, often, girl children.

2. Short Duration Marriages

Until 1960s, marriage ceremony normally took 3-4 days to be completed. Presently, this duration has been reduced to only 20 hours or less. Typical sequence of marriage events runs like this: bridegroom's party (*baraat*) or bride's party (a recent trend) reaches the would-be spouse's place in the evening, served early or late dinner as per local Jain community's regulations followed by marriage rituals during the night, departure of the couple after breakfast (*vidaai*) the next day. In case of day-time marriage ceremony, the departure takes place by the evening.

3. Only Day-time Marriage Ceremonies

In some cities or towns of Bundelkhand, only day-time marriage ceremonies are allowed by the Jain panchayats/communities. Monetary fines are imposed on those who violate this community regulation. The rationale behind this injunction is to avoid: i) violence to life of insects, etc. that hover around electricity poles or other sources of light that are used for lighting or decoration purposes, and ii) night-time eating.

4. Marriage Ceremonies by Jain Pandits

An increasing number of marriages these days are solemnised by Jain Pandits in Bundelkhand compared to the ones in earlier times in which a Brahmin *purohit* (pandit/astrologer) used to solemnise these ceremonies. This is due to the fact that there is an abundance of Jain *pandits/purohits* in Bundelkhand today. Secondly, it is a case of Jainisation process whereby through such moves, it is projected to show that the Jains are a self-sufficient community. Sociologically, doing away with Brahmin priests is also a case of the breakdown of *Jajmani* system in urban as well as rural areas.

5. Increase in Inter-Religion and Inter-Caste Marriages

Inter-religion marriages in the case of Jains in Bundelkhand mean for all practical purposes a marriage between Jains and Hindus only, as Jain-Hindu marriages were until recently unthinkable. Until recently, Jain-Hindu marriage was the rarest of rare cases and was confined to only urban areas. In the past few decades however, there has been a significant increase in the number of Jain-Hindu marriages. In our sample, whereas 8.3 per cent of the respondents reported that they had at least one inter-religion marriage in their families, 2.8 per cent respondents reported two cases of such marriages in their families (Table 5.4). Thus, about 90 per cent of our respondents have not witnessed any inter-religion marriage in their own or extended families. However, the acceptability of inter-religion marriage appears to be quite pronounced today in the region. This is clearly reflected in our study: as many as 27.2 per cent of the respondents support Jain-Hindu marriage in principle compared to 72.8 per cent who still oppose it (Table 5.3). Not only inter-religion marriages in Bundelkhand are on the increase, inter-caste marriages within the community are on the increase even at a more rapid pace. Though we do not have quantitative data to support the trend, ethnographic observations clearly suggest that caste endogamy—a phenomenon that strongly existed just a few decades ago in Bundelkhand, no longer exists today. The major factors behind the development of both these trends highlighted above is undoubtedly the skewed sex ratio, love marriage, and girls' desires and aspirations to get married to boys employed and living in bigger cities.

6. Acceptance of Widow/Divorcee Remarriage

In Digambar Jain tradition of North India, widow/divorcee remarriage is not allowed; instead, they are required to live an austere life and perform religious duties involving daily temple visits, scripture readings, listening to religious discourse, etc. Traditional Jain leaders like Ganesh Prasad Varni and a number of Jain associations like Akhil Bharatvarshiya Digambar Jain Parwar Sabha and Shree Bharatvarshiya Digambar Jain Mahasabha had been dead opposed to widow remarriage. This is however now changing, though very slowly. Our study found about 83.6 per cent respondents supporting the widow/divorcee remarriages. About 10.0 per cent of the respondents had reported to have been the witness of such marriages in their own or kin's families. The change is more visible in educated and service class families located in big cities and towns.

7. Marriage at a Convenient Place

Earlier marriage ceremonies invariably used to be performed at the bride's residence. In some cases where bride's home was not spacious enough to hold such a function, it used to be held at a nearby Jain *dharmashala*, hotel, school or any other available building. Groom's marriage party was also used to be lodged at a *dharamshala*, hotel, school, etc. The burden of marriage expenditure and dowry used to be borne by the bride's parents or family. With the ongoing marriage "crisis" in the Jain community of Bundelkhand, the brides have not only become dearer, the financial burden of dowry and other expenditures on marriage has shifted from the bride's to the groom's family. It is now the groom's family that arranges a suitable place for marriage ceremony to take place—often in their own town/city. They also make arrangements for the boarding and lodging of the brides and relatives and friends who are invited to attend the marriage. Thus, for all practical purposes, a key element in the age-old marriage ceremony has just been reversed: instead of groom's marriage party, it is now the bride's party that goes to the groom's place for the marriage ceremony to take place.

8. Changes in the System of Arranged Marriage

Arranged marriage system has undergone considerable changes. Due to time constraints, marriages are no longer arranged on one-to-one basis. Traditionally this was often done by the relatives, friends and well-wishers who used to exchange horoscope of the potential bride and groom. During the last quarter of the 20th century, in urban areas, they were briefly supplemented by matrimonial advertisements in newspapers and magazines. Presently, middlemen or marriage agencies have taken over this business of introducing the potential brides and grooms. These agencies named Sanjog, Milan, etc. organise conventions of Jain youth, both male and female, to get introduced to each other. Local/caste associations sometimes also organise such conventions. In one such convention called "Jain Yuvak Yuvati Parichay Sammelan" that I happened to witness in Sagar city, about 6,000 members of the Jain community must have taken part from 9 a.m. to 6 p.m. on 2 February 2014.

9. Decrease in Dowry Demand

Unlike in the past, dowry is no longer a problem in the Jain community of Bundelkhand today. This is largely due to the unavailability of marriageable girls on account of the skewed sex-ratio in the region. Dowry is voluntary now and no longer a hurdle for those who cannot afford it. This is particularly true in case of boys who are in the family business, lower rank services and/or living in small cities/towns. Dowry, however, is still prevalent and is demanded by boys who are in high class professions and living in big cities.

10. Increase in Show-Off and Wastage of Money

An increasing number of marriages today are being organised on a grand scale highlighting the show-off and wastage of money.

Problems of Marriage in Bundelkhand

Needless to add, it is mostly the youth that have been affected by these changes. Young men of marriageable age are the worst affected segment of the Jain population. As already mentioned, a significant number of them continue to remain unmarried due to these changes, and the number of unmarried youths is progressively on the rise. Neither the local Jain community or the caste associations, nor the national Jain associations such as Bharatvarshiya Digambar Jain Mahasabha, Digambar Jain Mahasamiti, etc. seem to have any collective action programme in order to combat this problem.

Table 5.3: Distribution of Supporters of Jain-Hindu Marriage

Supporter	*Percentage*
Yes	27.2
No	72.8
Total	100.0

Table 5.4: Number of Cases of Jain-Hindu Marriage in the Family

No. of Cases	*Percentage*
0	87.8
1	8.3
2	2.8
No Response	1.1
Total	100.0

Table 5.5: Changes in Marriage Institutions

Changes	*Percentage*
Show offs/high dowry	17.8
Day-time marriage	15
Short duration	5.6
Jain custom	12.2
At convenient place	41.7
Reduction in dowry	48.9
Inter-religious	9.4
Inter-caste	17.2
Other changes	3.3
No change	8.3
No response	7.8
Total	100.0

Social Stratification

Social scientists generally agree that social stratification—a horizontal division of society in high and low social strata or groups—is a universal and inevitable phenomenon. Lots of work all over the world has been done on the subject. Caste, class and estate have been recognised as the three major forms of social stratification in human societies. In most modern industrial societies, it is the class system that has emerged as the dominant form of social stratification. In case of traditional societies other indigenous forms of social stratification have to be additionally taken into account in order to understand the socio-economic dynamics in these societies. Thus, in the context of Africa and Middle East tribe has to be given its due importance, whereas in the context of South Asia in general and India in particular one has to recognise the centrality of caste system as a form of social stratification. Modernisation and social change have transformed these traditional forms of social stratification, and increasingly class stratification is gaining importance.

Jainism does not sanction caste system. It is, therefore, a social and not a religious institution for the Jains. At the time of Mahavir, Jainism was opposed to the Hindu caste system. The caste system among the Jains developed some time during the medieval period. Scholars have identified as many as 100 castes among the Jains in India today (*See* Singh, 1982; Sangave, 1980). Most of these castes however formed a very small groups, and therefore have been unable to sustain the rule of caste endogamy resulting in assimilation into other castes or further decline in their numerical strength. Presently only four or at the most five dozen Jain castes must be surviving in India. Whatever their number, they have created a segmental division within the community.

The working of caste system among the Jains is not as rigid as among the Hindus. According to Sangave (1980: 81), "among the Jains the castes were not arranged in a hierarchical order of respectability, no restrictions were put on social intercourse between different caste members and there was no lack of choice of occupation." The Jain caste/sub-caste endogamy which used to be rigidly practised earlier has also been fast disappearing now in many parts of India. As already discussed in Chapter Two, the Bundelkhand region is no exception in this regard, and inter-caste marriages between Parwar, Golapurav and Golalare are now quite common. Even inter-sub-sect marriages between these three castes and Samaiyas (Taranpanthis) are also taking place. Thus, the caste hierarchy within the Jain community of Bundelkhand is fast disappearing from the scene. Even when the caste stratification was at its zenith say about half a century ago, the above mentioned caste stratification within the Jain community of Bundelkhand should be considered quite simplistic as some other social groups such as seths, tyagis and pandits have not been considered here. When we take all these groups into account, the reality and thereby the social stratification system among the Jains of Bundelkhand gets quite different, and perhaps a little more complicated. Thus, this system cannot be explained by any single criterion like caste, class or honour/prestige, and a combination of them would have to take into account. Here Ganesh Prasad Varni's insights and observations into the Bundelkhand Jain community come handy. In the words of Professor Ravindra K. Jain (1999: 81), "Hence Varni coins and endorses the tripartite stratification of Jains in the Bundelkhund region as *Dhanik Varga* (the wealthy), the *Vidvad Jan* (pandits and tyagis) and the *Samanya Janata* (the common people)." Here *Dhanik Varga* includes former zamindar as well as wealthy and some very well off individuals. As already explained in Chapter Four, often this class also includes individuals who have been decorated with the traditional honourific titles of Singhai, Sawai Singhai, Seth and Srimant Seth.

The word *Singhai* is the distorted form of the Sanskrit word *Sanghpati*. In the context of Greater Bundelkhand, this title is given to those who have sponsored one *Panchkalyanak* and *Gajarath*. Those who sponsor two *Panchkalyanak* and *Gajarath* are given the title *Sawai Singhai,* in case of three Gajarath, the title is *Deodhria (Deodhe Singhai)*, in case of four *Gajarath* the title is Seth, and in case of five *Gajarath,* the title given is *Srimant Seth*. Later on, even in case of three *Gajarath* the title of *Srimant Seth* was given. These titles are given by the community members on the completion of the function. The tradition of *Gajarath*is unique to Bundelkhund and it is from here that it spread to other parts of the country. According to Siddhantacharya Pandit Phoolchandra Shastri (1992: 539), some 200 years ago, a grand Panchkalyanak was organisedat Chanderi in which the chariot was driven by elephants. Before this, there was no custom of elephant-driven chariots in *Panchkalyanak*. Subsequently the practice became commonplace in the entire Bundelkhad region, and then spread to some other parts of the country (Shastri, J. 1992: 15). Needless to say, the dhanikvarg functions as community leaders and as such wields considerable power.

Historically, in the context of Bundelkhand the discussion on caste/social stratification would not be complete without mentioning the existence of a group/caste called "Vinekabar", or "Vinekabal" (meaning "without unity" or deserters)—families who had gone against the customary norms and values, and rules and regulations of the mainstream Jain community, particularly regarding sexual alliance and/or marriage. This group included people who married a Jain widow, or a non-Jain woman, disobeyed community panchayat's rulings, etc. According to Pt. Phoolchandra Shastri (1992: 545), Vinekabals are divided into two-three sub-groups: some are the old ones who dissented in olden times, others were formed during medieval period, and in modern times have been added on by new ones. Due to their separation from the mainstream community, they were not allowed to enter the temple and do worship or any other religious activity inside the temple, in addition to a complete ban on their "*roti-beti vyavahar*" (inter-dining and inter-marriage relations). Eventually this resulted in construction of their own separate temples by *Vinekabals*. Presently the ban on the temple entry no longer exists, and the *roti-beti vyavahar* is also increasingly gaining acceptance of the wider Jain community of Bundelkhand.

Status of Women

Status of Jain women in the Indian society can be comprehended and analysed more or less within the same parameters which are applied to comprehend and analyse the status and roles of their Hindu counterparts. Some of these parameters in India vary in terms of religional-linguistic context. Thus, the Guajarati context differs from the Bengali or Tamil context. Other contextual factors that determine the status of Jain women are sect/sub-sect, caste and religiosity (*See* Jain, Prakash C., 2018c).

Status of women in contemporary Jain community of Bundelkhund can be looked at in terms of a number of indicators such as equality and liberty within the family and outside, educational and occupational achievements, religious freedom, freedom to choose one's life partner, lack of domestic violence and other kinds of exploitation etc. All these indicators can be better summed up by the phrase "dignified life" which was lacking in most of the traditional societies earlier. The Jain community in India in general and in the Bundelkhund region in particular was no exception in this regard. Only two generations ago, a vast majority of women were illiterate, lived under harsh patriarchal social order and enjoyed no choices in regard to occupation and/or marriage. Not only polygamy was in vogue, a number of Jain girls were forced to marry much older grooms giving rise to what was then known as '*Bemail Vivah*" or "*Vish Vivah*" (Poisonous marriages).Women faced domestic violence—physical, sexual, psychological and economic (e.g. dowry demand and/or expectation). Child marriage was rampant. There was no social approval for divorce. The attitude towards widows was particularly discriminatory in family as well as outside. Discrimination against girl-child was also there.

Since then the status of Jain women in Bundelkhund appears to have significantly changed for the better. Thus, patriarchal social order is slowly and steadily giving way to a democratic and liberal social order. Issues pertaining to marriage and family in the Jain community of Bundelkhand are discussed in detail in earlier part of this Chapter. Notwithstanding some anomalies regarding education and employment, the Jain women have been accorded much better status in religious/spiritual field.

Jainism grants considerable religious freedom and equality to women. Thus, they can join the ascetic order and follow the path of liberation. Even the widows are allowed this privilege. In fact, women have been an integral part of the Jain ascetic *sangh* (order) since the days of the 23rd Tirthankar Parshwanath. It is said that there were 20,000 women ascetics in the sangh of Lord Parshwanath and 36,000 in that of Lord Mahavir. It is also said that the women ascetics far outnumbered the male ascetics who, for example, numbered only 14,000 in Tirthankar Mahavir's sangh (Sangve, 1880). The prescribed ascetic rules are applied uniformally on both male and female ascetics. According to Prof V.A. Sangve (1980: 180), "as regards religious position of woman we can say with confidence that a yeoman service was rendered by Jaina Acharyas towards the suffering half of humanity by declaring open to it, all portals supreme spiritual domain and admitting it equally with the other half to the religious order for asceticism." Besides religious freedom, Shwetambar Jainism goes even one step further by declaring Tirthankar Mallinath as a female. Even today the situation in terms of the proportion of female participation in ascetic life continues to remain the same. According to one estimate of Jain mendicant population done in mid-1990s, of the total population of 11,518 mendicants there were 8,946 nuns and only 2,572 monks (Sethi 2012: 4). However, this situation has been different in the case of contemporary Digambar Jainism where, except until very recently, the monks always outnumbered the nuns (For details, *see* Jain, 2019: 249-51). In the Bundelkhand Jain community since at least the beginning of the 20th century, the monks have always outnumbered the nuns and continue to do so even today.

Most Jain women in Bundelkhand and elsewhere are not only well versed in religious and philosophical discourse—they are regularly busy in swadhyaya (self-study) of religious scriptures. Jainism liberally exhorts men and women to live an ascetic life—a call to which the Jain women, in spite of being subjected to some degree of patriarchy, have always responded positively at any given point of time in history.

In regard to "gender and salvation" issue, Digambar Jainism suffers from "doctrinal crisis" (*See* Balbir, 1994; Jaini, 1979; Kelting, 2003). And, therefore, the religious status of women in Bundelkhand too is not without pitfalls. Digambar Jainism questions the spiritual capacity and "integrity" of women and considers them inferior to men in annihilating karmic matter and achieving salvation. In Jain Sati narrative, women's body is usually treated as inferior and locus of violence and sexual desire and thereby a living and insidious threat to the monk's celibacy vow. In one of the worship hymns which is routinely sung in Jain temples of Bundelkhand, a woman is likened to a "poisonous creeper" (*vish bel*). Women are not allowed to worship by touching or anointing the idol with water, etc. As a partial compensation, however, they are allowed to have *darshan* and put offerings in front of the image. They are also allowed to do self-study of scriptures in the temple. As already mentioned, they are also allowed to become nuns and even independently head a female ascetic order/group.

On the whole however, except in the field of politics, the contemporary status of Jain women in Bundelkhand is not lagging behind vis-à-vis their counterparts in other Indian religious communities. Jain women have been able to take full advantage of modern education. Consequently, a number of them today have been employed as school teachers, college and university professors, doctors, engineers, lawyers, chartered accountants and management and information technology professionals, etc. It should not be out of place here to mention the name of Justice Vimla Jain of the Madhya Pradesh High Court (now retired a couple of years ago) who has the distinction of the first ever Jain woman to achieve this position. In the case of a majority of Jain women of Bundelkhand however, it can well be stated that corresponding to their level of literacy and education they have not been able to exploit employment opportunities for unknown reasons. Perhaps the relative family affluence does not motivate them to take up gainful employment in large numbers.

The demographic status of contemporary Jain women is not properly attuned with other aspects of their life. The gender ratio has not been in their favour since at least the late 19th century when the first systematic census of

India was undertaken in 1881. As per 2011 census, the sex ratio in population in Bundelkhand is about 1,000 males: 917 females. Besides the adult population, the problem of gender ratio is even more acute in child population comprising 0-6 year age group. This is further compounded by the fact that the Jains are relatively an affluent community and have begun to show clear evidence of low fertility behaviour. The 2011 census data further confirms this trend whereby the Jain population over the past decade grew by only 5.4 per cent. The decadal growth of Jain population in Bundelkhand is only about twice (about 9.6%) the national Jain population growth rate average.

Jain Associations

Following the growth of social reforms movements and the formation of associations like Arya Samaj, Brahmo Samaj, YMCA, etc. in the late 19th century, Jains were also inspired to have socio-religious reforms within their own community through appropriate associations. The earliest one to be formed in North India was Shri Bharatvarshiya Digambar Jain Mahasabha established in 1895 at Mathura (Kothari, 2004). Under the aegis of the Mahasabhaa a short-lived Jain Mahavidyalaya at Mathura, and a weekly news magazine "Jain Gazette" were also started. The Mahasabha and the magazine still continue to exist and operate from Lucknow and Delhi. The membership of the Mahasabha in the Bundelkhand region is nominal. Since its inception in 1895, only two of its 32 elected presidents so far have been from Bundelkhand. Seth Mohanlal of Khurai was elected president of the Mahasabha in 1925 and Seth Chandrabhan of Bamrana/Sadumal in 1932.

Subsequently, a number of national, regional and caste associations also began to be formed among the Digambar as well as Shwetambar Jains of India. Of these, mention must be made of Dakshin Bharat Jain Sabha (1899), Jain Young men Association (1899-1908), Bharat Jain Mahamandal (1910), Jain Political Conference (1917), Akhil Bharatvarshiya Digambar Jain Parishad (1923), and Digambar Jain Mahasamiti (1976). Of these the last two associations have some bearing on the Jains of Bundelkhand. These are highlighted below.

Digambar Jain Parishad

This association came into being in 1923 as a break-away group from Shri Bharatvarshiya Digambar Jain Mahasabha on the occasion of latter's annual convention in Delhi. The new association was supported by progressive and reformist leaders like Barrister Champat Rai, Kamta Prasad Jain, Ajit Prasad Jain and Br. Sheetal Prasad. In 1923 itself the Parishad began publishing its mouthpiece "Veer" monthly which was jointly edited by Br. Sheetal Prasad and Kamta Prasad Jain. The monthly magazine still continues to be published from

Delhi. In its initial phase of existence, the Parishad took up many social issues such as Jain womens' education and empowerment, remarriage of young widows, inter-caste marriage within the community, temple and worship rights for "*Dassas*", ban on death-feasts, and spread of Jainism to foreign lands, etc. The Parishad has significant presence in Bundelkhand.

Digambar Jain Mahasamiti

This association came into existence in 1976 on the eve of Tirthankar Mahavir's 2500th Nirvana (Salvation) anniversary celebrations. Late Shri Shanti Prasad Jain of New Delhi thought of having a Parliament of Digambar Jains—which should be a true representative of the entire Digambar Jain community. Its basic objectives were to spread the true principles of Jainism, to maintain harmony between different sects/sub-sects of the Jain community, and to assist in the preservation of Jain historical monuments, temples, and educational and other institutions. The Mahasamiti was founded with the hope that the then existing associations would join the newly created association. Unfortunately that did not happen and the community had to bear the burden of one more association. The association is still active with a sizeable membership all over India. One of its past presidents Shri Vijay Kumar Jain has started an educational programme called Jain "Siksha Samrudddhi Yojana" in January 2013 which aims at improving the academic standard of primary and lower secondary school Jain students in select towns and villages of Bundelkhand region.

Along with national Jain associations, regional associations too were taking shape in order to meet regional aspirations of the community. One of the regional associations taking care of the interests of Jains in central India was established on 31 March 1908 at Digambar Jain Siddhakshetra, Kundalpur. It was named Bundelkhand Madhyaprantiya Digambar Jain Sabha. In fact, it was founded on the occasion of Bharatvarshiya Digambar Jain Mahasabha's 12th convention which was held under the chairmanship of Seth Dev Kumar Raees of Arrah. Madhyaprantiya Sabha's 2nd convention was held at Nainagiri Siddhakshetra under the chairmanship of Seth Laxmi Chandra Jain, Bamrana. Its 3rd convention was held on 5 March 1911 at Lalitpur under the chairmanship of Seth Mathura Das Taraiya and the 4th convention was held at Dronagiri under the chairmanship of Pt. Ganesh Prasad Varni.

Parwar Sabha

The chairman of the 5th convention of Madhya Prantiya Sabha was Srimant Seth Mohanlal Khurai and it was held at Nainagiri, a major pilgrimage place in Bundelkhand. This convention became controversial in that the dominance of Parwar caste in the Association was questioned by members of another major Jain caste of Bundelkhand, and therefore an All-India Digambar Jain Golapurav

Mahasabha was established under the chairmanship of Seth Dhan Prashad of Banda, Sagar in 1918. According to Pt. Phoolchandra Shastri (1992: 542), after 2-3 years Shri Bharatvarshiya Digambar Jain Parwar Sabha was established in 1917 at Ramtek which was followed by Golalariya Sabha. In this way three major caste associations came into existence in Bundelkhund and the Madhyaprantiya Sabha ceased to exist. Much later an association called Taaran Taran Digamber Jain Samaj came into existence sometime in 1950s, which was short-lived and revived in 1977.

Bharatvarshiya Digamber Jain Parwar Sabha held twenty conventions in different places, namely Ramtek, Sivni, Jabalpur, Saugar, Papora, Bamora, Akaltara, Kurwai, Barchone, Beena-Barha, Khurai, etc. These conventions were chaired by the following distinguished Jains of Bundelkhund: (1) Seth Laxmi Chandra, Bamrana; (2) Sawai Singhai Garibdas, Jabalpur; (3) Singhai Pannalal, Amaravati; (4) Seth Pannalal Taraiya, Lalitpur (5) Shrimant Seth Lakshmichand, Vidisha; (6) Seth Ganpatlal Gurha, Khurai; (7) Shrimant Seth Puranshah, Sivni; (8) Shri Amritlal Advocate, Malthone; (9) Seth Bhagchandra, Doongargarh; (10) Shrimant Seth Rishabh Kumar, Khurai; (11) Sawai Singhai Dhanya Kumar, Katni; (12) Shri Panchamlal Tehsildar, Jabalpur; (13) Shrimant Seth Birdhi Chandra, Sivni; (14) Singhai Kunwarsen, Sivni. Besides these Seths, Pt. Devakinandan Siddhantshastri also chaired a number of regular and ad hoc conventions of the Parwar Sabha at various points in time.

The Parwar Sabha attempted to bring about a number of reforms in Bundelkhund Jain community, namely stopping of child, elderly and age-incompatible marriages, reforms in certain marriage rituals, promotion of Jain education and literature and renovation and restoration of Jain teerthkshetras, estabalishment of widow help funds, etc. The Sabha also tried to establish Parwar Jain panchayats in villages and towns but since Jain panchayats comprising all the Jain castes were already in existence in most places, it did not succeed in this venture and composite Jain castes panchayats continued to operate throughout Bundelkhund, both in rural and urban areas. The Parwar Sabha ceased to hold its annual conventions since 1953, nevertheless it was registered under Madhya Pradesh Trust Act in 1955 and is located at Jabalpur. Parwar Sabha also published a monthly news magazine named *Parwar Bandhu* which was edited by Pt. Jaganmohan Lal Shastri, and other scholars. The monthly magazine appeared during 1929-30 and then during 1939-44 only. Now the magazine is discontinued for a long time, whereas its other counterparts like "Golapurav Jain" and "Taaran Bandhu" still continue to get published from Sagar and Bhopal respectively.

In the early 1990s, Parwar Sabha's monumental achievement was the publication of a 650-page long book in Hindi entitled *Parwar Jain Samaj Ka Itihas* (*A History of Parwar Jain Society*) written by Siddhantacharya Pt. Phoolchandra Shastri (1992). The book details the 2000-year old history of the Parwar caste with numerous historical evidences based on *Pattawalis* of

Ascetics along with the literary as well as the archaeological evidences. Parwar community's past migratory movements and major settlement areas in present day Bundelkhand and beyond, its distinguished members including *munis, tyagis, pandits, seths* and their achievements in various walks of life are also highlighted in detail. For over forty years, the Sabha, in spite of its office at Jabalpur, is practically a defunct organisation now.

All-India Digambar Jain Golapurav Mahasabha

As already mentioned, it came into existence in 1918 and continued to operate for some time before it ceased to exist. The association was again revived in 2002 with the first convention held at Nainagiri. Since then regular conventions have been held at Drongiri, Banda, Shahgarh, Aharji, Pateriaji, Bahoriband, Nainagiri, Pateriaji, Sagar and Baragaon. The 11th convention was held at Kotma of Anooppur district in MP in 2015. (Jain Gazette, 28 September 2015). Its central office is located at Sagar and regional offices at Gwalior, Indore and Jaipur. Its mouthpiece *Golapurv Jain* was also revived in 2002 and has been regularly appearing since then from Sagar.

All-India Digambar Jain Organisations—Co-ordination Committee

As its name suggests this is a coordinating association of all the major existing Digambar Jain associations, namely Shri Bharatvarshiya Digambar Jain Mahasabha, Dakshin Bharat Jain Mahasabha, Digambar Jain Mahasamiti. It was founded in 1998 in Mumbai in order to bring about consensus of the member associations on certain issues and problems of importance to the Digambar Jain community in India. Presently its office is located at New Delhi. Its founder co-ordinator was Shri C.P. Jain, former chairman of National Thermal Power Projects. Since August 2015, Nirmal Kumar Jain Sethi is the co-ordinator. This association is mainly an advisory body. So far it has issued 18 appeals on various issues to the member associations as well as the Digambar Jain community at large. Some of the important issues are mentioned below.

1. Retaining various ways/systems of Jain worship, and not to impose one over the other.
2. Donating at least 2 per cent of the corporate profit for social empowerment of the Jain community.
3. Getting united in the face of Rajasthan High Court declaring Jain custom of *Santhara/Sallekhna* as suicide, and hence illegal.
4. Promoting 100 per cent literacy, higher education, computer and vocational training, and skill development and establishing boarding houses through community and individual efforts.

5. Requesting the local public as well as managing committees of *Tirth kshetras*/temples to seek prior consultation and advice of the Co-ordinating Committee before launching any renovation work.

Jain NGOs of Bundelkhand

Besides the various kinds of Jain associations discussed above, a number of NGOs have also been operating in Bundelkhand since around the 1930s. Most of these are involved in education sector promoting sacred education by establishing pathshalas and vidyalayas for Sanskrit and Jain studies and secular education through schools and colleges. Some of them also give away loans and scholarships to deserving students. Shri Veetrag Vani Trust, Tikamgarh is a good example of such NGOs that is running schools, a library and a research institution. Long ago the Sadumal Jain Sanskrit *vidyalaya* was established by trust funds created by Seth Laxmi Chand Jain of Bamrana/Sadumal. Shrimant Seth Sitabrai Laxmi Chand Parmarthic Trust Board, Vidisha (1935) runs several schools and colleges, healthcare facilities in the city, among other things. The Trust was also involved in financing the translation, editing and publishing of ancient Jain manuscripts including canonical work *Shatkhandagam* in several parts.

Healthcare activities, particularly the promotion of *Ayurvedic* system of medicine has been an important activity of a number of NGOs in the region. "BhagyodayaTeerth" at Sagar is one such endeavour. Eye camps for cataract removal is often organised by Jain NGOs in several cities and towns of Bundelkhand.

Inter-Ethnic Relations

Jains' sense of tolerance and peaceful coexistence with other communities can be related to their epistemological doctrine of relative pluralism (*nayavada*) which puts emphasis on non-ablolutism (*anekantvad*) in regard to seeking truth and knowledge. It states that the reality can be comprehended from an infinite number of standpoints which have been classified into seven types known as *saptabhanginaya* (seven-fold standpoint). In other words, no single proposition can express that whole of Reality. And even then "the truth of each affirmation is... only conditional, and inconceivable from the absolute point of view. To guarantee correctness, therefore, each affirmation should be preceded by the phrase '*syat*' ('may be')" (Dasgupta, 1963: 179). This doctrine is known as *syadavad* (doctrine of may be). In short, the doctrines of *anekant* and *syadavad* constitute one of the distinguishing features of Jainism. The Jains are particularly proud of this part of the Jain philosophy and in all probability, it reflects in their definition and perception of social reality.

As already mentioned, India is a multi-racial, multi-religious and multi-ethnic society with extreme economic and socio-cultural diversities. The Jains constitute only a very small community, though they are spread all over India. In the Bundelkhand region, the Jains have been mainly a trading community, and as such they have to interact with the members of the other communities. The patterns of these inter-ethnic relations of the Jains in Bundelkhand are briefly discussed below.

Hindus

In the wider context of the Indian socio-cultural diversity and pluralism, inter-ethnic relations of Jains vis-a-vis major religious and ethnic communities require anthropological/sociological investigation. Historically, the Jains had to suffer a lot, especially in the medieval period in South India when Hinduism was being revived. Not only hundreds of Jain *Munis* were put to violent death, Jain and Buddhist temples were destroyed and/or converted into Hindu places of worship. Many followers of Jainism were also converted to Hinduism.

Compared to these historical events in South India, religious intolerance on the part of Hindus against the Jains have been relatively mild. In the late 19th century when the Arya Samaj, a non-idolatrous break-away movement within Hinduism started by Swami Dayanand Sarswati (1824-1883), was being consolidated, it was quite critical of Jainism—at times leading to very acrimonious debates between the followers of the two religions. In this connection it is said that a Jain scholar Pt. Gopaldas Baraiya, the founder of Morena Sanskrit Jain Vidyalaya, was involved in a number of such *shashtrarths* (philosophical-religious debates) and was victorious on several occasions (Jain, Harish Chand, 2012: 232). In any case, these debates remained confined to scholars only, and did not have any major impact on inter-religious relations.

In more recent times only one incident is often recalled by the writers on this subject which happened in Jabalpur in 1959. According to one account, the Jain news magazine *Sanmati Sandesh* published from Jabalpur itself, brought out a special issue on "Ramcharit" (The Story of Lord Ram) in which Ram and Sita were described as Jain ascetics. In one of the articles it was also said that in the end of his life Ram chose *shivaramani (moksha)*. One sectarian-minded Brahmin writer Pt. Nathuram Vyas interpreted this to mean that Ram wedded Lord Shiva's *ramani* (consort) Parvati, and published this sensational news item in a right-wing Jan Sangh Party's daily newspaper. This led to minor communal riots in the city in which a Jain temple was damaged and a couple of shops (including one owned by the editor of the Jain Magazine Pt. Prakash Chand "Hiteshi") were looted by the mob. The publication of the news-magazine from Jabalpur was stopped and later on shifted to Delhi (*See* Sonrya, Bimal Kumar, 2013; 391 *also* Shastri, Pt. Phoolchandra, 1992: 288-89).

In modern times, with the exception of the above mentioned Jabalpur incident, the relations of Jains with the Hindus and other ethnic groups have by and large been cordial. Nevertheless, the Jains do maintain varying degree of social distance vis-à-vis rest of the communities in India. In different parts of India, Jains tend to behave like upper caste Hindus and as such they did and do practise untouchability against the Dalits. An experiment of integration of Dalits (Bhangis in Udaipur) into the Jain fold by Jain Acharya Tulsi could not go smoothly far enough (*see* Shyamlal, 1981). However, on the positive side of it, the Jains do maintain cordial relations including inter-marriages with Hindu *Banias* in many parts of India, particularly in Gujarat, Western Uttar Pradesh and most metropolitan towns. The services of Brahmin priests are utilised on the occasions of birth and marriage. And the Rajput and other Kshatriya castes are treated respectfully by the Jains. In village India, the Jains have been a part of the *Jajmani/kisani* system.

Christians

Christians are well tolerated by the Jains as the former are often associated with dispensing the quality education through convent schools and reliable health care facilities through well-established Allopathic hospitals. In fact, Lalitpur city hosts a centrally located and almost a century-old one such hospital popularly known as "mission hospital". In Jhansi there is a shrine of St. Jude, "a patron saint of the impossible" built in 1946 which is visited by thousands of devotees for its miraculous powers. During British days Jhansi was also a centre of missionary activities and hosts a sizeable population of Anglo-Indians.

Muslims

Muslims constitute the second largest community after Hindus throughout the Bundelkhand region. In 2001, the Muslim population averaged to 4 per cent in the region—5.3 per cent in UP-Bundelkhand and 3.7 per cent in MP-Bundelkhand. The 2011 data also suggest more or less the same composition of the Muslim community in the region. Comparatively the Bundelkhand average is three times less than the then national average of 13.4 per cent. If the Hindus in general and the Brahmins in particular are closest to the Jains in terms of the socio-cultural affinity, then the Muslim can be considered at the farthest end of the scale. This is mainly so as the Muslims as a group in general are invariably associated with non-vegetarianism. *Sharabi* (alcohol takers) and *Kababi* (*kabab*/meat eaters) are the common epithets that are applied by the Jain on Muslims. At inter-personal level, however, the situation is quite different. Individually, Muslim teachers (often called *maulvi saheb*), *hakeem* (Unani doctor), ascetics (*peer, faquir*, etc.) are treated with great tolerance and respect. Even short-term/casual/ad hoc Muslim employees/service providers such as masons, craftsmen and labourers, etc. are treated warmly. In the event of Hindu-Muslin riots, the Jains are almost always on the side of the Hindus.

Sikhs

There are very few Sikhs in Bundelkhand—mostly confined to bigger towns and cities. Invariably addressed as "Sardarji", the Sikhs are greatly admired by Jains for their sturdy physique, hard-working habits, entrepreneurship and religious orthodoxy.

Buddhists

There are very few Buddhists in Bundelkhand, except in Datia district where as per 2001 census data they constituted the third largest religious community after Hindus and Muslims at 1.5 per cent of the total population of the district. Educated Jains do know about the historical relationship between Buddhism and Jainism as fellow religions within the Shramanic tradition. But this kind of religious affinity does not carry much weight in lay Jain circles of Bundelkhand. So much so, that an average Jain perhaps would not be able to distinguish between a Buddhist monk and a Hindu monk.

Concluding Remarks

After discussing the changes in education and occupational structure in the previous chapter, social structural changes are highlighted in this chapter. Both micro and macro social structural features of the Bundelkhand's Jain community were taken into account. Whereas family, kinship and marriage and status of women were considered as micro social structures, caste system, social stratification, associational activities and inter-ethnic relations of the Jain community with wider society were treated as macro social structural features. It is found that both micro and macro social structural systems have varyingly been affected by the on-going social change. The kinship ties have been generally weakened over the generations. Notwithstanding the stage of family cycle, the average size of the family has been reduced. The family relations are now less patriarchal, and more democratic. The importance of daughters is increasingly being realised by most Jain families in Bundelkhand as married as well as unmarried daughters are more easily available in times of crisis or medical emergency.

The institution of marriage has too undergone numerous changes. There has been a drastic change in marriage duration—from 3-4 days to 12 to 20 hours only. There is some increase in inter-caste and inter-religion marriages. Attitude towards widow and divorcee marriages has changed resulting in wide acceptance for them. The agents of arranged marriage are no longer family members and/or relatives, but specialised marriage agencies. The custom of dowry has considerably declined. Other life cycle rituals mainly birth and death have also seen some changes over the generations.

Social stratification among Jains of Bundelkhand in terms of *dhanik varg*, *tyagis* and *jan sadharan* continues to remain more or less intact, but *dhanik varg's* sub-stratification as Shrimant Seth, Seth, Singhai, etc. is neither relevant now, nor in tune with the emerging reality of economic class formation based on education, profession and wealth. Education—both religious and secular has not only opened new avenues of professional careers but has also modernised businesses as discussed in the previous chapter. With harmonious inter-ethnic relations Bundelkhand provides a peaceful atmosphere for the Jains to live and work in the region. The overall regional economic development for several decades now, however, has not been very encouraging.

6

Continuity and Change in Jain Way of Life

This chapter focuses on the changes that are taking place in the Jain way of life which is mainly derived from Jain philosophy and religion, and more specifically from the doctrinally prescribed ethical code of conduct on the one hand, and the local customs and traditions on the other. In the early part of this chapter the Jain philosophy and its ethical principles are briefly presented, followed by some empirical findings about the Jain way of life in the Bundelkhand region.

The Jains primarily derive their identity as well as the way of life from religion, that is, Jainism. This has been so for centuries now. Time and again the unequivocal emphasis has been placed in Jainism on the *moksha-marg* as the true path of liberation. That the Jain social identity as well as the culture and the way of life are distinct from others is clearly highlighted by Prof. Vilas A. Sangave (1980: 350) in his celebrated sociological survey that was done in the late 1940s. He writes that "the features of Jaina culture are quite distinct from other cultures especially in matters like outlook towards life and world, insistence on spiritual progress, and observance of *Ahimsa* or creed of non-violence in all possible ways. The basic difference, it is stated, lies in the religious philosophy of Jainas and as religion moulds the entire way of life automatically becomes separate from other ways of life."

In most of India, the Jains maintain their distinct way of life and identity. This is not the case, perhaps, where certain Jain castes (e.g. Agrawal, Khandelwal and Oswal) closely interact with their Hindu counterparts leading to even matrimonial relations (e.g. Agrawal, Khandelwal and Oswal Jains in Gujarat, Delhi and parts of Western Uttar Pradesh). The consistent campaign since the early 1990s exhorting the Jains to return themselves as Jains in the 2001 and 2011 censuses has further been helpful in consolidating the Jain identity in terms of religion. It must, however, be added that the Jain identity cannot be divorced from its sect/sub-sect as well as the regional-linguistic context in which a particular Jain caste or community reside. Additionally, the divide between northern and southern Digambar Jainism can be fruitful in contextualising any sociological analysis (*See* Carrithers, 1988; Jain, Ravindra, K., 1999). More or less the same is true about other religious/ethnic communities in India, including the Hindus.

Jain Philosophy

In India Jainism as well as Buddhism has since long been recognised as a heterodox philosophical system. The traditional Indian philosophers regarded the two systems as *nastik* (non-believers, i.e., non-believers in the authority of the Vedas). As such, they are not part of the Hindu *Shad darshanas* (Six philosophical systems). Nevertheless, they have been recognised as formidable, autonomous and independent philosophical systems which merit attention in Indian philosophical discourses. In the West, however, a number of scholars until the late 19th century treated Jainism either as a sect of Hinduism or as an offshoot of Buddhism (Barth, 1969: 151; Weber, 1878; Wilson, 1861: 344). As Dasgupta (1963: 169) explained:

> Notwithstanding the radical differences in their philosophical notions, Jainism and Buddhism which were originally both orders of monks outside the pale of Brahmanism, present some resemblances in outward appearances, and some European scholars who became acquainted with Jainism through inadequate samples of Jaina literature easily persuaded themselves that it was an offshoot of Buddhism.

Thanks to the researches of a number of German Indologists (Buhler 1963; Jacobi 1946), Jainism is no longer considered merely a sect of Hinduism, or an offshoot of Buddhism. In the words of Pandit Jawaharlal Nehru (1969: 73): "Buddhism and Jainism were certainly not Hinduism or even the Vedic Dharma. Yet they arose in India and were integral parts of Indian life, culture and philosophy. A Buddhist or Jain in India is a hundred percent product of Indian thought and culture, yet neither is a Hindu by faith."

Jain Metaphysics

Jainism does not believe in the "Creator" of the universe. It believes in the entity of the world. It further believes that the reality (*sat*) is uncreated and is characterised by origination or appearance (*utpad*), destruction or disappearance (*Vyaya*), and permanence (*dhrauvya*). Every object of reality is also characterised by modes (*paryays*) and qualities (*gunas*) through which persist the essential sub-strata through all the times.

The Universe, according to Jainism, consists of six substances (*dravyas*): (i) living creatures or souls (*jiva*), (ii) matter (*pudgal*), (iii) medium/principle of motion (*dharma*), (iv) medium/principle of rest (*Aadharma*), (v) space (*akash*), and (vi) time (*kala*). These can be classified into two categories: living and non-living. Whereas *jiva* is the living substance, the rest of them are non-living. These *dravyas* are uncreated and undestructible. Their essential qualities remain the same; it is only their mode of condition (*paryay*) that can and does change.

Jain Ontology

The characteristic feature of *jiva* or soul is consciousness. The soul is the doer of all actions and is the enjoyer of the fruits of its actions. The souls are of two kinds: (i) *Sansarin* (mundane) or *Baddha* (in bondage), and (ii) *Siddha* (liberated) or *mukta* (free). Mundane souls are the embodied souls of living beings in the world and are still subject to the cycle of birth and death. On the other hand, *Siddha jivas* are the liberated souls and they will be embodied no more (Sangave, 2006: 30). The liberated souls in their pure condition possess the following four attributes: infinite perception, infinite knowledge, infinite power, and infinite bliss. In contrast, the mundane souls exist in the impure state as they are permeated with subtle psychosomatic matter called *karma.*

The Jain philosophy is based on the nature and interaction of the two constituent elements of the Universe, *Jiva* and *Ajiva.* The interaction is explained by the doctrine of Karma which is a remarkable feature of the Jain philosophy. According to Sangave (2006: 38), "The supreme importance of the doctrine of Karma lies in providing a rational and satisfying explanation to the apparently inexplicable phenomena of birth and death, of happiness and misery, of inequality in mental and physical attainments, and of the existence of different species of living beings."

Doctrine of Karma

In Jainism, Karmas are defined as a form of matter (*pudgala*) which are very fine and subtle and cannot be comprehended by any of the human senses. They are almost psycho-somatic in character and permeate the universe. Every phenomenon in the universe is the manifestation of Karmic energy.

All the existential conditions and enigmas of the world such as the all pervasive cycle of birth and death, suffering and happiness, wide variety of species of living beings, their differential mental and physical abilities and other characteristics can be explained by the doctrine of Karma which, as already mentioned, maintains that the soul is the doer of action and therefore has to bear the consequences of karmas. It further maintains that all the worldly souls are already in bondage of varying degrees. This bondage of karmas with soul obscures the innate qualities of the soul.

The doctrine further assumes the trans-migration of the soul after death into the next life. The balance sheet of the karmas in this life and the previous ones determine the kind and quality of next life. The doctrine further asserts that the *moksha* or liberation can be achieved only by completely destroying all the karmas. The structure and dynamics of the karma doctrine can be summed up in terms of the following seven *tattvas* or elements:

(i) *Jiva,* i.e., living substance,

(ii) *Ajiva*, i.e., non-living substance,
(iii) *Asrava,* i.e., the influx of karmic matter into the soul,
(iv) *Bandha,* i.e, bondage of soul by karmic-matter,
(v) *Samvara*, i.e., the stopping of asrava, the influx,
(vi) *Nirjara*, i.e., the gradual removal of karmic matter, and
(vii) *Moksha,* i.e., the attainment of perfect freedom from the karmas.

Whereas the first two items represent the structural elements of the universe, the last five unfold the dynamics of the Karma doctrine. "Stated briefly, *karma* is matter which 'flows in', *asrava,* and 'sticks', literally. What I do, sticks to me, and determines my character, the quality of my life and relationships. My thoughts, emotions and my speech are also 'acts'. They are called *bhavasrava.* They determine my perceptions, which lead me to act in the way that I do.... It is my thoughts and emotions, whether my own or inherited, that draw a veil over my perceptions. Untruth, delusion, and violence are its outcome. Jainism suggests to us that *anekanta-vada*, or the many-sidedness of truth; *a-parigraha*, or not-grasping; and *a-himsa*, or not-violence are the true basis of human freedom" (Badrinath, 1996).

Karma doctrine is a corner stone of the Jain philosophy. Jain scholars have gone into great details by classifying *karmas* into eight kinds and 148 sub-kinds. Based on the criterion whether a particular karma obstructs or destroys the essential attributes of the soul, the eight karmas are divided into the following two categories: (i) the *ghatia* (obstructive) and, (ii) the *aghatia* (non-obstructive) karmas. The former category consists of (a) *Jnanavarniya* (knowledge obstructing), (b) *darshanavarniya* (conation obstructing), (c) *vedaniya* (which causes feelings of pleasure and pain, etc.) and *mohiniya* (deluding) karmas. In the latter category are included the rest of the four karmas, namely: (a) *ayuh* (age), (b) *nama* (body making), (c) *gotra* (family determining) and (d) *antaraya* (karmas which hamper the innate qualities of the soul). It is easily clear that the *aghatia* karmas are mainly concerned with the state and particular conditions of embodiment (name, age, family, etc.).

A cursory look at the typology and functioning of *karmas* would suggest to their over-deterministic role in human life, but the Jain scholars emphatically maintain that theirs is not the doctrine of fatalism. Instead it is only a law of cause and effect. "Jainism does not fortify its followers by the terrors of *karma* nor does it make them languish in unhealthy, effeminate fatalism, as many people think all oriental religions do, but on the contrary, it trains the individuals to become a true hero on the battle field of self-conquest" (C. Krause quoted in Sangave, 2006: 44).

Jain Epistemology

Jain epistemology deals with the nature of objects of knowledge, means of knowledge, and the modes of comprehension and expression of reality. The objects of knowledge consist of all the six substances and associated phenomena as mentioned earlier. These substances not only display the properties of quality and modification, they are also extended over infinite space and time (past, present and future). Additionally, they are subject to origination, destruction and permanence. Moreover, when it comes to social phenomena, they are additionally complex by virtue of being subjective, symbolic and dynamic, and also diverse over space and time. Thus, according to Jain philosophers, the reality is complex and multifaceted (*anekanta)*. The recognition of this fact is summed up in the doctrine of *Anekantvad.* They further assert that such a reality can be fully comprehended only by an omniscient being, and not by ordinary human beings who have various kinds of limitations in their comprehension and expression of reality. This is more evident in the light of the fact that in terms of its means of acquisition, knowledge is classified by the Jain scholars into five categories: sense knowledge (*mati-jnan*), verbal or scriptural knowledge (*shruti-jnan),* extra-sensory perception or clairvoyant knowledge (*avadhi-jnan*), thought reading or telepathy (*manahparyay-jnan*), and ommiscience, absolute or perfect knowledge (*kevala-jnan*).

The fact that a human being can apprehend only partial reality led the Jain scholars to introduce the doctrine of *Nayavada* which is a system of describing reality from different points of view or stand-points (*nayas*). No single standpoint can be claimed as the only valid one. Thus, the doctrine recognises the relative validity of other standpoints. At the same time it provides a framework to introduce another doctrine, namely the doctrine of *Syadvada* which simply states that given the fact that our statements are only conditionally or relatively true, they must be "qualified with the term *Syat*, i.e. 'in some respects', or 'somehow', or 'in a way', with a view to emphasise its conditional or relative character" (Sangave, 2006: 48).

Jain Ethics

Jainism is basically a salvation religion—a religion that puts significant emphasis on attaining *moksha.* In terms of the karma doctrine, the complete freedom of the soul from *karmic* matter is called *moksha.* In Jainism *moksha* is not a place in heaven, but the attainment of the state of liberated soul, a final emancipation from the endless cycles of birth and death. According to German sociologist Max Weber, Jainism is a liberation religion of "cultured professional monks", and as such it requires considerable amount of spiritual education and training on the part of those who wish to follow the path of Jainism.

The Jain path to salvation consists of simultaneous pursuit of the right belief or perception, right knowledge and right conduct (*samyak-darshan, samyak-jnana* and *samyak-charitra*). The three together are known as *ratnatrayh* (three jewels) in Jain philosophy. The right belief consists in believing in the fundamentals of Jainism. According to Acharya Umaswami, "*Tattvarthasraddhanamsamyag-darsanam*", that is, right belief is the faith in the true nature of the substances as they are (*Tattvarthadhigama-Sutra*, Chapter 1, Sutra 2). At the same time, right belief also consists in believing in the true Jain God (deva), the true Jain scriptures (*shastras*), and the true Jain preceptors (*gurus*). The observance of right belief additionally requires the eight essential requisites, freedom from three kinds of superstitious beliefs (*mudhatas*), and freedom from eight kinds of pride or arrogance (*mada*). All these conditionalities are extremely difficult in practical observance as these are required to be rigorously followed by those who wish to advance on the path of salvation.

The second jewel of the *tri-ratna* of the liberation path, the right knowledge consists in having full comprehension of the real nature of soul and non-soul (i.e. matter) in such a manner that such knowledge should be free from doubt, perversity, and vagueness or wide finiteness" (Sangave, 2006: 58). We have already discussed the five kinds of means of acquiring such knowledge. How to do that has been deliberated upon at great length in Jain scriptures in terms of the right kinds of requirements that are again rigorous in observances. In short, "the right knowledge can be acquired by pursuit with devotion, by reading sacred scriptures, understanding their full meaning and significance in proper time and with punctuality, imbued with zeal, proper behaviour and open mind" (Sangave, 2006: 60).

The right conduct is the third integral component of the path of salvation. The right conduct is defined by Jain scholars as proper, appropriate and truly natural conduct of the soul which is conducive to its salvation. In practical terms, it comprises the ethical code and the rules, and disciplines which an aspirant is required to pursue. In Jainism, more or less common rules of conduct are prescribed for the laity and the ascetic of both sexes. Obviously, the rules prescribed for the laity are less rigorous compared to those for the ascetics for the simple reason that the householders have to earn their livelihood and maintain the family life. Looking at the rigorous conditionalities associated with right perception, right knowledge, right conduct, etc., it is difficult for a sociologist to escape the conclusion that there is a strong element of indoctrination in Jainism. It does allow free inquiry but only within the parameters set by itself.

Code of Conduct for the Householders

Four sets of ethical code are prescribed for Jain householders: Twelve *vratas*, eleven *pritimas*, six *Abshyakas*, and a number of appropriate conducts. It would appear that whereas the first two sets of conduct are more specific in nature in terms of their number as well as observance, the last two sets are general and perhaps flexible in practice. Thus, the fourth set of conducts known as *Bhadraka* (gentlemanly) or *marganusari* (accessory to the path) consists of 17, 21, or 35 rules according to different authorities.

Twelve Vows (Vratas)

The twelve vows prescribed for a Jain householder comprise the five *anuvratas*, three *gunavratas* and four *sikshavratas*. The five anuvratas, so-called because they are only lesser, partial, limited and qualified vows, and not absolute vows as prescribed for the ascetics, are *ahimsa* (abstention from violence or injury to living beings), *satya* (abstention from false speech), *achaurya* or *asteya* (abstention from theft), *bramhacharya* or *shil* (abstention from sexuality or unchastity), and *aparigraha* (abstention from greed for worldly possessions).

The first vow demands abstinence from intentional injury or killing of life for food, sport, pleasure or some other purpose. As much as possible, violence must be avoided in thought, words and deed. Defensive violence if necessary, however, is allowed for the householder in order to protect his country, society, family, religious institutions, and property. Injury to life is also permitted to householders who might commit it during their vocational calling such as agricultural, industrial or other occupational activities. Injury should be limited to the minimum possible extent.

The second vow demands that one must not only abstain from telling lies, but also avoid using harsh or abusive language. Language that hurts the feelings of others or amounts to ridiculing, backbiting and flattery should also be avoided. The third vow *achaurya-anuvrata* demands abstaining from stealing, robbing, or misappropriation of others' property. It also includes abstinence from cheating and using dishonest or illegal means in acquiring any worldly possessions. The fourth vow, *shilanuvrata* demands abstention from having sexual relations with anyone except one's own lawfully wedded spouse. The fifth, *parigraha-parimana-anuvrata* requires the imposition of a limit on one's needs, acquisitions and possessions.

During the course of observing the above discussed five vows, a householder has to guard himself/herself against committing certain infringements and transgressions:

> such as tying up living beings or keeping them in bondage, mutilating them, beating them, overloading them and starving them, in the case of the first vow; preaching falsehood, divulging other people's secrets, forgery, misappropriation, and disclosure of a man and wife's secret talk, in the case of the second vow; adulteration, abetment of theft, receiving stolen property, violation of government laws, and use of false weights and measures, in the case of the third vow; avoidable match making, intercourse with an unchaste married person, prostitution, unnatural offence or sex perversion and inordinate sex

> desire, in the case of the fourth vow; and to exceed the limits set by oneself with regard to landed property, movable effects and riches, servants, pet animals, and other worldly goods, in the case of the fifth vow (Jain, J. P., 1983: 86-87).

In addition to five *anuvratas*, a householder is required to practise three *guna-vratas* (the multiplicative vows) that enhance the effect and value of the *anuvratas* manifold. These are: (1) *dig-vrata*, taking a life-long vow to limit one's worldly activities to fixed points in different spatial directions, (2) *desa-vrata*, taking a vow to limit the above also to a limited area, and (3) *anarthadanda-vrata*, taking a vow not to indulge in purposeless moral offences.

Besides five *anuvratas* and three *guna-vratas*, a householder is also required to practise four disciplinary vows *(siksha-vratas)* which are intended to prepare the aspirant gradually for the discipline of ascetic life. These are *samayika*, *prosadhopavasa*, *upabhoga-paribhoga-parimana*, and *atithi-samvibhaga*. The first one requires the householder to contemplate or meditate preferably thrice a day for about forty-five minutes each. The second vow requires him to fast on two days of the lunar fortnight, namely, the eighth and the fourteenth. The third requires a householder to limit on daily basis his or her enjoyment of consumable and non-consumable items. And the fourth vow requires the householder to share food with the guest including ascetic, recluse, pious or needy person.

Observance of five *anuvratas* and abstention from wine, meat and honey together constitute eight *mulagunas*, that is, basic or primary virtues of a householder. Simlarly, the three *guna-vratas* and four *shiksha-vratas* combine to form seven *shila-vratas* that supplement the *anuvratas.*

In addition to the twelve vows, a householder is expected to undergo in the last days of his/her life the process of *Sallekhna*, that is, peaceful or voluntary death which is different from suicide in that the latter is regarded in Jainism as a cowardly act and even a sin (Streefkerk, 1997). For Jains *Sallekhna* is an equanimously-planned preparation for the inevitable death, and therefore a religious act (Baya 'Sreyas', 2007).

That *sallekhna/santhara* has been a living tradition is borne out by the findings of a recent study (Baya 'Sreyas', 2007) which is based on the sample size of 350 cases of 'voluntary peaceful death' (extrapolated figure 2,400 cases) in Udaipur district during the period 1994-2003. The study suggests (i) that compared to Digambaras (26%), about three times more (74%) Shvetambars Jains practise*santhara*; (ii) that overall householders, both males and females, embrace the vow of voluntary peaceful death in much greater number than their ascetic counterparts (p. 263); (iii) that within the Digambar tradition the practise was found to be five-times less prevalent among the householders (4.3%) than among the ascetics (22.3%). The situation was found to be reverse in Shvetambar Jainism with 62.3 per cent householders and only 11.1 per cent ascetics practicing *santhara*. The incidences of voluntary peaceful death were reported more from the urban areas (62.9%) than from the rural areas (37.1%). The study further suggests that maximum number of such incidences take place in the 61-90 years age-group with average age of the practitioners being 77 years. Old age and/or incurable disease was found to be the main cause of death. The overwhelming majority of people took the vow of *santhara* when they were fully conscious and remained on the death-bed for more than one day (p. 267).

Eleven Stages (Pratimas)

Shravaka-Pratimas consisting of eleven steps plan chart out the course of spiritual journey prescribed for the householders. Each step like a rung in the ladder progressively leads to the higher stage of spiritual progress. These are briefly presented below.

1. *Darsana Pratima:* At this first stage the householder is required to observe all the practical aspects of the Right Belief. He is also supposed to have given up eating meat, wine and honey and five *udumbara* fruits. Hunting, gambling, prostitution and adultery are strictly prohibited.
2. *Vrata Pratima:* The householder is required to observe without transgression the twelve vows discussed earlier.
3. *Samayika Pratima:* It consists of self-contemplation and meditation in general for fortyeight minutes, three times daily so that one could concentrate on spiritual values and purify one's ideas and mind.
4. *Prosadhopavasa Pratima:* It involves regular fasting twice a fortnight in each lunar month, accompanied by meditation, hearing of religious discourse and study of scriptures.
5. *Sachitta-tyaga Pratima*: This pratima consists in abandoning the use of animate items such as roots, fruits, seeds, etc. without getting them sterilised by boiling etc. One is also refrained from serving such food to others. A householder should also not trample upon any growing plant or pluck fruits from a tree.
6. *Ratri-*Bhojan*Tyag Pratima*: At this stage the householder is required to give up forever eating or drinking anything after sunset. To offer food and drinks to others at night is also prohibited.
7. *Brahmacharya Pratima*: At this stage the householder leads a life of absolute continence and gives up sexual gratification in any manner even with own spouse. It also includes avoidance of personal decorations.
8. *Arambha-tyaga Pratima*: This stage requires the householder to renounce all occupational activities—agriculture, business, service, or profession.

9. *Parigraha-tyaga Pratima*. At this stage the householder is required to give up almost all the worldly possessions, except bare minimum necessary for the preparation of an ascetic life.
10. *Anumati-Tyag Pratima*: The householder in this stage refrains from showing any concern about family affairs. "He would not even express his agreement or disagreement, approval or disapproval in such matters. He is for all purposes an anchorite, or recluse, only that he is still living in the home with other members of his family" (Jain, J. P., 1983: 90).
11. *Uddista-tyag Pratima*. At this stage the householder becomes a wandering monk after leaving his home. He lives in the forest or a lonely place in the company of an ascetic.

On attaining the eleventh stage the householder can choose to become either a "*Kshullaka*" or an "*Ailaka*" depending on his preference for dress and style of meal-taking, etc. Thus, whereas the *kshullaka* uses a loincloth and an upper garment, the *ailaka* uses only a loin-cloth. The former applies instruments for cutting his hair, keeps a broom in place of a *picchi*, takes his meal once a day either in the palm of his hands or in some pot in a sitting posture, and observes fast on every *parvan* day. The latter pulls out his hair and takes his meals in the palm of his hands" (Bhargava, 1968: 145).

Accessory Rules

A number of rules, known as *bhadraka* (gentlemanly) or *marganusari* (accessory to the path), are advocated for the guidance of a lay follower in his day-to-day practical conduct and behaviour. Their exact number—seventeen, twenty-one, or thirty-five—differs from prescribing authority to authority, but many of the qualities advocated are common.

> These rules are: to earn one's living lawfully; to pursue one's economic and religious activities without conflict; to keep one's expenditure within the limits of his income; to avoid misuse of money; to undertake a task according to one's capacity; to specialise at least in some one branch of learning, art or industry; to take proper and wholesome food; to observe cleanliness of person and environment; to live in a proper and suitable house; to avoid residing in a habitation or locality which is not peaceful and congenial to one's own way of living; to spouse a suitable person; due respect and care of one's parents; due care, protection and maintenance of wife, children and other dependents; to have love for one's country and to uphold national character, ideologies and culture; to avoid doing things contrary to the customs of one's country, social group or family; to adopt fashions of the place and times one lives in, that is, adaptability; to follow the lead given by old and

> experienced persons; to respect the wise and the pious; to have love for the god; to avail opportunity of listening to religious discourse; fear of sin., i.e, to fear from committing sinful acts; to cultivate a sense of duty and responsibility; to be ready to serve fellow human beings; to develop manners, decent behaviour and proper conduct; to avoid talking ill of others; to refrain from wickedness; to avoid being cruel; to be amiable and sweet in speech; to be amicable; to be impartial; to be tolerant; to have a yielding disposition, as opposed to obstinacy or stubbornness; hospitality; charitability; generosity of heart; gentility; popularity, i.e., to try to win the love and esteem of others; to be kind and compassionate; gratefulness; prudence; modesty; humility; to avoid being vain, proud, conceited, arrogant or haughty; honesty and truthfulness; to avoid hatred; to refrain from being jealous; to try not to give way to anger, greed, or abnormal sexual passion; to try to practise sense-control; to save oneself from being deluded; and to have a comprehension of one's ultimate goal (Jain, J.P., 1983: 84-85).

It is clear that the cultivation of these qualities paves the path of spiritual progress.

Code of Conduct for Ascetics

"The ascetics, whether male or female, are those fully dedicated souls who have renounced worldly life and pleasures, adopted a life of renunciation and asceticism, and devote themselves to the pursuit of *moksa* or liberation, by attending primarily to their own spiritual wellbeing and secondarily to the moral welfare of the society in general" (Jain, J.P.,1983: 81-82). Thus, the ascetics are not only the spiritual self-seekers but also the "community builders" (Folkert, 1993). They are in regular interaction with the laity—the interaction being especially intense during the four-month rainy season (*chaturmas*). In the Bundelkhand region this is especially so. Thus, for example, Acharya Vidyasagar, one of the most celebrated Digambar Jain ascetics, had done 51 chaturmas during 1968 and 2018 (http://www.vidyasagar.net/chaturmas/ Last accessed on 28.07.2019). Of these 16 (about 31%) were held in Bundelkhand and 27 (about 53%) in "Greater Bundelkhand".

As in other religions, in Jainism too the ascetics constitute a tiny minority, perhaps numbering about 17,000, including women ascetics. The number of Digambar Jain ascetics is much smaller—estimatedly only about 1,400 (*See* Jain, Prakash C., 2019: 249-51). However, their authority and influence over the laity is extra-ordinary. Apart from the personality factor, much of their institutionalised legitimacy and authority is derived from their spiritual attainment along the path of salvation (*See* Carrithers, 1989; Cort 1991; Flugel, 2011; Fohr, 2001; Goonasekera 1986; Sethi 2010; Vallely 2003). The Digambar tradition prescribes the following twenty-eight essential qualities of a monk which are known as *Mulagunas:*

1-5. Five great vows (*panchamaha-vratas)*,
6-10. Five-fold path of vigilance (*pancha-samitis*),
11-15. Control of five senses (*Indriya-jaya*),
16-21. Six essential duties (*Sad-avashyakas*),
22. Pulling out of the hair (*Kesa-lunchana*),
23. Nudity,
24. Non-bathing,
25. Sleeping on the ground,
26. Not cleaning the teeth,
27. Taking food in standing posture,
28. Eating only once in twenty-four hours (*Ekabhukta*).

The Shvetambar tradition, as already mentioned, does not take nudity to be an essential quality of a monk. Besides this, there are a couple of more variations in the essential qualities of a monk.

It would be observed that in the Digambar tradition the ethical codes of conduct for both the ascetics and the householders are more or less common, though in the case of ascetics it is more rigorous for obvious reasons. There is also a gradation in both the codes, and the householders and the ascetics are required to follow a graduated course of conduct keeping in mind the individual capacity of the person. Moreover, it must also be kept in mind that "though the rules of conduct as prescribed by Jainism appear to be too elaborate and sometimes even superfluous, yet the basic idea behind these rules is that of self-realisation. When there is a feeling-realisation of the true nature of the self and when one is completely lost in the bliss of self-meditation, the observance of all the moral rules becomes spontaneous coming from within and not being an imposition from without" (Bhargava, 1968: 220).

Religious Orthodoxy

Scriptural reading of Jainism and particularly that of its ethical codes of conduct establishes the salvation or *moksha-marg* discourse as central to Jainism. The *moksh-marg* ideology exhibits all the characteristic features of a religious orthodoxy which can be defined as the way of life involving regular interaction with ascetics, observance of rituals, "recitation of prayers and mantras, full acceptance of the authority of Mahavir and his teachings, and a concern with correct practice and sectarian exclusivity, all typically associated with women and old-people" (Dundas, 1992: 233). It was, therefore, quite appropriate for Max Weber and many other scholars to characterise Jainism as soteriological religion (Jaini, 1979; Sangave, 1980; Weber, 1958).

Recent fieldwork-based studies of Shvetambar Jains in Gujarat and Rajasthan, however, do not entirely support this view (e.g. Banks, 1992; Cort, 2001; Laidlaw, 1995). Thus, in his ethnographic study of Shvetambar Murtipujak Jains in Jamnagar, Marcus Banks (1992) points out "the lack of knowledge about doctrines and also the lack of modeling of the lay behaviour after ascetic ideals" (cited in Jain, R.K., 1999: 51). According to Banks, "Jainism in practice, therefore, is a collaborative project undertaken by both lay and ascetic (rather than the graduated project implied by P.S. Jaini's (1979) account of lay and ascetic paths, where the former is seen as wholly subordinate to the latter" (Banks 1992: 3).

In his study of Shvetambar Jains in Jaipur, Laidlaw also examines the practicality of Jain asceticism, and argues that the "asceticism which lay Jainism exudes comes not from uniform adherence to a set of socially enforced rules" (1995: 170). "There is no single view expressed either in ancient sacred texts or in religious debate and practice today" (p. 191). The numerous vows including those of fasting and dietary practices that Jain laity undertakes are often voluntary and based on personal decisions "which Jain teachers have charted out, and around which contemporary asceticism tends to move" (p. 191). Laidlaw further argues that "the self that Jainism proposes for its followers to make of themselves is fragmented and incomplete, torn between conflicting ideals and focused ultimately on an impossible one" (1995: 20-21).

Similarly, John Cort (2001: 186) in his study of Shvetambar Murtipujak Jain community of Patan, Gujarat argues that the *moksha-marg* ideology, spelled out some two thousand years ago in such works like *Tattvarth Sutra* and *Uttradhyan Sutra,* "has remained remarkably consistent throughout the Jain history." It is, however, mainly practised only by ascetics and a few Jain laypersons, and for the vast majority of laity it is not compelling. For the latter the realm of wellbeing is more important which involves "a mix of health, contentment, peace and prosperity". Furthermore, "the *moksha-marg* ideology and the value of wellbeing are held in unresolved tension because of the multivocality of the symbols by which the two are expressed. According to the *moksh-marg* ideology, an individual has to make a choice between wellbeing and the *moksh-marg*. In practice the two are held in tension, and people act and live on the assumption that one can have it both ways; following practices of the *moksh-marg* brings wellbeing, and pursuit of wellbeing (within certain boundaries) advances one at least a small way along the *moksh-marg*" (Cort 2001: 200).

These studies need to be contextualised in terms of the sectarian monastic organisation in that the Shevetambar lay Jains are not generally stratified along the path of *moksha-marg* unlike their Digambar Jain counterparts. As Cort (1989: 663) himself remarks elsewhere, "The principal hierarchical differentiation among Digambar occurs *before* full initiation as a *muni*, in the level of advanced householdership of *brahmachari*, *kshullak* and *ailak*, while the mendicants consists mainly of the single level of *munis*, with hierarchy determined by seniority of initiation. The Shvetambars, on the other hand, exhibit uniformity among the laity—they are all just *shravaks* (men) and *shravikas* (women)—but a graduated hierarchy of initiatory ranks among the mendicants".

The sect-specific monastic organisation in Jainism becomes more clear when we contrast these studies with two studies of north Indian Digambar Jains done by Ravindra K. Jain—one based on the autobiography of *Kshullak* Ganesh Prasad Varni (1949) that describes in detail the organisation of Jains in the Bundelkhand region of central India and the other, a brief ethnography of Digambar Jains of Baraut of Meerut district in Uttar Pradesh (Jain, R. K., 1999: 50-82 and 83-100). These studies maintain that in Varni's accounts of Digambar Jain communities of Bundelkhand, the "doctrine and practice are closely tied up with each other" and that there is "a continuous and ever-increasing stress on the path of purification among Digambar Jain householders" (Jain, R. K., 1999: 51), which manifests in hierarchical differentiation of laity in the form of *brahmachari*, *kshullak* and *ailak* (collectively called *tyagis*). Along with *tyagis,* Jain pandits (teachers and scholars) form a significant intermediate layer between the ascetics and the laity in Bundelkhand region. The sectarian context thus puts the *moksh-marg* ideal and ascetic-laity interaction in some perspective. However, Cort's thesis cannot be dismissed lightly. Indeed, it provides deeper insight into the world of Jain laity as rightly argued by Peter Flugel (2006) in his review article of *Jains in the World*. Undoubtedly, more studies are required on the issue before we discover the underlying sociological patterns.

Whether the salvation ideology and its twin pillars, namely *mulachara* and *shravakachara* require any change or modern reinterpretation in the context of the contemporary life is a moot sociological question. The orthodox Jains would obviously support the *status quo* in this regard. The reformists, on the other hand, would certainly insist on some changes. Inconclusive seminars have also been held on *Shravakachar* and *Mulachara* with no concrete plan to modify or even reinterpret the old codes of conduct, although the need for doing something about this situation has been underlined in the face of increasing laxity in observing the prescribed codes of conduct by ascetics.

Shithilachara, or the laxity in observance of the *mulachara* on the part of the *sadhus* has been an old problem in Jain community. A majority of our respondents (64.4%) agree with the observation that there have been changes in the conduct of munis over a period of time. The rigorous code of conduct is not appropriately followed by some of the ascetics. A number of them have not been able to control even such basic impulses as anger, greed, pride and envy. Some of these behavioural traits are extended to intra-group and inter-group levels. A subtle under-current of rivalry and politics can easily be discerned among the various *muni-sanghas.* So much so, that they avoid sharing the public meeting platforms with each other. Some of them are also accused of *ekal-vihar* (moving or living alone, and not with the *sangh*), inviting criticism from many quarters in the Jain community. Seeking name and fame has also been a weakness with some *sadhus* and *aryikas*—something which is strictly prohibited in Digambar Jain ascetic code of conduct. There has been an increased tendency among them to getting celebrated their birthdays and *deeksha* days, etc. Patronage is also provided by most *sadhus* to rich *shrawakas (Seths and Shrimants, etc.)* for getting new temples built, and for getting published their own religious discourses in book forms, or CDs, etc. The munis also patronise pandits and other scholars by getting them awards and fellowships of various foundations/trusts/NGOs run by the Jain Seths.

Table 6.1: Some Aspects of Jain Religiosity

	Yes	*No*	*No Respons e*	*Total (%)*
Observe shradha/varsi of diseased	6.7	92.2	21.1	100
Jainism is the best of all religions	92.8	6.1	21.1	100
Change in conduct of Jain monks	64.4	21.1	14.4	100
Differentiate between *Nishchay and Vyavahar Naya*	30.6	63.3	6.1	100
Supporter of Kanji Swami Panth	19.4	76.7	73.9	100
Supporter of Baal-Diksha	10	86.1	73.9	100

Kanji Swami Panth: A Challenge to Orthodoxy

The origin and basic tenets of Kanji Swami Panth (KSP) are briefly discussed in Chapter Two. It is essentially a variation in Digambar Jain moksha-marg ideology. In the context of Bundelkhand, it challenges the religious orthodoxy at least on two points: (i) In the face of the problem of *shithilachar* among Digambar Jain *munis*, the Kanji Panth appears to sideline the very institution of naked asceticism by emphasing the point that there is no possibility of becoming an ideal muni in present times; (ii) Its focus on the soul and self-realisation from the standpoint of *nishchaynaya* makes religious rituals unnecessary and redundant. The two attempt to strike at the very roots of orthodoxy in Digambar Jainism in that the devotion to ascetics *(muni-bhakti)*, idol worship and allied rituals are no longer considered necessary for the attainment of liberation. Over the years, the ideological contestation got so bitter that a number of Jain temples put up sign boards barring the Kanji Panthi religious literature from being displayed or studied in the temple premises. In response, separate Kanji Panthi temples were built in major cities and towns of Bundelkhand including Sagar, Lalitpur, Damoh, Tikamgarh, Chhatarpur and Khaniadhana.

Dr. Hukam Chand Bharill and his brother Pt. Ratan Chand Bharill are the well-known supporters of the Kanji Panth among Bundelkhandi pandits. They live in Jaipur and propagate the KSP ideology through Pandit Todarmal Smarak Trust, Jaipur. Among the other supporters of KSP ideology, mention must be made of Pt. Gyan Chand Jain, Vidisha; Dr. Suddhatm Prakash, Mumbai; Prof. Sudeep Jain,

Delhi; Pt. Shreyansh Singhai, Jaipur; Pt. Abhay Kumar Jain, Jabalpur; Pt. Uttam Chand Jain, Siwni and Pt. Hem Chand Jain "Hem", Jabalpur.

In our survey, Kanji Swami Panth is supported by about 20 per cent of the respondents and its influence in the Bundelkhand region was reported to be slowly growing. Some scholars, however, believe that the influence of the KSP ideology has significantly been neutralised by the rise of Acharya Vidyasagarji Maharaj who is extremely popular in the region since at least the turn of the 21st century.

It is interesting to note here that in a way Kanji Panth comes closer to Taaran Taran Panth of 15th century A.D. that emphasised on absolute spirituality sans idol worship. Not surprisingly, Kanji Swami greatly admires Taaran Taran Swami's views on spirituality. In his words: "Muni TaaranTaran Swami was a great spiritualist saint on account of the fact that deep mysteries (of spiritualism) are present in *shastras* written by him" (quoted in Bharill, R. C., 2010: viii).

Neo-Orthodoxy and Heterodoxy

Contemporary Jain studies in modern Indian as well as diasporic Jain contexts have thrown up two variant concepts and practices of orthodoxy in Jainism, namely neo-orthodoxy and heterodoxy (Banks, 1992, Dundas,1992, Jain, Yogendra, 2007, Mardia, 2003, Kachhara 2005, Rankin 2007). According to Dundas (1992: 233), neo-orthodoxy "presents itself as modern and progressive with an emphasis on those aspects of Jainism which can be interpreted as scientific and rational and can therefore be accommodated to and encompass western modes of thought." Again to quote Dundas (1992 : 233):

> Heterodoxy involves an interpretation of Jainism as theistic and frees from the metaphysical complexities which many feel to be a feature of the religion, with the ford-makers being viewed as in some way the manifestation of a supreme deity and endowed with the capacity to intervene directly in human affairs and offer assistance. Here God-focused devotion plays an important part in the Jains who have espoused this heterodoxy see no incongruity in, for example, worshipping in Hindu or Sikh temples.

In the context of the Bundelkhand Jain community, whereas the adherents of neo-orthodoxy appear to be in great majority, there are very few takers of heterodoxy. In this study, it was confirmed by asking a few questions. Thus, when asked, "is Jainism the best of all religions?", an overwhelming majority of respondents (92.8%) replied in the affirmative. Although the respondents were not asked to explain their replies, my fieldwork observations and casual talk on the subject would often bring the conversation towards the scientific nature of Jainism and its antiquity.

In highlighting the scientific nature of Jainism, the most frequently mentioned themes/sub-themes that are integral parts of Jain philosophy and religion are: Jain cosmology, especially the notion that the universe is self-supporting, infinite and not created by God, concepts of atom and molecule, the existence of *jiva* (life) in even plants, benefits of vegetarianism and avoiding eating food after sunset, moral implications of the ethical principles of Ahimsa, *aparigraha* and *anekantvad/syadvad*, a religion open to all, irrespective of caste, class, creed or colour, and so on.

As per the definition of heterodoxy mentioned above, a majority of Jains in Bundelkhand do not believe in heterodoxy. Two questions were asked to find out the extent of heterodoxy present among the Jains of Bundelkhand: (i) Do you worship any family deity?, and (ii) "Do you have faith in Gods of other religions?" The reply to both these questions was given in the negative by a great majority of respondents (85.0% and 86.7% respectively). Thus, only about 15 per cent of respondents tend to support heterodoxy. The data thus clearly support the contention of Ganesh Prasad Varni (1949), Pt. Phoolchandra Shastri (1992) and other scholars (Jain, Ravindra K., 1999) that Bundelkhand Jain community still continues to carry on the original unbridled tradition (*moolamnaya*) of Lord Mahavir, Acharya Kundkund and other Digambar Jain acharyas.

***Dincharya* (Daily Routine)**

Daily routine of Jains in Bundelkhund does not seem to have changed for over a century. Writing about the daily *dincharya* of Bundelkhund Jains of the early twentieth century, Ganesh Prasad Varni (1949: 27) wrote: "Followers of this religion (Jainism) practise compassion, use only filtered water, do not eat after sunset, maintain cleanliness, visit temples everyday…there is daily discourse in the temple… and carefully scrutinise all food materials before use." Although these practices are only the externals but they are inexplicably woven with the "Jain path of Purification" (Jain, Ravindra K., 1999: 69). True to his time, Varni could not mention self-study (*swadhyay*) as another daily activity of majority of Jains of Bundelkhand which is now possible because of the easy availability of published scriptural material.

In response to a question: "As a follower of Jainism, what is your *dincharya* from morning till evening?", an overwhelming majority of respondents in our study narrated the following sequence of activities: getting ready for the day, temple visit of varying duration, ranging from 10 minutes to two hours during which the recitation of *namokar mantra*, *samayik* (meditation), worship and/or self-study of scripture(s), are done; breakfast/early lunch; attending shop/office; meal before sunset; early night temple visit for listening to religious or philosophical discourse from a *Tyagi*/Pandit or Muni. Author's field observations suggest that the complete sequence of this *dincharya* is followed by elderly males, most of the females and only a few male youngsters.

Heavily loaded schedule of daily routine puts enormous pressure on women's life in Bundelkhand. This is particularly so in those households which are dependent on business and trade for livelihood. Though a majority of women continue to bear the extra burden of household chores, the upcoming generation of educated girls have revolted against the traders' life style and prefer to marry salaried-class boys working in bigger towns and cities. This obviously amounts to coming out of "only domestic" domain and going out and see the world.

Laxity in observance of this *dincharya* and an overall indifference towards religion on the part of Jain youth has caused a considerable concern within the Jain community of Bundelkhand in recent decades. Thus, over 76 per cent of our respondents have said "Yes" in reply to the question "Are Jain children becoming indifferent to their religion?" About 21.7 per cent maintained an attitude of status quo in this regard, whereas about 2 per cent respondents did not reply to the question (*see* Table 6.2). An overwhelming majority of respondents (97.7%) were, therefore, in favour of giving compulsory religious education in one form or the other to the youngsters, both male and female.

Table 6.2: Jain Children's Indifference Towards Religion

Response	*Percentage*
Yes	76.1
No	21.7
No Response	2.2
Total	100.0

Table 6.3: Should Jain Children Be Given Compulsory Religious Education?

Response	*Percentage*
Yes	97.7
No	1.7
No Response	0.6
Total	100.0

When asked how, a number of suggestions were offered by the respondents. Although it was a structured question, and respondents were required to give only one response, almost all of them gave two or more responses and therefore it was not possible to quantify the responses. A very significant number of respondents were in favour of parents or some other senior family member educating and training their children in Jain way of life. A little lesser number of respondents thought that children should be given religious instructions during or as part of the evening religious discourse in the temple. Still others suggested that children be sent to Jain *pathshalas* on part-time basis. A fourth option endorsed by a large number of respondents was to organise religious camps of a short duration to impart education and training about Jainism.

This fourth option also appears to be the preferred option of the various Jain associations and leaders. In many parts of north India including Bundelkhand, the Jain religious camps have been in vogue for the past two decades or so. These are generally organised by local or regional chapters of national Jain associations, and are quite popular with the community. One such programme that is being continuously held since 2009 in Bhopal is known as "Sanskar Education Camp", and is organised by the regional chapter of Bharat Varshiya Digambar Jain Mahasabha, Delhi. In 2015, the camp was organised during May 10-20 at 21 centres in the city which was attended by about 1,000 youngsters. The daily activities started with temple visit, idol worshipping, education and training sessions in the forenoon and afternoon and religious discourse late in the evening. These programmes were held in temple premises (*See Jain Gazette*, 22 June 2015: 8).

Diet and Dietary Regulations

A few individual exceptions apart, Jains all over India in general, and in the Bundelkhund region in particular, are strictly vegetarian. In this study, we deliberately did not ask any question about vegetarianism. An overwhelming majority of Jains of Bundelkhand show zero tolerance towards non-vegetarian food items. This, however, does not mean that a few youngsters occasionally may not have been taking non-vegetarian food outside their homes, away from the gaze of the family and community members. More or less the same situation exists about alcohol and some other intoxicants like ganja, charas etc. Besides these two taboo food items, scriptures also do not permit the following food items but the Jains in Bundelkhund do consume them with varying degree of openness: garlic, onion, potato, brinjal, arvi, radish, carrot and tomato.

Most Jains in Bundelkhand do not prefer even occasionally to eat out in hotels, restaurants, etc. This is so because most such establishments are run by non-Jains who do not use cloth-filtered water for cooking or drinking purposes. Use of garlic, onion, etc. in many cooked food items also puts off Jains from consuming such food. Strong sense of purity and pollution, and lower caste background of cooks and waiters further act as deterrents for the Jains to visit such places. The overall perception is that hotel's/restaurant's food is generally unhygienic and therefore must be avoided at any cost. This perception and practice is slowly changing in case of younger generation when they are travelling long distances, or are using hostel facilities of educational institutions.

The above discussion clearly suggests that ordinarily Jains in Bundelkhand not only pay considerable attention to the distinction of eatable and non-eatable food items, but also to the details of how to prepare and cook them. Even more care is taken in preparing and cooking food for the spiritually inclined members in the family. The following 16 kinds of purity-precautions have been prescribed in Jainism for preparing such a food which is thereby known as '*solah ka khana*'. It is particularly taken by *tyagis* and spiritually inclined elderly men and women. Food prepared under the similar conditions is offered to the ascetics with far more ritually prescribed precautions. The sixteen kinds of precautions are as follows:

1. *Material purity*: (1) food items' purity, (2) water purity, (3) fire purity, (4) cook's purity.
2. *Place/Space purity*: (1) light purity, (2) air purity, (3) space purity, (4) odourless environment.
3. *Time Purity*: (1) avoiding eclipse time, (2) avoiding mourning time, (3) avoiding festive time, (4) avoiding religious festivity time.
4. *Purity of Intensions*: (1) child-like intensions, (2) compassionate intensions, (3) devotion (*vinaybhav*), (4) giving away (*dan bhav*).

Thus, food should not only be prepared with utmost attention and cleanliness at proper place and time, but also be consumed with and/or offered with good intensions. *Solah ka Khana* is an idealistic prescription and the concerned people try to follow the precautions as much as possible. However, in the Bundelkhand context, where there are a number of constrains regarding kitchen and dining space, availability of water, drainage system and electricity, etc. much is left to be desired. This is more so on the occasions of marriage and other group functions.

Festivals and Pilgrimage

Jains generally celebrate all the major Hindu festivals such as Rakshabandhan, Dashahra, Deepawali, and Holi. Different reasons are given for celebrating them. Thus Deepawali, for example, is celebrated by the Jains not so much because that day Lord Rama returned to Ayodhya after the victory over the Lanka king Ravana, but because Tirthankara Mahavira attained *Nirvana* on the same day. The birthday of Lord Mahavira (Mahavira *Jayanti*) has been a public holiday in India since the late British days for which the Jains had to indulge in some politics.

Other important festivals celebrated by Jains are *Paryushan Parva/Das Lakshan* (last eight/ten days of *Bhadra*) and *Ashthanika* (the last eight days of *Kartika*). These are regarded very auspicious by the Jains. During these days, the atmosphere in most Jains families is charged with high spirituality and almost all the Jains make it a point to go to the temples for worship and recite or listen to the scriptures. In many temples or *Sthanakas,* Pandits are also engaged to deliver religious discourses in the evenings. Most Jains in Bundelkhand observe fast during these 10 days. In our survey about 83.3 per cent of respondents said yes to keeping fast during *paryushan parva*, whereas this figure came down to only 26.11 per cent when asked if they kept fast on every *ashtmi* and *chaturdashi* (eights and fourteenth day of lunar fortnightly cycle) (*See* Table 6.4). Needless to say, keeping fast at regular intervals and/or on auspicious days is an important component of Jain spiritual practices. At the conclusion of *Paryushan/Das Lakshan, Pratikraman or Kshamavani* ceremony is held in which repentance of faults and forgiveness is asked for and given to all. Some Jains do the same thing through newspaper advertisements, and/or through sending hand-written or printed letters by post, or through emails.

Table 6.4: Some Other Indicators of Jain Religiosity

Religiosity	*Yes*	*No*	*No Response*	*Total (%)*
Fast during Duslakshan	83.3	16.7	0	100
Fast on Ashtami/Chaturdasi	26.1	73.3	0.6	100
Worship of any family deity	14.4	85	0.6	100
Faith in deity of any other religion	12.7	86.7	0.6	100

Jains have a vast network of pilgrimage places (*Teerth Kshetras*) all over India. These can broadly be classified into four categories. "The *Kalyanaka Kshetras*, associated with the birth and other memorable events in the life of the Tirthankaras; the *Siddha Kshetras,* where the Tirthankaras or other saints attained *Nirvana;* the *Atishaya Kshetras,* associated with some miracle or myth; and *Kala Kshetras*, reputed for their artistic monuments, temples, and images" (Jain, J. P. 1983: 128). There are at least 238 Digambar Jain Tirth kshetras in India (*See* Jain, Anupam 2015). Of these the following pilgrimage places are frequently visited by the Jains: Ayodhya, Mathura, Varanasi, Champapur, Hastinapur, Patna, Rajgrahi, Kundalpur, Pawapur, Sammed Shikharaji, Giranara, Khandagiri, Sonagiri, Deogarh, Khajuraho, Gwalior, Chanderi, Mahavirji, Chittor, Ajanta-Ellora, Ranakpur, Mount Abu, Dharmasthala, Mudhabidri, Sravanabelagola, etc.

Jains often go on pilgrimage in groups. During the winter months a large number of Jains can be seen traveling from place to place in the reserved buses, jeeps, and cars. Others travel by trains and some even by air. Air-conditioned vehicles, hotels, and *dharmashalas* have facilitated the pilgrimage even during the summer months. In recent years, some temple sites in Nepal, Japan, Singapore, Thailand, Malaysia, Kenya, the U.K., Canada and the U.S., etc., have been fast emerging as the new pilgrimage places, at least for those who can afford to visit them.

Table 6.5: Any Family Member Gone on Pilgrimage?

	Percentage
Yes	93.9
No	4.4
No Response	1.7
Total	100.0

From the point of view of Bundelkhand Jains, Jain teerth kshetras can be classified into two categories: (i) distant teerthkshetras, and (ii) local/regional teerthkshetras. In the first category the most visited ones are: Sammed Shikharjee (Jharkhand), Mahavirji (Rajasthan), Sravanbelgola (Karnataka), Hastinapur (Uttar Pradesh) and Giranarji (Gujarat). In the second category, one can put three to four dozen of pilgrimage places, of which Deogarh, Sonagiri, Chanderi, Aharji, Papauraji, Nainagiri, Kundalpur are the important ones. In response to a question whether any family members have gone on pilgrimage in recent years, the overwhelming majority of respondents (93.9%) replied in the affirmative (*See* Table 6.5). Planned family pilgrimage occasions for visit of pilgrimage places also occur when *panchkalyanak, siddhachakravidhan, kesh lonch*, and other such religious ceremonies are held there. Most Jains from Bundelkhand also go to pilgrimage places for *mundan sanskar* of the male or female child. In some cases, marriage ceremonies are also held at places of pilgrimage.

All over India Jain pilgrimage places are being renovated and modernised with better boarding as well as lodging facilities. So much so that many such places have now also begun to double up as convention, seminar and conference venues, in addition to chaturmas places for ascetics. Thus, All-India Digambar Jain Newspaper Editors' Association held its convention on 12th April 2015 at Parshwanath Digambar Jain Atishay Kshetra Karguvanji (Jhansi). In the presence of Acharya Vimarsh Sagarji Maharaj, a Jain youth convention was held on Saturday 17th October 2015 at Shri Digambar Jain Atishaya Kshetra Paporaji (Tikamgarh). Similarly, Shri Digambar Jain Siddha Kshetra Sonagiri was witness to five international conferences of Jain engineers, doctors, bankers, etc. during the months of October, November and December 2015.

Mass media have also added additional dimensions of religiosity in the Jain way of life in India. Presently there are three Jain Television channels, namely Paras, Jinvani and Kalash that continuously relay programmes related to Jain events, religion and rituals. In most Jain homes of Bundelkhand these channels are regularly watched with due reverence and faith. Elderly men and women are particularly glued to these programmes daily for several hours on end.

Life-Cycle Rituals

Birth and Naming Ceremonies. The Jains observe many life-cycle rituals of which the birth, marriage and death are the most important ones. During the seventh month of pregnancy of a woman, they observe a ritual called *Sad* in which the pregnant woman is offered sweets, fruits, flowers, etc. by the women of the family and relatives. In some areas this ritual is known as *Athwan* which is observed in the eighth month of pregnancy. The pregnant woman goes to the temple and worships the deity. A feast is organised on this occasion. Childbirth usually takes place in a hospital or at home under the supervision of a doctor. On the tenth day of the child's birth the *nahavan* ritual is preformed when the house is cleaned and the mother takes a bath. Birth pollution remains for 40 days. The pollution period is followed by *Namkaran Sanskar* in which the child is named after consulting the horoscope prepared by a Brahmin or Jain astrologer.

Cereals are fed to the child, for the first time when he is about six months old. The child is bathed, dressed in new clothes and taken to the temple to worship the idol. On his return, he is fed *khir* (made of milk, sugar and rice) by the eldest member of the family.

The *mundan* (tonsure) ceremony of a male child is observed in the 3rd, 5th or 7th year. This is generally done at a pilgrimage place, at a local temple, or in a specified temple for which a vow was taken. It is optional in case of a girl child. The *Hajjam* (barber) cuts the hair for which he is paid in cash and/or kind. The child is given a bath and taken to the deity. A swastika mark is made on his skull. An offering of some cash is given to the deity.

Marriage. The marriage ceremony is preceded by *sagai.* The bride's parents and some elder members of the girl's family go to the bridegroom's house and place fruits in the lap of bridegroom. The bridegroom's party goes to the bride's house for *godbharai.* Appropriate gifts including clothes, cosmetics, sweets and fruits are given to the bride.

At the auspicious time, the marriage rite is performed by a Brahmin or a Jain priest, amidst the chanting of hymns. *Saptadigaman* or *Saptapadi* (walking seven times around the sacred fire) is an essential ritual. The ritual of *Kanyadan* (giving away of the bride) is performed by the father, brother, or the guardians of the bride. The wedding rituals usually come to a close after *sindurdan* (application of vermilion by the bridegroom on the forehead of the bride). On the following day, the bride goes to her husband's house. We already discussed in detail in Chapter Five the changes that have been taking place in the institution of marriage in the Bundelkhand region.

Death. After death, the body is cremated on a fixed burial place, on the bank of a river, lake or pond. The last rites are generally performed by the eldest son. The person who lights the pyre is called the *karta* (chief mourner). He has to observe several restrictions for a period of thirteen days. On the day after the cremation, the male members of the family and other relatives get their head shaved, and thereafter they go to collect the ashes of the diseased and disperse/submerge them in the nearby water body, dry stream or bushes. This is followed by the *Pagdi* ceremony in which a headgear is tied on the head of the *karta* declaring him the head of the family.

On the thirteenth day of the death *(terahvin)* the death-feast is given to friends, relatives and well-wishers of the deceased. In a major change due to shortage of time, *Terahvin* is increasingly being held now on the fourth day of the death and called *Chautha.* Although Jain scriptures do not sanction death feast, the practice is wide-spread among the Jains of Bundelkhand, particularly in small towns and villages. So much so that in some cases the number of guests can run into one thousand persons or more. On such occasions not only the Jains but select members of the other communities also come to participate. The custom of death-feast continues for two important sociological reasons: (i) death as well as marriage are the two occasions when the Jains who have traditionally been merchants and traders can sort of gratify their real or potential clients by serving them food, and (ii) it is also a reciprocal practice on the part of the Jains as the custom is universal among upper caste Hindus.

Conclusion

Jain way of life and identity is primarily derived from Jain philosophy and religion, particularly from its ethical codes of conduct. In the case of the Jain community of Bundelkhand, Terapanth Digambar Jainism is the basis of the Jain way of life. In this orthodox sub-sect of Digambar Jainism the adherents are guided by moksha-marg ideology of *samyak darshan, samyak gyan* and *samyak chaaritra*. Accordingly, Tirthankars, ascetics and scriptures are worshipped and venerated.

For generations, religious orthodoxy continued to hold sway on the Jain community of Bundelkhand. This can be seen not only in the daily routine (*dincharya*) of Jain men and women, but also in many other aspects of their religiosity. Morning and evening daily visits to a Jain temple, celebration of *Paryushan Parv* and other festivals, keeping periodic fast on auspicious days, regular interaction with ascetics, etc. have been very much intact in varying degrees among the Jains of Bundelkhand. Needless to say, women's participation in all these activities is much more vigorous than that of their male counterparts. Jain women of Bundelkhand are also quite knowledgeable about Jain philosophy.

Vegetarianism is the trademark of the Jains in Bundelkhand. They are also very particular about using cloth-strained water for drinking and cooking purposes. Dietary regulations require them not to use garlic, onion, potato, etc. Consumption of alcohol, and other intoxicants are also a taboo. The famed Bundelkhandi Jain *chowka* (kitchen) and *solah ka khana* (food prepared with 16 precautions) are also the integral parts of the Jain religiosity.

During the past few decades the religious orthodoxy in Bundelkhand Jain community has been challenged from both within and without. While the KSP ideology and activities can be considered a challenge from within, the on-going socio-economic changes and modernisation pose a major threat to it from without. The indifference and "drift" of a section of youth is a clear manifestation of this latter development which can be observed in the form of significant laxity in "daily routine" and dietary rules and regulations. Needless to say, more systematic studies are required to fully understand the changes and continuity in the religiosity among the Jains of Bundelkhand.

7

Summary and Conclusion

In this study an attempt has been made to analyze the educational, occupational, socio-cultural and religious changes in the Jain community of Bundelkhand within a span of two-three generations. Historically, Jains have constituted a unique economic niche for themselves in the Bundelkhand region which has been underdeveloped since the British colonial days. Uncertain climatic conditions, frequent famines, lack of irrigation facilities, un-egalitarian social structure, and increasing population pressure on agricultural land have further added to the economic woes of the region. Not surprisingly, until about a couple of generations ago the Jain community of Bundelkhand also suffered from some of these socio-economic characteristics of the region. Compared to Jains of other parts of the country, a majority of Jains of Bundelkhand were relatively less affluent and progressive. The vast majority of them were involved in small-time trading and commercial activities. Their socio-religious attitude was characterized by conservatism and religious orthodoxy. However, during the past couple of decades this over-all situation of the community has significantly changed for the better. The Jains of the region have been showing significant amount of predisposition to social change and modernisation, particularly in regard to education and occupational aspects.

Socio-economic background of the respondents clearly indicate two major trends: (i) a majority of Jains in Bundelkhand today are engaged in services and professions than in trade and commercial activities, and (ii) there has been a significant improvement in the levels of education, occupational mobility and economic wellbeing. This is reflected in better living standards, healthy and balanced diet and expenditure on a variety of cosumer goods.

In the economy of Bundelkhand, for centuries the Jains have generally been associated with the whole sale as well as retail trade. While they still continue to dominate these sectors, newer economic and occupational opportunities have also been opened up for them during the past few decades. To begin with, trade and commercial activities have expanded to include newer products and services related to construction and housing, mechanisation of agriculture, irrigation, information technology, processed and fast food, etc. Thus, quite a number of Jains have shifted to wholesale and retail sale of hardware, water pumps, tractor parts, photocopiers, mobiles, TV sets, ACs, washing machines, motor cycles parts and so on. In the textile sector readymade garments have emerged as major items of trade in both rural and urban areas. Thus trading activities have gone beyond supplying only household and provision goods, and in the Bundelkhand region the Jains appear to have taken full advantage of this transformation. Besides expanding and consolidating their class position as traders, some of the Jains have moved to entrepreneurship in areas like flour, rice and dal mills, saw mills, manufacturing of readymade garments and school uniforms, operation of petrol pumps, buses and trucks, etc. A few of them have also gone into taking up contracts for construction of bridges, roads and housing colonies.

Crystalisation and consolidation of a class segment of highly educated professionals is another development that has taken place among the Jains of Bundelkhand during the past three-four decades. Earlier, this class segment was confined to only male school and college teachers, village land record-keepers (*lekhpals*), higher or middle-ranked government servants, and a minuscule number of engineers, doctors and lawyers. Today however, it has not only expanded multi-fold but also includes university professors, information technology personnel, business management and banking professionals, etc. During the past half a century the role of Jain Sanskrit *vidyalayas* in raising three or four generations of traditional Jain scholars (*Pandits*) and in contributing towards the growth of college and university teachers of Jain Philosophy and Religion, Indology, Sanskrit, Pali, Prakrit and Hindi languages has been remarkably significant. The service class among Jains appears to have numerically strengthened during the past couple of decades.

Income levels of Jains in Bundelkhand have gone up during the past couple of decades. This is clearly reflected in better living standards, increased use of home appliances and consumer goods such as refrigerators, cooking gas cylinders, washing machines, motor cycles, etc., better diet and better housing facilities in rural as well as urban areas. A vast majority of Jains in Bundelkhand now have their own *pucca* houses equipped with in-house toilet facilities.

The economic stratification of the community is increasingly acquiring the form of a modern class system. This is obviously based on modern education, occupations, income/wealth and the attendant life style and the patterns of consumption. In the process the traditional hierarchy of Shrimant Seth, Seth, Singhai, etc. no longer correspond with the emerging economic stratification system and therefore losing its relevance. The community has never been economically homogeneous; it has been quite stratified and continues to be so in spite of undergoing modernisation and social change, and becoming relatively affluent by local Bundelkhand standards.

Data from our study suggest the small size family norm of 4-5 members. Age of marriage also appears to have gone up by a few years in recent decades. Our field work data also suggest a considerable number of boys beyond marriageable age remaining unmarried, particularly in villages and towns due to skewed sex ratio and other sociological factors. In spite of some improvement in sex and child sex ratios in 2011 census, both the indicators continue to remain far below the Jain national average. Their direct or indirect impact on the marriage institution and eventually on the population dynamics of the community has emerged as a matter of serious concern. Among other demographic changes, literacy and education figure prominently whose levels have certainly gone up. There appears to be a fair amount of out-migration of Jains from the region, particularly of highly educated professionals as many of them happen to be getting education outside the region and thereby easily getting suitable jobs there itself. A number of Bundelkhandi Jains have also settled abroad, particularly in North America.

In spite of practising a distinct religion for centuries, the Jain community has so much affinity with the wider Hindu society and culture that the Jains are often considered as upper caste Hindus. Until about a century ago a large majority of Jains themselves believed in this. This self-perception began to change with the activities of Shri Bharatvarshiya Digambar Jain Mahasabha (1895) and other regional and caste associations established during early decades of the 20th century. The change was further strengthened over the decades by the consistent efforts of the Jain community leaders, *pandits*, press as well as *munis* and *tyagis* with the result that today a great majority of Jains consider themselves as distinct and separate religious minority – something which the British Indian government had recognised by enumerating the Jains as a distinct religious minority since the 1881 census, and which the Government of India confirmed by eventually granting them the minority status in January 2014. Although the Jains being a relatively affluent community do not require economic benefits or reservations in government jobs, the minority status accorded to them would certainly go a long way in protecting the Jain cultural heritage.

High levels of education, occupational mobility, and associated out-migration of Jains from Bundelkhand have deeply affected their key social structural institutions such as family, kinship and marriage, caste and class. In Bundelkhand, as in other parts of India, not only the kinship system has weakened, the structure and functions of family have also undergone changes which can be summarized as follows: small size, assertion of individuality in regard to choice of education and career and choice of marriage partner, democratisation of family relations, decrease in discrimination against girl child, etc. An ever increasing number of Jains have begun to realize that daughters are more dependable and reliable than sons, particularly in times of healthcare emergency. Even otherwise, unlike their Hindu counterparts, the Jains were not required to have a son for any religious or spiritual purpose.

Of all the social institutions, perhaps the marriage has undergone the most changes in the Jain community of Bundelkhand. To begin with, "poisonous" or "bad" marriages (*vish vivah*) in the form of child marriage, polygamy and age-incompatible marriages that were prevalent until about the middle of the 20th century have completely disappeared. Among other changes, mention must be made of significant increase in the number of inter-religion as well as inter-caste marriages, acceptance of widow and divorcee remarriages and decrease in dowry demand. The duration of marriage ceremonies has been reduced from three-four days to about 24 hours or even less over a period of about two generations. An increasing number of marriages are now solemnized by Jain *pandits*, and often during day time.

The system of arranged marriage has more or less become a thing of the past. Instead, most marriages today are arranged either through newspaper advertisements or increasingly by professional marriage agencies or marriage bureaus. Perhaps more radical change has occurred in regard to the customary bride groom's party going to bride's place for the marriage to get solemnised. In most cases this is no longer so; instead marriage now takes place at a mutually-agreed-upon place which often happens to be the groom's town or city. Depending on the mutual negotiations, the financial implications of this arrangement for both the parties vary accordingly. In most marriages expenditure on decoration and food has gone up many-folds in recent decades. In the process, the specificity of Bundelkhandi style of Jain marriage has given way to Indian "filmi" style of marriage with the accompanying dance, music and multi-cuisine food, etc.

Besides marriage, two more important life cycle rituals, namely birth and death have also undergone some significant changes. The time constraint on the part of kinsmen and relatives who now live in distant towns and cities due to employment reasons has curtailed elaborate rituals associated with birth as well as death to the bare minimum. Thus, *Terahvin* of the deceased is often held on 3rd or 4th day after the death. Naming of both male and female babies has changed remarkably in that more and more Sanskritic names are now given to them.

The social status of Jain women has undergone significant changes over the decades. Only three generations ago a large majority of women were either illiterate or were poorly educated. There was no question of their employment. Patriarchy as a social order prevailed and girls were routinely discriminated against in the Jain community. As discussed in detail in Chapter Five, some of them were subjected to "bad" marriages. Fortunately, all of this has now changed. Today Jain women are relatively free to have their say in the family, and to have choice in education, vocation and marriage. Not surprisingly, most Jain women have emerged as individuals capable of performing roles befitting a modern society. The problematic aspects of Jain women's life in Bundelkhand include skewed sex ratio, lower work participation rate, and practically non-existent political participation. Notwithstanding the increased use of kitchen appliances and other gadgets, their share in the burden of household chores has also not lessened significantly.

Our study suggests both continuity and change in various aspects of the Jain way of life in the region. One aspect of Jain way of life that has shown remarkable stability and continuity over perhaps the centuries is the daily routine of life (*dincharya*). This involves morning and early night visits to a Jain temple, meditation, contemplation and/or self-study of scriptures while inside the temple, use of cloth-strained water for drinking and cooking and taking dinner before sunset. These practices are widespread in the region. So much so that this daily routine is considered the very identity of a Jain. A daily visit to temple even for a few minutes is a must for Jains in the region; only in exceptional circumstances such as sickness it is avoided.

Religious orthodoxy typified in the above described daily routine, dietary observances, religious rituals and devotion to tyagis/ascetics continue to be quite high among the Jains of Bundelkhand. Even the spread and consolidation of Kanji Swami Panth ideology during the past half-a-century has not been able to erode this religious orthodoxy. With the spread of education, neo-orthodoxy is also gaining ground among the new generation of scholars and lay Jains who often interpret Jainism as a scientific religion. Thus, as per our sample, about 80% of the followers of Jainism are orthodox/neo-orthodox; only about 15% of them can be considered as heterodox — simultaneously having faith in mainly Hindu gods and goddesses and/or worshiping family deity.

Celebrating Jain festivals, observing fast on auspices occasions and visiting pilgrimage places are important indicators of Jain religiosity and the way of life. Thus, almost all the Jains in Bundelkhand celebrate the 10-day Paryushan parva and a vast majority of them varyingly keep fast on this occasion. Again, almost all the Jains of Bundelkhand pay visits to both local/regional and national pilgrimage places. Every individual Jain aspires to visit some of the national pilgrimage centres like Sammed Shikharji, Mahavirji and Girnarji at least once in their life-time. Last but not the least, diet and dietary regulations on the day-to-day basis are very strictly observed by Jains of Bundelkhand. Most of them are not only teetotallers, they also do not consume any kinds of intoxicants. Most Jain families in the region avoid taking food in market place, hotels and restaurants; instead they prefer to prepare most food items at home for reasons of purity, cleanliness and cloth-strained water.

Typical of a generational gap, the elders of the Jain community of Bundelkhand do not consider the younger generation as much religious and even socially responsible as they would have liked. A majority of our respondents echo this viewpoint and agree with the idea that the younger generation is generally indifferent towards religion which is reflected in their daily routine, food habits, attitude towards ascetics, etc. Lack of care of the elderly members of the family, on the part of male youth is also regarded as the proof of this indifference. Their preoccupation with television, mobile phones and Internet is mentioned as additional cause of concern. Not surprisingly, a large majority of our respondents support the idea of strengthening moral education and training for youngsters through schools, moral educational/spiritual camps, etc.

A comparative account of socio-economic change in various aspects of the Jain community of Bundelkhand clearly brings out the uneven nature of social change and development. Thus, economic, educational and occupational aspects have changed relatively much faster than socio-cultural and religious aspects underlining the well-known theory of culture lag which states that material aspects of a culture change much faster than non-material aspects. Perhaps social changes in a community or society too follow a similar law. Needless to say, a few more systematic studies would be required in order to fully understand the course of development of the Bundelkhand Jain community. In the final analysis, however, its future is certainly tied up with the over-all socio-economic development of the region.

Appendices

Appendix-1

Some Prominent Bundelkhandis

- Goswami Tulsidas, 16th century author of *Ramcharitmanas*, born in Rajapur, Banda.
- Keshav Das. 16th century poet.
- Rani Lakshmibai, (1828–1858) Maratha Queen of princely state of Jhansi, one of the key figures in the India's First Independence Movement of 1857.
- Maithili Sharan Gupt (1886-1964), Author of *Bharat Bharati*, National Hindi Poet.
- Pandit Nathuram Premi (1881–1960), Prominent publisher of Hindi, Sanskrit and Urdu literature as well as Jain literature. Independent scholar, Jain historian and editor of several Jain works. Founder of the publishing house Hindi Granth Ratnakar Karyalay, Bombay (1912), Manikachandra Digambara Jain Granthamala and *Jain Hitaishi* magazine.
- Dr. Hari Singh Gaur (1870-1949), Member of Indian Constitution Draft Committee, and founder of the University of Saugar.
- Padma Bhushan Vrindavan Lal Verma, Hindi novelist and playwright (*Mrig Nayani, Jhansi Ki Rani*).
- Hockey wizard Dhyan Chand (Singh) (1905-1979), the Olympic and Indian national hockey player.
- Indeevar (Shyamlal Babu Rai) (1924-1997), one of the leading Hindi film lyricists during 1960s and 1970s.
- Maharishi Mahesh Yogi, of Transcendental Meditation fame.
- Phoolan Devi, (1963–2001) popularly known as "Bandit Queen", was an Indian dacoit and later a politician.
- Uma Bharti (b. 1959), Prominent BJP politician, Ex-Chief Minister of MP and ex-Minister and MP from Jhansi Lok Sabha seat.
- Pradeep Jain Aditya (b.1962), Politician, Lok Sabha member from Jhansi seat (1914-19) and ex-Minister of State for Rural Development in Dr. Manmohan Singh's cabinet.

- Kailash Satyarthi (b. 1954), Nobel Peace prize winner for working against child labour.
- Anurag Sharma (b. 1964), CEO of Baidyanath Ayurveda Bhawan Pvt. Ltd., and the Member of the 17th Lok Sabha from Jhansi-Lalitpur constituency.
- Raja Bundela (Rajendra Pratap Singh).(Age about 60 years), actor, film maker, civil activis and politiciant; president of Bundelkhand Mukti Morcha.

Appendix–2

List of Prominent Jain Pandits/Scholars from Bundelkhand

1. Guru Gopaldas Baraiya (?-1917, Morena)
2. Pt. Banshidhar Shastri Nyayalankar (1890-1994, Mahroni, Lalitpur)
3. Pt. Devkinandan Siddhantshastri (1853-1950, Baruasagar, Jhansi)
4. Pt. Ghanshyamdas Nyayteerth (1888-1924, Mahroni, Lalitpur)
5. Kshullak Ganesh Prasad Varni (Hansera, Lalitpur, 1874-1961)
6. Pt. Nathuram Premi (1882-1960, Devari, Sagar; Bombay)
7. Pt. Kundan Lal Jain Mody (1891-1965, Deorikalan, Sagar)
8. Pt. Munna Lal Randheliya (1893-1993, Patan, Sagar)
9. Pt. Nanhein Lal Jain Shastri (1894-1978, Servas, Jhansi)
10. Pt. Dharam Das Shastri (1896-1956, Sadumal, Lalitpur)
11. Pt. Tulsiram, Kavyatirth, (Lalitpur)
12. Pt. Thakurdas Shastri (1897-1965, Mahroni, Lalitpur)
13. Pt. Jeevandhar Shastri, Nyaytirth (?-1974 Shahgarh, Sagar)
14. Pt. Hazari Lal Nyaytirth (1899-1933, Parson, Sagar)
15. Dr. Hira Lal Jain (1899-1973, Gangai, Narsighpur)
16. Pt. Khunni Lal (Pt. Gyananand) (1900-?, Tikamgarh)
17. Pt. Kastoor Chand Jain (1900-1966, Noorbarkheda, Raisen Dist,)
18. Pt. Phoolchandra Siddhantshastri (1901-1991, Silawan, Lalitpur)
19. Pt. Jagan Mohanlal Shastri (1901-1995, Shahdol))
20. Pt. Hazari Lal (1903-1932, Parson, Sagar)
21. Pt. Hira Lal Siddhantshastri (1904-1981, Sadumal, Lalitpur)
22. Pt. Manik Chandra Jain (1904-1986, Shahpur, Sagar)
23. Pt. Bhagwandas Jain Shastri (1904-?, Sadumal, Lalitpur/Raipur)
24. Pt. Shobhachandra Bharill (1904-?, Khairana, Sagar)
25. Pt. Sumer Chandra "Diwakar" (1905-?, Seoni)
26. Pt. Vansidhar Vyakarnacharya (1905-?, Sonrai, Lalitpur)
27. Pt. Balchandra Siddhanthastri (1905-1985, Sonrai, Lalitpur)
28. Pt. Barelal Jain Rajyavaidya (1905-1981, Samri, Tikamgarh)
29. Pt. Moolchand Shastri (vs 1960-?, Malthon, Sagar)
30. Pt. Pannalal, Dharmalankar (?-?, Malthon, Sagar)
31. Pt. Parmanand Shastri (1907-1977, Niwar, Chhatarpur)
32. Pt. Parmeshthi Das, Nyayacharya (1907-1978, Mahroni, Lalitpur)
33. Pt. Moti Lal Fauzdar (1907-1970, Drongiri, Chhatarpur)
34. Pt. Shrutsagar, Nyaytirth (1908-1992, Shahpur, Sagar)

35. Pt. Mohan Lal Shastri, Kavyatirth (1908-?, Baraytha, Sagar)
36. Pt. Gore Lal Shastri (1908-?, Sendpa, Drongiri)
37. Pt. Panna Lal Shastri (1909-2004, Khaniadhana, Shivpuri)
38. Dr. Panna Lal Jain Sahityacharya (1911-2001, Parguan, Sagar)
39. Dr. Darwari Lal Kothia, Nyayacharya (1911-?, Sonrai, Lalitpur)
40. Pt. Daya Chandra, Siddhantshastri (1899-?, Bandri, Sagar)
41. Pt. Nathu Lal Shastri (1911-2007, Indore)
42. Shri Gyan Chand Jain (1913-1992, Seoni)
43. Pt. Hira Lal "Kaushal" (1914-1997, Lalitpur)
44. Pt. Jambu Prasad Shastri (1914-?, Khurai)
45. Dr. Raj Kumar, Sahityacharya (1917-?, Gundarapur, Lalitpur)
46. Prof. Khushal Chandra Gorawala (1917-?, Madawra, Lalitpur)
47. Dr. Gulab Chandra Chowdhry (1917-1974, Silodhi, Jabalpur)
48. Prof. Mahendra Kumar Nyayacharya (1919-1959, Khurai)
49. Pt. Babulal "Aakul" (1919-1998, Nihani, Sagar)
50. Pt. Amrit Lal, Shastri (1919-?, Bamrana, Lalitpur)
51. Pt, BabuLal Jain Jamadar (1922-?, Lalitpur)
52. Pt. Kapoor Chandra Jain, Shastri (1922-1996, Ramtoria, Chhatarpur)
53. Prof Udai Chandra Jain, Sarvadarshnacharya (1923-?, Piprauda, Khaniadhana)
54. Pt. Gulab Chandra "Pushp" (1924-1914, Kakarwaha, Tikamgarh)
55. Dr. Narendra Vidyarthi (1924-?, Dhanguan, Chhatarpur)
56. Pt. Niraj Jain (1926-2013, Reethi, Katni)
57. Prof. L. C. Jain (1926, Sagar)
58. Dr. Nemi Chandra Jain (1927-?)
59. Dr. Nand Lal Jain (1928-2007, Shahgarh, Chhatarpur)
60. Dr. Harindra Bhushan Jain (1929-1989, Naryavali, Sagar)
61. Dr. Mahendra Kumar Jain (1929-1989, Bhagwan, Chhatarpur)
62. Pt. Uttam Chand Rakesh (1929-?, Lalitpur)
63. Prof Rajaram Jain Shastri (1929, Malthon, Sagar)
64. Pt. Rajmal Jain (1930, Khurai, Sagar)
65. Pt. Kanchedi Lal Jain, Sahiyacharya (1929-1996, Bilari (Patharia), Damoh)
66. Pt. Anand Kumar Jain (1931-2000, Badagaon, Dhasan, Tikamgarh)
67. Dr. Sagarmal Jain (1932, Shajapur)
68. Pt. Ratan Chand Bharill (1932, Baroda Swamy, Lalitpur)
69. Pt. Mool Chand Shastri (1933-1998, Varmatal, Tikamgarh)
70. Dr. Devendra Kumar Shastri (1933, Chirgaon, Jhansi)
71. Dr. Jay Kumar Jain "Jalaj" (1934, Lalitpur)
72. Prof. Gokul Chandra Jain (1934-2016, Pidrua, Sagar)
73. Shri Lal Chandra Jain Rakesh (1934, Silgan, Lalitpur)
74. Prof Komal Chandra Jain (1935-2012, Bina)
75. Pt. Gopi Lal Amar (1935, Padwar, Sagar)

76. Prof. Bhag Chandra Jain "Bhaskar" (1936, Bamhori, Chhatarpur)
77. Dr. Shekhar Chandra Jain (1936, Ahmedabad)
78. Dr. Hukam Chand Bharill (1937, Baroda Swamy, Lalitpur)
79. Dr. Bhag Chand Jain Bhagendu (1937, Reethi, Katni)
80. Dr. Rajendra Kumar Jain (1938, Chanderi, Ashok Nagar)
81. Pt. Abhay Kumar Jain (1938, Bina)
82. Dr. Dev Kumar Jain (1939-?, Sadumal, Lalitpur)
83. Prof. Dharam Chand Jain (1940, Sagar)
84. Prof. Prem Suman Jain (1942, Sinhudi, Jabalpur)
85. Pt. Nihal Chand Jain (1942, Madawra, Lalitpur)
86. Shri Suresh Chand Jain Saral (1942, Jabalpur)
87. Prof Sudarshan Lal Jain (1944, Damoh)
88. Prof. Lal Chandra Jain (1944, Kishangarh, Chhatarpur)
89. Dr. Ramesh Chand Jain (1945, Madawra, Lalitpur)
90. Dr. Udai Chandra Jain (1947, Bamhori, Chhatarpur)
91. Prof. Phool Chand Jain Premi (1948, Dalpatpur, Sagar)
92. Dr. Shital Chand Jain (1948, Madawra, Lalitpur)
93. Dr. Suresh Chand Jain (1948-?, Kotma, Shahdol)
94. Prof. Kamlesh Kumar Jain (1950, Piparia, Tikamgarh)
95. Dr. Shreyans Kumar Jain (1952, Dumduma, Tikamgarh)
96. Dr. Kapoor Chand Jain (1954, Bardhuwan, Datia)
97. Prof Vijay Kumar Jain (1956, Basaura, Panna)
98. Dr. (Mrs) Jyoti Jain (1958, Sagar)
99. Prof. Ashok Kumar Jain (1959, Madawra, Lalitpur)
100. Br. Jay Kumar Jain Nishant (1959, Kakarwaha, Tikamgarh)
101. Pt. Vinod Kumar Jain (1959, Rajvans)
102. Dr. Kamlesh Kumar Jain (1960, Kakrari, Lalitpur)
103. Dr. Rishabh Chandra Jain Fauzdar (1960, Sendpa, Chhatarpur)
104. Dr. Mahendra Kumar Jain Manuj (1960, Khutaguan, Lalitpur)
105. Pt. Mahendra Kumar Jain (1960, Kakrari, Lalitpur)
106. Dr. Jitendra Kumar Jain (1962, Sinhudi, Jabalpur)
107. Dr. Surendra Kumar Jain Bharti (1963, Madawra)
108. Dr. Bare Lal Jain (1963, Hata, Tikamgarh)
109. Dr. Kastoor Chand Jain Suman (1963, Bansatarkheda, Damoh)
110. Pt. Pawan Kumar Jain Deewan (1964, Chanderi, Ashoknagar)
111. Dr. Anekant Kumar Jain, (1978, Dalpatpur, Sagar)

Appendix-3

Jains of Bundelkhand in Literature

1. Laxmi Chandra Jain (1909-1999, Chhatarpur)
2. Gyan Chandra Jain "Swatantra" (1912-1990, Bahadurpur, Guna)
3. Damodar "Chandra" (1916-?, Ghuwara, Chhatarpur)
4. Champalal Singhai "Purandar" (1919-?, Chanderi, Guna)
5. Hazari Lal "Kaka" (1919-?, Sakrar, Jhansi)
6. Hukam Chand Bukharia "Tanmaya" (1921-1997, Lalitpur)
7. Laxmi Chand Jain "Saroj" (1925-1991, Sirgam, Jhansi)
8. Pt. Dhanya Kumar "Sudesh" (1927-?, Nagod, Satna)
9. Lal Chandra Jain "Rakesh" (1934, Silgan, Lalitpur)
10. Dr. Jay Kumar Jain "Jalaj" (1934, Lalitpur)
11. Sarman Lal "Saras" (1937, Sakrar, Jhansi)
12. Suresh Chand Jain "Saral" (1942, Jabalpur)
13. Padma Shri Kailash Chand Madbaiya (1944, Banpur, Lalitpur)
14. Mahendra Kumar Jain "Manuj" (1960, Khutguwan, Lalitpur)
15. Niraj Jain, (1926-2013, Satna)

Appendix-4

Major Bundelkhand Jain Tirth Kshetras

Madhya Pradesh-Bundelkhand

- Bandhaji: Shri Ajitnath Digambar Jain Atishaya Kshetra Bandhaji
- Maksi Parsvanath: Shri Dig. Jain Atishaya Kshetra Maksi Parsvanath
- Beena (Barha): Shri Digambar Jain Atishaya Kshetra, Beena (Barha)
- Kundalgiri (Koniji): Shri Digambar Jain AtishayaKshetraKundalgiri (Koniji), Patan
- Muktagiri (Mendhagiri): Shri Digambar Jain Siddha Kshetra Muktagiri (Mendhagiri)
- Patnaganj–Rahli: Shri Digambar Jain Teerth Kshetra, Patnaganj–Rahli
- Khajuraho: Shri Digamber Jain Atishay Kshetra, Khajuraho.
- Chanderi: Shri Digamber Jain Atishaya Kshetra Choubeesee Bara Mandir, Chanderi.
- Gopachal: Shri Digamber Jain Atishaya Kshetra Gopachal.
- Khandargiri: Shri Digamber Jain Atishaya Kshetra Khandargiri.
- Panagar: Shri Digamber Jain Atishaya Kshetra Panagar
- Papouraji: Shri Digamber Jain Atishaya Kshetra Papouraji
- Thuvonji: Shri Digamber Jain Atishaya KshetraThuvonji.
- Banediaji: Shri Digamber Jain Atishaya Kshetra, Banediaji,
- Aharji: Shri Digamber Jain Siddha Kshetra Aharji.
- Chulgiri (Bawangaja): Shri Digamber Jain Siddha Kshetra Chulgiri (Bawangaja)
- Drongiri: Shri Digamber Jain Siddha Kshetra Drongiri.
- Kundalgiri (Kundalpur): Shri Digamber Jain Siddha Kshetra Kundalgiri (Kundalpur),
- Nainagiri (Reshandigiri): Shri Digamber Jain Siddha Kshetra Nainagiri (Reshandigiri)
- PavagiriUna: Shri Digamber Jain Siddha Kshetra Pavagiri Una.
- Siddhaverkoot: Shri Digamber Jain Siddha Kshetra Siddhaverkoot.
- Sonagiri: Shri Digamber Jain Siddha Shetra Sonagiri.
- PisanhariMadiya, Jabalpur: Shri Parshvanath Digamber Jain Mandir Pisanhari Madiya, Jabalpur,
- Pateria: Shri Parsvanath Digamber Jain Atishaya Kshetra, Pateria.
- Nougaja: Shri Shantinath (Nougaja) Digambar Jain Atishaya Kshetra

- Bhojpur: Shri Shantinath Digambar Jain Atishaya Kshetra Bhojpur
- Ishurvara: Shri Shantinath Digambar Jain Atishaya Kshetra Ishurvara
- Bajrang Garh: Shri Shantinath Digamber Jain Atishaya Kshetra Bajrang Garh.
- Sinhoniyaji: Shri Shantinath Digamber Jain Atishaya Kshetra Sinhoniyaji.
- Karitoran: Shri Digambar Jain Atishaya Kshetra, Karitoran, Tikamgarh

Uttar Pradesh-Bundelkhand

- Pawagiriji: Shri Dig. Jain Siddha Kshetra Pawagiriji, Lalitpur
- Devgarh: Shri Digambar Jain Atishay Kshetra Devgarh, Lalitpur
- Madanpur: Shri Digambar Jain Atishay Kshetra Madanpur, Lalitpur
- Todi Fatehpur: Shri Digambar Jain Atishaya Chamatkari Kshetra Todi Fatehpur
- Nava Garh (Nabai): Shri Digambar Jain Atishaya Kshetra Nava Garh (Nabai)
- Kakandi: Shri Digambar Jain Teerth Kshetra Kakandi
- Rishbhanchal: Shri Digambar Jain Teerth Rishbhanchal
- Banpur: Shri Digamber Jain Atishaya Kshetra Banpur
- Karguvanji: Shri Digamber Jain Atishaya Kshetra Sanvaliya Parasnath Karguvanji.
- Marsalganj (Rishabh Nagar) Shri Marsalganj (Rishabh Nagar) Diagambar Jain Atishaya Teerth Kshetra.
- Serona Shri Shantinath Digamber Jain Atishaya Kshetra, Serona.
- Bateshwar/Shri Shouripur—Bateshwar Digambar Jain Siddha Kshetra,

Appendix-5

A List of Select Jain Sanskrit Vidyalayas

1. Shri Gopal Digambar Jain Siddhant Mahavidylaya, Morena
2. Shri Syadvad Digambar Jain Sanskrit Mahavidyalaya, Varanasi
3. Shri Ganesh Digambar Jain Vidyalaya, Sagar
4. Shri Mahavir Digambar Jain Vidyalaya, Sadumal
5. Shri Hukum Chand Digambar Jain Vidyalaya, Indore
6. Shanti Niketan Jain Sanskrit Vidyalaya, Katni
7. Shri Nabhinandan Digambar Jain Sanskrit Vidyalaya, Bina
8. Shri Gurudatta Digambar Jain Pathshala, Dronagiri
9. Shri Parshwanath Digambar Jain Gurukul, Khurai
10. Shri Digambar Jain Sanskrit Vidyalaya, Aharji
11. Shri Mahavir Digambar Jain Vidyalaya, Papaura
12. Shri Digambar Jain Vidyalaya, Baruasagar
13. Shri Samantbhadra Digambar Jain Vidyalaya, New Delhi
14. Shri Veer Seva Mandir, New Delhi
15. Shri Shantiveer Digambar Jain Purv Praveshika Sanskrit Vidyalaya, Shri Mahavirji
16. Trilok Shodh Sansthan, Hastinapur
17. Jain Sanskriti Shodh Sansthan, Indore
18. Kundkund Bharti, Indore
19. Gyanodaya Foundation, Indore
20. Pratibhasthali Gyanodaya Vidyapeeth, Jabalpur
21. Shri Varni Digambar Jain Pathshala, Damoh
22. Shri Pushpadant Digambar Jain Sanskrit Vidyalaya, Shahpur

Appendix-6

*Martyrs and Freedom Fighters of Bundelkhand**

A. Martyrs

S.No.	Name	Place of Birth	Year of Hanging
1.	Amar Chand Banthiya	Gwalior	1858
2.	Choudhary Bhaiya Lal	Damoh	1922
3.	Kandhi Lal Jain	Indore	1930
4.	Singhai Prem Chand Jain	Damoh	1941
5.	Mulayam Chand Jain	Jabalpur	1942
6.	Sabulal Jain Baisakhiya	Gadhakota, Sagar	1942
7.	Chauth Mal Bhandari	Ujjain	1943

B. Freedom Fighters

S.No.	Name	Place of Birth	Year of Arrest
1.	Kanchhedi Lal Jain	Banda Sagar	1942
2.	Kapur Chand Jain	Gadhakota, Sagar	1942
3.	Dr. Kapur Chand Jain	Sagar	
4.	Kaluram Jain	Sagar	1932
5.	Singhai Kunji Lal Jain	Sagar	1930,1932
6.	Kundanlal Jain Nayak	Devary, Sagar	1942
7.	Keval Chand Jain	Gaurjhamar	1942
8.	Kailash Chand Jain	Bandri, Sagar	1942
9.	Khuman Jain	Dalpatpur, Sagar	1942
10.	Khub Chand Jain	Devadiya, Shahgarh, Sagar	1942
11.	Khub Chand Vaisakhiya	Rahli, Sagar	1942
12.	Khem Chand Jain	Baleh, Sagar	1942
13.	Gatote Lal Bhavji	Sagar	1929, 1942
14.	Girdhari Lal Seth	Gadhakota	1930, 1932, 1942
15.	Guljhari Lal Jagati	Tada, Sagar	1942
16.	Guljari Lal Jain	Sihora, Sagar	1942
17.	Gulab Chand Jain	Sagar	1942
18.	Gulab Chand Jain Vaidya	Dhana, Sagar	1941

S.No.	Name	Place of Birth	Year of Arrest
19.	Gulab Chand Jain Pushp	Sagar	1949
20.	Gopi Lal Jain	Sagar	1942
21.	Chintaman Jain	Tada, Sagar	1942
22.	Chunni Lal Jain	Vinaika, Sagar	1942
23.	Chhotelal (Ratan Chand Malaiya)	Gadhakota, Sagar	1942
24.	Jinendra Kumar Malaiya	Sagar	1942
25.	Tikamram Jain	Sagar	1942
26.	Tara Chand Jain	Sagar	1942
27.	Dayal Chand Jain	Sagar	1942
28.	Dal Chand Jain	Sagar	1942
29.	Dal Chand Singhai	Gadhakota, Sagar	1933
30.	Deep Chand Malaiya	Gadhakota, Sagar	1942
31.	Nanhe Lal Jain	Sagar	1942
32.	Nanhe Lal Jain	Karrapur, Sagar	1942
33.	Dharam Chand Jain 'Mast'	Panna, Sagar	1942
34.	Narain Das Jain	Sagar	1942
35.	Panchamlal Baisakhiya	Rahli, Sagar	1932
36.	Padam Kumar Jain	Sagar	1941,1942
37.	Parmanand Singhai	Devarikalan, Sagar	1942
38.	Panna Lal Vasal	Mandibamora, Sagar	1942
39.	Puran Chand Jain Bhaiji	Sagar	1942
40.	Phool Chand Jain 'Madhur'	Sagar	1942
41.	Babu Lal Jain	Karrapur, Sagar	1942
42.	Babu Lal Jain	Sagar	1942
43.	Babu Lal Jain	Gaurjhamar, Sagar	1931
44.	Babu Lal Jain	Sagar	1932
45.	Babu Lal Jain Modi	Rahli	1942
46.	Babu Lal Singhi	Gadakota, Sagar	1930, 1932
47.	Bal Chand Jain	Sagar	1941
48.	Dr. Bal Chand Jain	Sagar	1942, 1943
49.	Pt.Bhuvanendra Kumar Shastri	Sagar	1942
50.	Bhaiyalal Jain	Banda, Sagar	1942
51.	Bhaiyalal Jain	Gaurjhamar, Sagar	1942
52.	Mitthulal Jain	Sagar	1942
53.	Munnalal Jain	Sagar	1942
54.	Mulayam Chand Jain	Tada, Sagar	1942
55.	Pt. Moti Lal Jain Shastri	Band, Sagar	1942

S.No.	Name	Place of Birth	Year of Arrest
56.	Ratan Lal Malviya	Sagar	1942
57.	Rajdhar Jain	Shahpur, Sagar	1942
58.	Roop Chand Jain	Sagar	1942
59.	Laxmi Chand Jain	Sagar	1942
60.	Laxmi Chand Jain	Sagar	1942
61.	Sukhlal Jain	Sagar	1942
62.	Suresh Chand Singhai	Devary	1942
63.	Sumat Chand Sondhiya	Sagar	1942
64.	Swaroop Chand Singhai	Sagar	1942
65.	Harish Chandra Jain	Sagar	1942
66.	Dr. Harindra Bhushan Jain	Nariyavali, Sagar	1942
67.	Hukam Chand Bukharia 'Tanmay'	Lalitpur,	1940; 1942

* This list is only indicative and not exhaustive.

For the source and full details about the Jain martyres and freedom fighters, *see* Kapoor Chand Jain and Jyoti Jain, 2006.

Appendix-7

*Jain Monks and Nuns from Greater Bundelkhand** *(With Year and Place of Birth)*

1. Acharya Shri Arajavsagarji Maharaj, 1967. Futerakalan (Damoh)
2. Ailacharya Shri Pragyasagarji Maharaj, 1978 KumbhiSatdhara (Jabalpur),
3. Acharya Shri Chandrasagarji Maharaj, 1967, Malthone (Sagar)
4. Balacharya Shri Yogindrasagarji Maharaj, 1961, Laskar (Gwalior)
5. Acharya Shri Sunilsagarji Maharaj, 1977, Tigora (Sagar)
6. Acharya Shri Devnandi, 1963, Shahgarh (Sagar)
7. Acharya Shri Kumudsagarji Maharaj, 1963, Shahgarh (Sagar)
8. Acharya Shri Viragsagarji Maharaj, 1963, Patharia (Damoh)
9. Acharya Shri Vishuddhasagarji Maharaj, 1971, Rur Gram (Bhind)
10. Acharya Shri Vishadsagarji Maharaj, 1964, Kupi (Chhatarpur)
11. Acharya Shri Vibhavsagarji Maharaj, 1976, Kashanpura (Sagar)
12. Acharya Shri Vimarshsagarji Maharaj, 1973, Jatara (Tikamgarh)
13. Acharya Shri Vikarshsagarji Maharaj, 1970, Bina (Sagar)
14. Acharya Shri Vimadsagarji Maharaj, 1976, Shahgarh (Sagar)
15. Acharya Shri Vinamrasagarji Maharaj1963, Bhind
16. Acharya Shri Vinishchaysagarji Maharaj, 1973, Patharia (Damoh)
17. Muni Shri Prarthnasagarji Maharaj, 1970, Gadhakota (Sagar)
18. Acharya Shri Suryasagarji Maharaj, 1883, Premsar (Gwalior)
19. Acharya Shri Vijaysagarji Maharaj, 1881, Sirali (Gwalior)
20. Acharya Shri Vimalsagarji Maharaj, 1892, Mohna (Gwalior)
21. Acharya Shri Sumatisagarji Maharaj, 1917-2004, Shyampura (Morena)
22. Acharya Shri Sanmatisagarji Maharaj, 1949-2013, Barbai (Morena)
23. Acharya Shri Bharatsagarji Maharaj, 1950-2014, Gudargram (Shivpuri)
24. Sarakoddharak Achaya Shri Gyansagarji Maharaj, 1958, Morena
25. Acharya Shri Viveksagarji Maharaj, 1961, Laskar (Gwalior)
26. Acharya Shri Viveksagarji Maharaj, 1972, Ghisoli, Jakhora (Lalitpur)
27. Acharya Shri Vineetsagarji Maharaj, 1971, Mahroni (Lalitpur)
28. Muni Shri Amitsagarji Maharaj, 1963, Khurai (Sagar)
29. Muni Shri Abhaisagarji Maharaj, 1960, Patan (Jabalpur)
30. Muni Shri Arunsagarji Maharaj, 1963, Sahajpur (Jabalpur)
31. Muni Shri Ajitsagarji Maharaj, 1968, Simaria, Garhakota (Sagar)
32. Muni Shtri Kshamasagarji Maharaj, 1957, Sagar

33. Upadhyay Shri Nirbhaisagarji Maharaj,1963, Dhaboli (Sagar)
34. Muni Shri Pragyasagarji Maharaj, 1972, Pidrai (MP)
35. Muni Shri Pulaksagarji Maharaj, 1970, Dhantari (Chhatarpur)
36. Muni Shri Prateeksagarji Maharaj, 1980, Bhind
37. Muni Shri Prakarshsagarji Maharaj, 1967, Brajpur (Panna)
38. Muni Pungav Shri Sudhasagarji Maharaj, 1958, Ishurwara (Sagar)
39. Muni Shri Samtasagarji Maharaj, 1962, Nanhi Devri (Sagar)
40. Krantikari Muni Shri Tarunsagarji Maharaj, Guhanchee (Damoh)
41. Muni Shri Vishrantsagarji Maharaj, 1977, Kunwarpur (Panna)

NUNS

1. Aryika Shri Buddhimati Mataji, 1910, Jabalpur
2. Aryika Shri Vimalmati mataji, 1905, Mungawali, Shahgarh, MP
3. Aryika Shri Vishuddhamati Mataji, 1928, Rithi
4. Aryika Shri Siddhamati Mataji, 1933, Bhopal.
5. Ganani Aryika Shri Vishuddhamati Mataji, 1948, Gwalior
6. Ganani Aryika Shri Syadvadmati Mataji, 1953, Indore
7. Aryika Shri Vishuddhamati Mataji, 1954, Jabalpur
8. Aryika Shri Vinatmati Mataji, 1963, Shivpuri
9. Aryika Shri Gunamati Mataji, 1964, Shahgarh
10. Aryika Shri Dhaarnamati Mataji, 1964, Shahgarh
11. Aryika Shri Annanyamati Mataji, 1969, Lar (Tikamgarh)

* This list is only indicative and is not complete.

Source: R. K. Jain (2015).

Appendix-8

Some Prominent Jains of Bundhelkhand

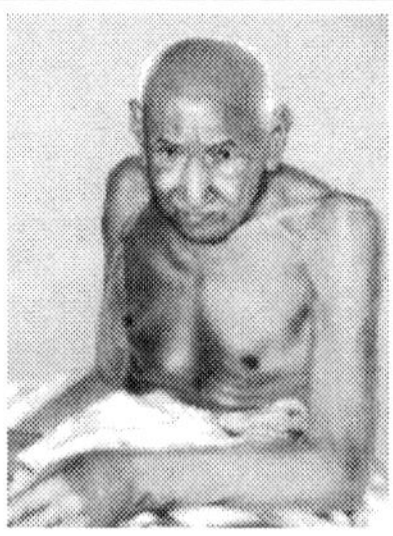

Kshullak Ganesh Prasad Varni

Siddhantacharya
Pt. Phoolchandra Shastri

Dr. Hukam Chand Bharill

Raibahadur Shrimant Seth
Mohan Lal Jain, Khurai

Seth Chandra Bhan Jain,
Bamrana/Sadumal

Seth Laxmi Chand Jain,
Bamrana,/Sadumal

Shrimant Seth Bhagawan Das Jain, Sagar

Seth Shiv Prasad Malaiya

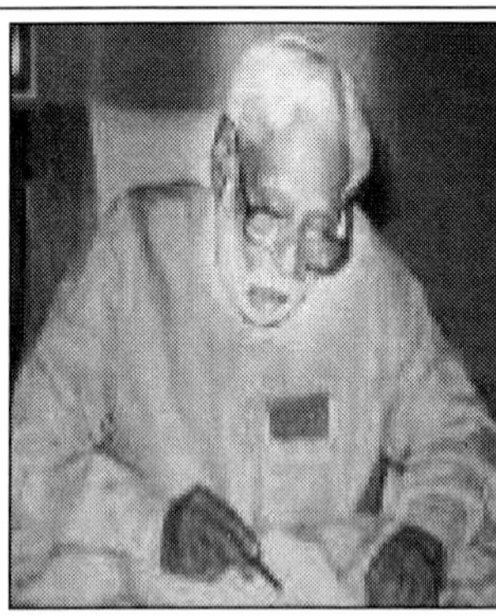

Dal Chand Jain, Ex-M. P.

Pradeep K. Jain 'Aditya', Ex-M.P.

Hukam Chand Bukharia "Tanmay", Poet

Padmshri Kailash Madbaiya, Poet, Author

Bibliography

Babb, Laurence A. (1998) *Absent Lord: Ascetics and Kings in a Jain Ritual Culture*. New Delhi: Motilal Banarsidass.

Bajpai, Madhulika (1989) *Development of Jain Religion in Madhya Pradesh* (Since the Earlier Time to c. 1200 A.D.). New Delhi: Ramanand Vidya Bhawan.

Banks, Marcus (1986) "Defining Division: An Historical Overview of Jain Social Organisation", *Modern Asian Studies*, 20(3): 447-60.

Banks, Marcus (1992*) Organising Jainism in India and England*. Oxford: Clarendon Press.

Barth, A. (1969). The Religion of India. Sixth Edition. New Delhi: S. Chand & Co.

Baya "Shreyas", D.S. (2007) *Death with Equanimity: The Pursuit of Immortality*. Jaipur: Prakrit Bharati Academy.

Bharill, Ratan Chand (2010) *"Prastavna", in Kanji Swami, Adyatma-Vaani* (in Hindi). Sagar: Shrimant Seth Bhagwandas Shobhalal Jain Parmarthik Sansthan.

Buhler, Johann George (1963) (1903) *The Indian Sect of the Jainas* (Translated and edited by J. Burgess). Calcutta: Susil Gupta (India) Pvt. Ltd.

Caillat, Collette and Nalini Balbir (eds) (2008) *Jaina Studies*. Delhi: Motilal Banarsidass.

Carrithers, M. (1989) 'Naked Ascetics in Southern Digambar Jainism', Man (NS) 24: 210-235.

Carrithers, M. (1991) 'The Foundations of Community among Southern Digambar Jains: An Essay on Rhetoric & Experience", pp. 261-286, in M. Carrithers & C. Humphrey (eds.) *The Assembly of Listeners: Jains in Society*. Cambridge: Cambridge University Press.

Census of India 1961 (1963) Paper No. 1 of 1963, Religion. New Delhi: R. G. Office.

Census of India 1971 (1972) Paper No. 2 of 1972, Religion. New Delhi: R. G. Office.

Census of India 1981 (1984) Paper No. 4 of 1984, Household Population by Religion of Head of Household. New Delhi: R. G. Office.

Census of India 1991 (1995) Paper No. 1 of 1995, Religion. New Delhi: R. G. Office.

Census of India 2001 (2005) First Report of Religion Data. New Delhi: R. G. Offfice.

Chanchreek, K. L. and Mahesh K. Jain (eds) (2004) *Jaina Economic Life: Ancient and Medieval India*. New Delhi: Shree Publishers & Distributors.

Chanchreek, K. L. and Mahesh K. Jain (eds) (2004) *Jaina Social Life*. New Delhi: Shree Publishers & Distributors.

Chapple, Christopher Key (1993) *Nonviolence to Animals: Earth and Self in Asian Tradition*. Albany: State University of New York Press.

Chapple, Christopher Key (2002) Jainism and Ecology: *Nonviolence in Web of life*. Cambridge: Harvard University Press.

Cort, John E. (1991) 'The Shvetambar Murtipujak Jain Mendicant', Man, 26(4): 651-671.

Cort, John E. (1998) *Open Boundaries: Jain Communities and Cultures in Indian History*. Albany: State University of New York Press.

Cort, John E. (2001) *Jains in the world: Religious Values and Ideology in India*. New York and Delhi: Oxford University Press.

Cort, John E. (2004) "Jains, Caste and Hierarchy in North Gujarat", Contributions to Indian Sociology 38 (1&2): 73-112.

Cort, John E. (2006) "A Fifteenth-Century Jain Mystic and His Followers", in Peter Flugel (ed) *Studies in Jain History and Culture: Disputes and Dialogues*. London: Taylor & Francis.

Dakle, Sunita P. (2011) Socio-Economic Study of Jain Women Entrepreneurs: With Reference to Pune District. Ph.D. Thesis. Pune: Department of Economics, Tilak Maharashtra Vidyapeeth.

Dasgupta, Debendra Chandra (1996) (1942) *Jaina System of Education*. Delhi: Motilal Banarsidass Publishers Ltd.

Dasgupta, Surendranath (1963) *A History of Indian Philosophy*. Cambridge: Cambridge University Press.

Davis, Kingsley (1951) *Population of India & Pakistan*, New York: Russell & Russell.

Deo, S.B. (1956) History of Jaina Monachism from Inscriptions and Literature. Deccan College Dissertation Series 17. Poona: Deccan College Postgraduate and Research Institute.

Desai, P.B. (1957) *Jainism in South India and Some Jaina Epigraphs*. Sholapur.

"Diwakar", Pt. Sumeru Chandra (2006) *Charitra Chakravarti Shanti Sagarji Maharaj*. 8th Edition. New Delhi: Shri Bharatvarshiya Digambar Jain Mahasabha.

Diwan, Mohan Kishor (ed) (2000) *Nepathya Nayak: Laxmi Chandra Jain* (in Hindi). New Delhi: Bhartiya Jnanpith.

Dundas, Paul (1992) *The Jains*. London & New York: Routledge.

Flugel, Peter (2006) "Jainism and Society", *Bulletin of SOAS* 68: 91-112.

Flugel, Peter (ed) (2006) *Studies in Jain History and Culture: Disputes and Dialogues*. London: Routledge.

Folkert, Kendal W. (1993) *Scripture and Community: Collected Essays on the Jains*. Atlanta: Scholars Press.

Gandhi, M.K. (1940) *An Autobiography, or the Story of My Experiments with Truth*. Ahmedabad: Navjivan Press.

Gopal, Surendra (1984) "Jain Merchants in Eastern India under the Great Mughals", pp. 69-81, in Dwijendra Tripathi (ed) *Business Communities of India: A Historical Perspective*. Delhi: Manohar Publishers & Distributors

Goyaleeya, Ayodhya Prasad (1964) *Jain Jagaran ke Agradoot* (in Hindi). New Delhi: Bhartiya Jnanpith.

Gupta, Dipankar (2000) *Interrogating Caste: Understanding Hierarchy and Difference in Indian Society*. New Delhi: Penguin Books.

Hardiman, David (1996) *Feeding the Bania: Peasants and Usurers in Western India*. Delhi: Oxford University Press.

Humphrey, C. (1991) "Local Jain Communities", pp. 69-73, In M. Carrithers and C. Humphrey (eds.) *The Assembly of Listeners*. Cambridge: Cambridge University Press.

Humphrey, Caroline and James Laidlaw (1994) *Archetypal Actions of Ritual: A Theory Illustrated by the Jain Rite of Worship*. Oxford: Clarendon Press.

ISJS (2019) *National Report: A Sociological Study of the Jain Community in India*. New Delhi: International School for Jain Studies.

Jacobi, Hermann (1946) *Studies in Jainism*. Ahmedabad: Jaina Sahitya Samshodhaka Karyalaya.

Jain, Anupam (Ed) (2015) *Digambar Jain Tirth Nirdeshika* (in Hindi). 9th edition. Indore: Kundkund Bharati.

Jain, Bhag Chand (1972) Jainism in Buddhist Literature. Nagpur.

Jain, Deepak (2001) "Taaran Taran Jain Samajki Jangadna", *Taaran Bandhu* 25(1): 105-108.

Jain, Dheeraj (2017) *Jain Population in India: A perspective from Census 2011*. Delhi: International School for Jain Studies.

Jain, Harish Chandra (2012) "Pandit Gopaldas Varaiya", pp. 229-234, in Shital Chand Jain and Phool Chand Jain Premi (eds) *Beesvin Shatabdi ke Jain Vidwano ka Avdan*. Burhanpur: Shri Akhil Bharatvarshiya Digambar Jain Vidvatparishad.

Jain, Hiralal and A.N. Upadhye (1975) *Mahavira: His Times and his Philosophy of Life*. New Delhi: Bhartiya Jnanpith.

Jain, J.C. (1947). *Life in Ancient India as Depicted in the Jaina Canons*. Bombay: New Book Company.

Jain, Jyoti (1997) *Swarajya aur Jain Mahilayen* (in Hindi). Khatauli: Shri Kailash Chand Jain Smriti Nyas.

Jain, Jyoti Prasad (1983) *Religion and Culture of the Jains*. 3rd Edition. Delhi: Bhartiya Jnanpith.

Jain, Jyoti Prasad (2005) (1964) *The Jaina Sources of the History of Ancient India, 100 B.C.-A.D. 900*. Delhi: Munshiram Manoharlal Publishers.

Jain, Mahendra Kumar (ed.) (1986) *Chhatarpur Zila: Jain Samajik va Sanskritik Survekshan* (in Hindi). Bhagwan, Chhatarpur: Akhil Bharatvarshiya Digambar Parishad Zila Sakha.

Jain, Narendra Kumar (ed) (2017) Smarika: Centenary Year 1917-2017: Shri Mahavir Digambar Jain Sanskrit Uchchtar Madhymik Vidyalaya. Sadumal: Centenary Committee.

Jain, Niraj (2010) *Songarh Sameeksha* (in Hindi). Delhi: Shri Bharatvarshiya Digambar Jain Mahasabha.

Jain, Prakash C. (2005) "Syadvad Mahavidyalaya: Ek Smriti-Chitra", *Shri Syadvad Mahavidyalaya Centenary Yearbook, 1905-2005* (in Hindi). Varanasi: Centenary Celebrations Committee.

Jain Prakash C. (2010a) "For a Sociology of the Jain Community", *Tulsi Prajna* 37 (146): 63-76.

Jain, Prakash C. (2010b) "Status of the Contemporary Jain Community", *Arhat Vachan* 22(1 &2): 71-83.

Jain, Prakash C. (2011) *Jains in India and Abroad: A Sociological Introduction*. New Delhi: International School for Jain Studies.

Jain, Prakash C. (2018a) "Jain Community of Bundelkhand: A Sociological Introduction", *Arhat Vachan* 30 (1): 53-64.

Jain, Prakash C. (2018b) "Education and Occupational Mobility among the Jains of Bundelkhand", *Shramana* 68 (3): 68-85.

Jain, Prakash C. (2018c) "Status of Contemporary Jain Women: A Sociolocal Analysis", *Women's Link Jurnal*, vol. 25, No. 3, pp. 3-11.

Jain, Prakash C. (ed) (2019) *Studies in Jain Population and Demography*. Jaipur: Rawat Publications.

Jain, Prakash C. and H. C. Jain (2017) "Status of Jain Youth of Bundelkhand: A Sociological Survey", *ISJS-Transaction* 2 (4): 11-18.

Jain, Prem Chandra and Asha Jain (2018) `*Vidvat-Trayi: Pt. Phoolchandra Shastri, Pt. Kailash Chandra Shastri and Pt. Jaganmohanlal Shastri* (in Hindi). Shri Ganesh Varni Digambar Jain Sansthan, Varanasi.

Jain, R. K. (2015) *Jain Digambaracharya: Prerak Sant evem Sadvichar* (in Hindi). Kota: Shri Sakal Digambar Jain Samaj Samiti (Reg).

Jain, Ravindra K. (1999) The Universe as Audience: Metaphor and Community among the Jains of North India. Shimla: Indian Institute of Advanced Study.

Jain, Ravindra K. (2006) *Between History and Legend: Status and Power in Bundelkhand*. New Delhi: Orient Blackswan.

Jain, Satish Kumar (1987) *Progresive Jains*. New Delhi: Shraman Sahitya Sansthan.

Jain, Shalin (2017) *Identity, Community and State: The Jains under the Mughals*. Delhi: Primus Books.

Jain, Shital Chand and Phoolchand Jain Premi (2012) *Beesvin Shatabdi ke Jain Vidwano ka Avdan*. Burhanpur: Akhil Bharatvarshiya Digambar Jain Vidwatparishad

Jain, Shugan C. and Prakash C. Jain (eds) (2014) *Social Consciousness in Jainism*. New Delhi: New Bharatiya Book Corporation.

Jain, Surendra Kumar (1996) *Golapurav Jain Samaj: Itihas evam Sarvekshan* (in Hindi). Sagar: Paras Shodh Sansthan.

Jain, Suresh (2018) "Baba Daulatram Varni "Nainagiri" kee Terah Rachnayen", *Shrut Sambardhini*, January: 18-20.

Jain, Yogendra (2007) *Jain Way of Life*. Getzville, New York: Federation of Jain Associations in North America.

Jain "Bharati", Surendra Kumar (2004) "Jain Patrakarita ka Vikas". *Shrut Sambardhini*, October and November, pp. 6-9 & 12-16.

Jain "Premi", Phool Chand (2005) *Syavad Smarika*. Varanasi: Shri Digambar Jain Syadvad Sanskrit Mahavidyalaya.

Jain "Premi", Phool Chand (Ed) (2006) *Saraswat Maneeshee: Samagat Vidwano ka Sankshipt Parichay* (in HIndi). Shravanbelgola: Mahamatabhishek Mahotsav Samiti.

Jaini, Padmanabh S. (1970). "Shramnas: Their Conflict with Brahminical Society", pp. 39-81, in J.W. Elder (ed.) *Chapters in Indian Civilization, I. Dubuque,* Iowa: Kendall Hunt.

Jaini, Padmanabh S. (1979) *The Jain Path of Purification*. Delhi: Motilal Banarasidass.

Jaini, Padmanabh, S. (1980) 'The Disappearance of Buddhism and the Survival of Jainism: A Study in 'Contrast'", pp. 81-91, in A. K. Narain (ed.) *Studies in Buddhism*. New Delhi: B. R. Publishing Corporation.

Jaini, Padmanabh, S. (2000) *Collected Papers on Jaina Studies*. Delhi: Motilal Banarsidass.

Kapadia, K.M. (1966) *Marriage and Family in India*. Bombay.

Karve, Irawati (1965) *Kinship Organization in India*. Second edition. Bombay: Asia Publishing House.

Kavyateerth, Pt. Mohanlal Jain (1941) Shri *Akhil Bharatvarshiya Digambar Jain Golapurv-Directory* (in Hindi). Baraytha, Sagar: The Author.

Kavyateerth, Pt. Tulsiram (editor) (1924) *Digambar Jain Parwar Directory*. Amravati: Singhai Banshilal Pannalal Parwar Jain.

Kothari, Trilok Chand (2003) *Akhil Bharatvarshiya Digambar Jain Mahasabha ka Ateet, 1895-1980*. Kota: Trilok Institute of Higher Studies and Research.

Kumar, Bhuvanendra (1996) *Jainism in North America.* Missisauga, Ontario: Humanities Press.

Laidlaw, James (1995) *Riches and Renunciation: Religion, Economy and Society among the Jains*. Oxford: Clarendon Press.

Long, Jeffery D. (2009) *Jainism: An Introduction*. London and New York: I. B. Tauris.

Mahaprajna, Acharya (2002) *Anekanta: The Third Eye*. Ladnun: Jain Vishwa Bharati University.

Mahmood, Tahir (1993) "Hindus, Buddhists, Jains and Sikhs: Religious Identity, Beliefs and Practices under the Indian Legal System," *Religion and Law Review* 2 (2): 5-28.

Malaiya, Yashwant K. (1996) "Golapurava Anvaya: Ek Parichaya", pp. 32-44, in Surendra K. Jain (ed) *Golapurava Jain Samaj: Itihas evam Sarvekshan* (in Hindi). Sagar: Paras Sodh Sansthan.

Marett, Paul (2000) *Jainism Explained*. Leicester: Jain Samaj Europe Publication.

Mehta, D. (n.d.) *Shrimad Rajchandra: A Life*. Ahmedabad: Shrimad Rajchandra Janma Shatabdi Mandal.

Mehta, M. and D. Tripathi (1991) *Business Houses in Western India*. New Delhi: Manohar Books.

Mittal, A. C. (2006) *Economic Aspects of Jainism*. New Delhi: Vista International Publishing House.

Mukhtar "Yugvir", Jugal Kishor (1963) *Yugvir Nibandhavali*—Part I. Delhi: Vir Sewa Mandir Trust.

Nehru, Jawaharlal (1961) *The Discovery of India*. Bombay: Asia Publishing House.

Nevaskar, Balwant (1971) *Capitalists without Capitalism: The Jains of India and the Quakers of the West*. Westport, Conn.: Greenwood Publishing Corporation.

Nevaskar, Balwant (ed.) (1978) *Sramana Tradition: Its Contribution to Indian Culture*. Ahmedabad: L. D. Institute of Indology.

NITI Ayog (2018) *Human Development Report of Bundelkhand 2012*. (UNDP). http://www.undp.org/content/india/bundelkhand report, 23 Jan. 2018. Pdf. Accesed on 15th April 2019.

Patil, Padmaja A. (2014) "A Century of Boarding Houses under Dakshin Bharat Jain Sabha", pp. 128-38, in Shugan C. Jain and Prakash C. Jain (eds) *Social Consciousness in Jainism*. Delhi: New Bharatiya Book Corporation.

Premi, Nathuram (1992) "Parwar Jatike Itihas par Kuchh Prakash", pp. 150-83, in Siddhantacharya Pt. Phoolchandra Shastri (ed) *Parwar Jain Samaj ka Itihas* (in Hindi). Jabalpur: Shri Bharatvarshiya Digambar Jain Parwar Sabha.

Radhakrishnan, Sarvapalli and Charles A. Moore (ed.) (1957) *A Source Book of Indian Philosophy*. Princeton: Princeton University Press.

Rankin, Aidan (2007) *The Jain Path: Ancient Wisdom for an Age of Anxiety*. New Delhi: New Age Books.

Reynell, Josephine (1985b) "Renunciation and Ostentation: A Jain Paradox", *Cambridge Anthropology* 9(3): 20-33.

Reynell, Josephine (1991) "Women and the Reproduction of the Jain Community", pp. 41-68, in M. Carrithers and C. Humphrey (eds.) *The Assembly of Listeners*. Cambridge: Cambridge University Press.

Rivers, W.H.R. (1932) *Social Organisation*. London.

Russell, Robert Vane and Hiralal (1975) (1916) *The Tribes and Castes of the Central Provinces of India*. Delhi: Cosmo Publications.

Sangave, Vilas A. (1976) *Daksin Bharat Jain Sabhaka Itihas*. Sangli: Daksin Bharat Jain Sabha.

Sangave, Vilas A. (1980) (1959) Jain *Community: A Social Survey*. Second Edition. Bombay: Popular Prakashan.

Sangave, Vilas A. (1991) "Reform movements among Jains in Modern India", pp. 233-40, in Michael Carrithers and Caroline Humphrey (eds.) *The Assembly of Listeners: Jains in Society*. Cambridge: Cambridge University Press.

Sangave, Vilas A. (1992) *Jain Society through the Ages*. Delhi: R.K. Jain Charitable Trust.

Sangave, Vilas A. (2001) Facets of Jainology: Selected Papers on Jain Society, Religion and Culture. Mumbai: Popular Prakashan.

Sangave, Vilas A. (2006) (1990) *Aspects of Jaina Religion*. New Delhi: Bhartiya Jnanpith.

Sethi, Manisha (2012) *Escaping the World: Women Renouncers among Jains*. New Delhi: Routledge.

Shah, C. J. (1932) *Jainism in North India*. London: Green & Co.

Shah, Natubhai (1998) *Jainism: The World of Conquerors*. 2 Vols. Blighton: Sussex Academic Press.

Shah, Sneh (1977) "Who Are the Jains?" *New Community*, 7: 369–75.

Sharma, Jagdish P. (1976) "The Jains as a Minority in History and Society", *Jain Journal* 5 (April): 137-148.

Sharma, Jagdish P. (1999) "The Jinasattvas: Class and Gender in the Social Origins of Jaina Heroes", in Wagle, N.K. and Olle Quarnstrom (eds) *Approaches to Jain Studies: Philosophy, Logic, Rituals and Symbols*. Toronto: The Centre for South Asian Studies, University of Toronto.

Shastri, Jaganmohanlal (1992) "Prastawna", pp. 13-36, in Siddhantacharya Pt. Phoolchadra Shastri (author and editor), *Parwar Jain Samaj ka Itihas* (in Hindi). Jabalpur: Shri Bharatvarshiya Digambar Jain Parwar Sabha.

Shastri, Pt. Kamal Kumar (1967) *Papauraji ka Sankshipt Parichay* (in Hindi). Third Edition. Tikamgarh: Shri Digambar Jain Atishaya Kshetra Paporaji Management Committee.

Shastri, Pt. Phoolchandra (1990?) *Varna, Jati aur Dharma* (in Hindi). Second Edition. New Delhi: Bharatiya Jnanpith.

Shastri, Siddhantacharya Pt. Phoolchandra (1992) *Parwar Jain Samaj ka Itihas* (in Hindi). Jabalpur: Shri Bharatvarshiya Digambar Jain Parwar Sabha.

Shethia, Tara (ed) (2002) *The Lessons of Ahinsa and Anekant for Contemporary Life*. Delhi: Motilal Banarsidass.

Siddhantashastri, Pt. Kailash Chandra (2014) Shri Syadvad Mahavidyalaya ka Arambhik Itihas", *Shrut Sambardhini*, April, pp. 19-22.

Singh, K.S. (1998) "Jain", pp. 1327-1338, *India's Communities, H–M* (People of India National Series, Vol. V). Delhi: Anthropological Survey of India and Oxford University Press.

Singh, R.N. and R.P. Chaturvedi (1984) "Dynamics of Population Growth: Bundelkhand Region—A Case Study", *Population Geography* 6 (1-2): 53-65.

Singh, Yogendra (1973) *Modernisation of Indian Tradition*. Delhi: Thomson Press.

Singhi, N.K. (1987) *Studies in Jainism: Ideal, Ideology, and Practice*. Jaipur: Printwell Publishers.

Spratt, P. (1966) "Jainism", pp. 300-314, in *Hindu Culture and Personality: A Psycho-Analytic Study*. Bombay: Manaktalas & Sons.

Stevenson, Sinclair (1995) (1915) *The Heart of Jainism*. 3rd Edition. Delhi: Munshiram Manoharlal Publishers Pvt. Ltd.

Syamlal (1992) "The Jain Movement and Socio-Religious Transformation of the "Bhangis" of Jodhpur, Rajasthan", *The Indian Journal of Social Work* LIII (1): 59-67.

Thornton (2003) (1898) *Parsi, Jaina, and Sikh: Or Some Minor Religious Sects in India*. New Delhi: Mittal Publications.

Timberg, T. A. (1978) *The Marwaris: From Traders to Industrialists*. Delhi: Vikas Publishing House.

Titze, Kurt (1998) *Jainism: A Pictorial Guide to the Religion of Non-Violence*. Delhi: Motilal Banarsidass.

Tobias, Michael (1991) *Life Force: The World of Jainism*. Berkley: Asian Humanities Press.

Tod, James (1839) *Travels in Western India*. London: W. H. Allen.

Tod, James (1920) *Annals and Antiquities of Rajasthan*, 3 vols. London: Oxford University Press.

Tripathi, Dwijendra (ed) (1984) *Business Communities of India: A Historical Perspective*. Delhi: Manohar Publishers & Distributors.

Tyagi, Raj Kumar (1997) *Grassland and Fodder Atlas of Bundelkhand*. Jhansi: Indian Grassland and Fodder Research Institute.

Upadhye, A.N. (1946) "Studies in Jaina Gotras", *Jain Antiquary* II (3): 61-69.

Vallely, Anne (2002) "Ethical Discourses among Orthodox and Diaspora Jains" in Michael Lambek (ed) *A Reader in the Anthropology of Religion*. London: Blackwell Publishing.

Varni, Ganesh Prasad (1949) *Meri Jeevan Gatha* (in Hindi). Kashi: Bhargava Bhushan Press.

Weber, Albrecht (1878). *The History of Indian Literature*. London.

Weber, Max (1958) "The Heterodox Soteriologies of the Cultured Professional Monks", pp. 192-204, in *The Religion of India: The Sociology of Hinduism and Buddhism*. New York: The Free Press of Glencoe.

Williams, R. (1963) *Jaina Yoga: A Study of the Medieval Sravakacharas*, London: Oxford University Press.

Wilson, H.H. (1861). *Works of Wilson*, Vol. 1. London: Trubner & Co.

Index